SAVING
Faith

SAVING
Faith

How Families Protect, Sustain, and Encourage Faith

JOHN GEE

Published by the Religious Studies Center, Brigham Young University, Provo, Utah, in cooperation with Deseret Book Company, Salt Lake City, Utah. Visit us at rsc.byu.edu.

Printed in the United States of America by Sheridan Books, Inc.

DESERET BOOK is a registered trademark of Deseret Book Company. Visit us at DeseretBook.com.

Cover and interior design by Carmen Durland Cole.

ISBN 978-1-9443-9493-6

Library of Congress Cataloging-in-Publication Data
Names: Gee, John, 1964- author.
Title: Saving faith : how families protect, sustain, and encourage faith / John Gee.
Description: Provo, Utah : Religious Studies Center, Brigham Young University, [2020] | Includes index. | Summary: "Narratives about Latter-day Saint youth and young adults losing faith in droves are examined in the context of data from the longitudinal National Study of Youth and Religion and other studies. These narratives are largely unsupported by the data and overemphasize the role that doubt plays in the loss of faith by ignoring other factors. Weekly church attendance, daily prayer, frequent scripture study, and avoiding sexual activity outside of marriage make a difference in maintaining and preserving faith"-- Provided by publisher.
Identifiers: LCCN 2019050968 | ISBN 9781944394936 (hardcover)
Subjects: LCSH: Church of Jesus Christ of Latter-day Saints--Doctrines. | Christian life--Mormon authors. | Parenting--Religious aspects--Christianity. | Belief and doubt. | Mormon Church--Doctrines. | Problem children.
Classification: LCC BX8656 .G44 2020 | DDC 289.3/3208350973--dc23
LC record available at https://lccn.loc.gov/2019050968

For my family

CONTENTS

| PREFACE

Behind every book is a story about why it was written, and knowing that story can sometimes help the reader make sense of the book.

This book was written because there is a need for it.

Like many members of The Church of Jesus Christ of Latter-day Saints, I listened as President Gordon B. Hinckley said the following in the April 2005 general conference:

> I have been reading a new book, recently published by the Oxford University Press, which has received considerable attention among us. It contains a study conducted by members of the faculty of the University of North Carolina at Chapel Hill. It deals with the religious and spiritual lives of American teenagers. Those who conducted the study questioned young people of various faiths and traditions.[1]

They reached the conclusion that our LDS youth know more about their faith, are more committed to it, and abide more closely by its teachings concerning social behavior than do their peers.

One of the researchers stated, "The LDS Church asks a lot of its teenagers, and . . . more often than not, they get it."[2]

Our young people were found to be more likely to hold the same religious beliefs as their parents, to attend religious services once a week, to share their faith with others, to engage in fasting or some other form of self-denial, and to have less doubt about their religious beliefs.

Commentators on the study speak of our youth arising early in the morning to attend seminary. "It is hard to get up so early," one seminary student said. "But there are blessings that come from doing it. It is a wonderful way to start the day."

The researchers point out that not all of our youth are perfect, but by and large they excel in a most remarkable way. I should add that there is no time to play poker for these high school students.[3]

This report intrigued me and so I too bought the book and read it. I started following the National Study of Youth and Religion and reading the books as they were published, occasionally going back to do my own research in the data. Even though I have been studying the processes involved in apostasy for more than three decades,[4] in this case I was mainly satisfying my own curiosity as a parent. I have seen the patterns, both good and bad, revealed by the research play out in my extended family.

I also noticed something else. Those concerned with apostasy in the modern Church and with supporting and defending the Church in various disciplines do so almost entirely on the basis of anecdotal evidence. Much of what has been produced has been sound scholarship, on target, and helpful because it deals with specific cases of known problems. Some of it has been counterproductive; truth is not well served by a bad argument. Almost all of it has been produced without the benefit of data detailing which threats are real and which are largely illusions and which approaches are helpful or hurtful. A substantial body of literature based on data does deal with the topics, but those engaged in defending the faith have largely been ignorant of it and thus have not utilized it. This book, besides providing information to parents and family members, provides data to those interested in supporting and defending the Church.

Over the years I have shared some of the things I have learned with friends and others in various venues.[5] A couple of bishops I know told me that they found my summaries helpful for them. In 2015 at an archaeological conference (of all places), Charles Wilson, a graduate student at another university, told me how helpful he had found some of these discussions and that some of his local leaders had found them useful too.

It was then I decided that if my notes have proven beneficial to people, I might try to share them more broadly—hence the book. I have since received encouragement from a number of people to publish these notes. The book is a synthesis of existing research rather than a new investigation. The lead investigator of the National Study of Youth and Religion himself argued that such compilations were necessary and helpful.[6] Since this book is a synthesis of other research for the benefit of nonspecialists, I have not found it needful to include a section on methodology. My interest has been to summarize and organize the research of others and to point out some places where it ties into scriptures and counsel given by apostles and prophets. The organization looks at how many youth and young adults we are keeping in the faith and how many we are losing (chapter 1), where those we lose are going (chapter 2), different categories (that may be more useful than active and less active) of classifying youth (chapter 3), the role that doubts play in the loss of faith (chapter 4), what causes youth to leave (chapter 5), what the major intellectual issues that cause a loss of faith are (chapter 6), what impact sexual behavior has on loss of faith (chapter 7), what has been shown statistically to help youth retain faith (chapter 8), and what parents can do to preserve the faith of their children (chapter 9). The data have been the main driver (even when the data took me places I would rather not have gone), but I have tried to view the data through a gospel lens and to be explicit about that lens. Though I have deliberately juxtaposed secular and sacred sources, I did not do this in an effort to dilute sacred sources or make them depend on secular sources for validity but rather to show that in many cases they use different lines of reasoning to come to the same conclusion.

Most of the data deals with younger individuals in the years from about 12 to 26. This divides into categories of about 12 to 18 and 18 to 26. The former group is variously called teenagers and youth and is associated with being in high school. The latter group might be called young adults, emerging adults, or college students, even though not all of them are actually enrolled at a college or university. I will employ these terms within each age division synonymously for easier reading since phrases like "younger adults who are of the age that is usually associated with attending college or university but might also include those who for whatever reason might not actually be enrolled" become awkward in normal prose.

In certain cases the discussion tries unsuccessfully to keep up with a moving target. I wrote the manuscript in early 2016 and late 2017, before and after a sabbatical. For a year it underwent peer review. In the meantime the Church announced it was in the process of replacing its youth programs. The final version of the manuscript went to the publishers before the new program had been announced, so the analysis given is that of the old program.

A number of the topics discussed are sensitive to various people, usually because of past personal experiences that have been quite painful. With Martius from Shakespeare's *Coriolanus*, they say, "I have some wounds upon me, and they smart / To hear themselves rememb'red."[7] The data lead one "to enlarge the wounds of those who are already wounded, instead of consoling and healing their wounds; and those who have not been wounded, instead of feasting upon the pleasing word of God have daggers placed to pierce their souls and wound their delicate minds" (Jacob 2:9). Others have sensitivities because "the guilty taketh the truth to be hard, for it cutteth them to the very center" (1 Nephi 16:2); we do not like having our pet sins pointed out or poked. Nevertheless, the data are there and just because we do not like what they have to say is not reason in itself to avoid discussing them honestly. It seems to me to be more important to save faith than to save face. I hope the reader might find something useful in what follows. At least the reader can take comfort in the fact that he or she does not necessarily need to be a statistic.

A number of people have made comments at various stages along the way and provided encouragement. I would like to thank two who will remain anonymous because I do not think that they would want their encouragement of dealing with the information to be mistaken as an endorsement of my particular effort. The anonymous reviewers of the volume were very helpful, and I have taken those recommendations seriously. Laurence Gee, Sydney Gee, and Rebecca Lambert read early drafts and provided helpful comments. Scott Esplin at the Religious Studies Center has been unfailingly encouraging. Brent Nordgren helpfully handled distribution, coordination, and legal aspects. Devan Jensen not only kept production on track, but served as a sounding board on various issues. Throughout my career I have been blessed by and benefited from the expert editing of Shirley Ricks, in this book even more than usual as she has a PhD in the subject and located a number of sources that I had despaired of finding again. Sarah Whitney Johnson and Emily Cook assisted in the editing and occasionally served as sparring partners for my arguments. Fortunately, Carmen Cole has been involved in the production of every one of my books and lent her talents to the design of the volume. Although this book was mostly written in my spare time, it could not have been done at all without the support of the William (Bill) Gay chair, and I am grateful to the Gay family for providing the financial support that made this book possible. Brad Neiger, James Rasband, Noel Reynolds, and Martin Tanner helped solve some bureaucratic problems at a key stage of the book production. Finally, I thank my wife, Kathleen, who not only has provided the essential support for writing the book but also read through the penultimate draft to ensure readability and improved it significantly. My children supplied the inspiration for the volume. None of these individuals should be held accountable for the errors that remain in the present work. The unquoted opinions expressed are mine.

Notes

1. See Christian Smith and Melinda Lundquist Denton, *Soul Searching: The Religious and Spiritual Lives of American Teenagers* (Oxford: Oxford University Press, 2005).
2. In Elaine Jarvik, "LDS Teens Rank Tops in Living Their Faith," *Deseret Morning News*, March 15, 2005, p. A3.
3. Gordon B. Hinckley, "Gambling," *Ensign*, May 2005, 61.

4. Some of the fruits of this research have been published in John Gee, "La Trahison des Clercs: On the Language and Translation of the Book of Mormon," *Review of Books on the Book of Mormon* 6, no. 1 (1994): 51–120; John Gee and Daniel C. Peterson, "Graft and Corruption: On Olives and Olive Culture in the Pre-Modern Mediterranean," in *The Allegory of the Olive Tree*, ed. Stephen D. Ricks and John W. Welch (Salt Lake City: Deseret Book; Provo, UT: FARMS, 1994), 186–247; John Gee, "The Hagiography of Doubting Thomas," *FARMS Review of Books* 10, no. 2 (1998): 158–83; John Gee, "The Corruption of Scripture in Early Christianity," in *Early Christians in Disarray: Contemporary LDS Perspectives on the Christian Apostasy*, ed. Noel B. Reynolds (Provo, UT: FARMS, 2005), 163–204; John Gee, "James, First and Second Peter, and Jude: Epistles of Persecution," in *The Life and Teachings of the New Testament Apostles: From the Day of Pentecost to the Apocalypse*, ed. Richard Neitzel Holzapfel and Thomas A. Wayment (Salt Lake City: Deseret Book, 2010), 171–90.

5. Among which are John Gee, "On Corrupting the Youth," *FARMS Review* 22, no. 2 (2010): 195–228; and John Gee, "Of Tolerance and Smoked Fish," *Issues in Religion and Psychotherapy* 37 (2015): 17–20.

6. Christian Smith, "Five Proposals for Reforming Article Publishing in the Social Scientific Study of Religion (Especially Quantitative): Improving the Quality, Value, and Cumulativeness of Our Scholarship," *Journal for the Scientific Study of Religion* 49, no. 4 (2010): 588–89.

7. William Shakespeare, *Coriolanus* act 1, sc. 9, lines 28–29.

1 | **HARDLY PERFECT**

In 2011 and 2012 rumors circulated around the internet that a General Authority of The Church of Jesus Christ of Latter-day Saints had claimed that the Church was losing young people; they were "leaving in droves."[1] Whether the particular General Authority actually said that is not something that particularly interests me.[2] I am interested in assessing how true the statement might be, and if it is true, what can be done about it.

The Church certainly has the statistics to verify or falsify the claim and recently did so. Elder Quentin L. Cook addressed this issue in the April 2015 general conference: "Some have asserted that more members are leaving the Church today and that there is more doubt and unbelief than in the past. This is simply not true."[3] As an apostle, Elder Cook has access to the Church's statistics and we do not. That, however, does not mean that we do not have access to certain publicly available statistics. These statistics tell an interesting story that allows us to assess the validity of certain statements and figure out what we can and should be doing. The statistics show that while there is need for concern, there is not necessarily need for alarm. They also show that following the gospel and the counsel given by prophets and apostles for at least forty years is the best way to experience happy outcomes.

THE PROMISE AND PROBLEMS OF STATISTICS

How does an average Latter-day Saint teenager act? That depends, of course, on what we mean by *average*. In statistics there are three types of averages: mean, median, and mode. The mean is the arithmetic average where all the numbers are added together and then divided by the number of individual data points. The median is found by arranging all the numbers in order of size and selecting the one in the exact middle. The mode is simply the most frequent number in a set of data.

An example might illustrate how this works: Suppose you go into a store to buy a watch. The store has a number of watches that vary in price from cheap to expensive. You find that the watch prices are $10, $20, $25, $30, $35, $40, $40, $40, and $2,010. What is the average price of a watch? The mean is $250; but one exceptionally priced watch has skewed the average so that the mean is significantly higher than every watch but one. In this case, if you wanted to convey the average price, you would probably not want to use the mean. You might, in this case, choose the median, the price in the exact middle, which is $35. In some cases, what you want is the most common price, which in this case is $40; if you picked a watch at random, you are more likely to come up with one that cost $40 than any other price. Each of these averages has its uses. In most cases in our discussion I will specify the type of average where it is relevant.

In small samples—such as the last one considered—a small number of outliers can skew the results. In larger, randomly selected samples, outliers have less of a chance of skewing the data. They tend to follow what is called a standard, or normal, distribution of data. In a normal distribution, the mean, the median, and the mode will correspond. Half of the data will be above average and half will be below. A normal distribution also has some other properties. Any set of data has a standard deviation, which is a numerical measure of how much a random item of data will vary (or deviate) from the average. In a normal distribution, about two-thirds of the data (68%) will be within one standard deviation of the average. The vast majority of the data (95%) will be within two standard deviations of the average. Almost all of the data (99.7%) will be within three standard deviations of the average. Most large-scale random samples of measurable human characteristics (like height, weight, or intelligence) will tend to approximate a normal distribution.

To see how this works, consider the following example: Scaled down to twenty-four individuals following a normal distribution, we would expect one individual to be between two and three standard deviations below average. Three individuals would be between one and two standard deviations below average. Eight would be within one standard deviation below average. Those above average would display the reverse pattern. Eight would be within one standard deviation above average. Three would be between one and two standard deviations above average, and one would be between two and three standard deviations above average. In a normal distribution, about two-thirds of the sample are centered on the mode. Most people are average and fall in the middle of the distribution. One thing that makes data interesting is when they do not follow a normal distribution. While in some respects Latter-day Saint youth are average, in others they are not.

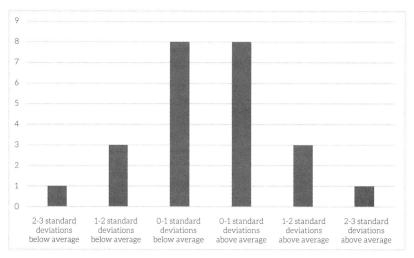

FIGURE. A HYPOTHETICAL NORMAL DISTRIBUTION OF 24 INDIVIDUALS

One of the more interesting sets of statistical data on youth in the Church comes out of the National Study of Youth and Religion (NSYR). This project followed more than three thousand youth in the United States for over a decade. The youth (and their parents or guardians) not only filled out many lengthy questionnaires, but a significant percentage also participated in extensive personal interviews. The process was repeated in multiple waves every few years. The study began at the University of North Carolina in 2001 under the direction of Christian Smith and ended in 2015 after he moved to the University of Notre Dame. The result is a rich and extensive collection of data about teenagers and young adults. Much of the information I will use comes from the NSYR, though I will take advantage of a number of other data collections as well. This provides a treasure trove of useful information for parents, information that tells us both where we stand and what we can do about our position.

The NSYR data set has several advantages and some disadvantages that the reader should be aware of. One advantage is that it is publicly available in several published reports, and the raw data are also publicly available.[4] The information in those reports can be plowed through and pored over, dissected and discussed in ways that the Church's internal statistics cannot.[5] (The Church has good reasons for not releasing that data to the public; even if I do not know all of them, I am satisfied by the reasons I can think of.) Some might also see the fact that the information was not gathered by the Church as a distinct advantage because they consider the Church's internal statistics to be biased or tainted in some way. I doubt that the Church's statistics are deliberately biased or tainted since it is in the Church's own best interest to have an accurate assessment of things as they really are.

Another advantage with the NSYR data set is its large sample size. A typical ward—if there is such a thing—might have a few hundred members and few dozen youth. A ward might have a few really good youth, a few with major problems, and a whole lot in between. A typical stake might have a few thousand members and a few hundred youth. The exceptional youth would stand out more than in the typical ward, and the problems might be more severe than those of a typical ward. It would take several stakes of the Church to have as many youth as were in the NSYR sample. The NSYR data set comprises the results of basically a whole stake made up of nothing but youth. That allows researchers to see the whole range of youth from the exceptional to the abysmal and everything in between. It allows them to see what is typical and what is unusual much more than a normal bishop or a parent can.

A third advantage of the NSYR data set is that it was gathered in a longitudinal study. Rather than just taking a large sample at one point in time, it followed the same youth for over a decade into their young adult years, allowing us to see changes over time in the lives of youth, the harvest of the seeds sown in youth, and whether an individual's status improved or not over time or stayed more or less the same.

A fourth advantage of the NSYR data set is that its sample cut across society, allowing us to compare how youth from different religious traditions fared and to see the effect of different belief systems on the youth and young adults.

This last advantage, however, is also a disadvantage, at least from the perspective of considering Latter-day Saint youth. Because the sample was representative of the population at large, it is not as fine-grained when it comes to Latter-day Saints in particular.[6] This provides a challenge when assessing where Latter-day Saints stand and what we should do about that stance. Sometimes the patterns of the NSYR data reflect the population as a whole and not the situation of the Latter-day Saints, which sometimes varies significantly from national norms, particularly in the area of sexual morality, but also, somewhat paradoxically, in obesity.[7] To be sure, the data of Latter-day Saints are contained in the larger data set but may not necessarily reflect the general trend. The data from the others in the study may simply swamp out the data on Latter-day Saints.

A story might help illustrate this. I once took a linear algebra class from Paul Yearout. At the beginning of the class, one of the students asked if we were going to be graded on the curve. He walked to the board and wrote the equation $y = e^{-x^2}$. "That," he said, "is the equation of the normal curve." If you took all the grades of all the students in all the classes of all the colleges in the whole country over the last century, it might approximate the curve, but there was no way that one upper division math class of thirty students would do so. So, no, he would not be grading on the curve. I have never forgotten Professor Yearout's answer.

Statistics can be great at pointing out general patterns for most people, but they can be terrible at predicting behavior of any one individual or a smaller group of individuals. Courtesy of Free-Photos/Pixabay.

Sometimes the data on Latter-day Saints may be the thirty students compared to the rest of the country. This needs to be kept in mind when considering some of the statistical results, but there are usually good reasons for taking recommendations from those results seriously.

This is another way of pointing out the problem of statistics in general. Statistics are great at pointing out general patterns for most people, but statistics may be terrible at predicting the behavior of any given individual or a smaller group of individuals. A. E. Housman once quipped that "if a dog hunted for fleas on mathematical principles, basing his research on statistics of area and population, he would never catch a flea except on accident. They require to be treated as individuals."[8] The individual has his or her agency and needs not follow the general path of the majority. One pair of sociologists concluded, "Human bodies and social life are complicated. Nothing is necessarily predictable or guaranteed in any given instance, even if the overall pattern of associations and causes is pretty clear for the population. We are dealing here, in other words, with probabilities, likelihoods, and tendencies that apply to most people, not with universal laws or formulas that work for everyone."[9]

The parent or bishop may see in the statistics the story of a particular child or youth, and the statistics might help the parent or Church leader understand better what is going on. But, this might not be true in any particular case. Statistics deal with the general rule, not necessarily the exceptions. Still, the statistics should reflect the majority of cases.

Another factor that we need to be aware of is that while in some parts of their lives Latter-day Saints follow national norms,

It is also possible that individuals do not give truthful answers but tailor their answers toward social expectations. Latter-day Saints are the least likely of religious groups to give socially desirable answers.

in other areas their teachings, attitudes, and practices go very much against the norms, as in some cases they certainly should. One researcher was struck with how Latter-day Saints differed from the rest of her sample in what the Saints consider spiritual aspects: "Mormons are distinctive among our participants for the relative absence of spiritual language that moves beyond theism. . . . Mormons inhabit a spiritual world saturated with symbols and experiences that focus on a clearly identified deity, and they have a long list of things one can do to be in relation to that deity. What happens in the natural world—as well as in their own souls—has specific theological significance and does not depend on any broader, generic spiritual language."[10]

Another concern that might be raised about the data is its accuracy. The data do little good if they are not accurate and honest. Accuracy can be affected by sample size, and given the relatively small percentage of Latter-day Saints among the general population, this can be a legitimate concern. It is also possible that individuals do not give truthful answers but tailor their answers toward social expectations; that is, they give the answers to the questions that they believe are appropriate rather than the ones that are true. This phenomenon has been studied, and the effects of religion have been noted. Latter-day Saints are the least likely of religious groups to give socially desirable answers. "Indeed, the odds of Mormons giving socially desirable responses are one-third that of evangelical Protestants."[11] Latter-day Saints stood out as so much of an outlier that the researchers thought it worthy of comment:

> It is worth noting the inverse association between Mormons and socially desirable response bias. While not strong (due likely to the small number of Mormons in the sample), it affirms the validity of the measures, since Mormon youth might be popularly thought to be prone (in general) to less arguing or criticizing. However, they are least likely among all religious adolescents to suggest that they entirely avoid these, or never get sad. Perhaps they are simply the *most* aware of such forms of human frailty.[12]

While the integrity of the data is a concern, the data from Latter-day Saints seems likely to be honest.

There is another way to skew data: not having a representative sample. A number of studies of Latter-day Saints have obtained their data by snowball sampling or chain-referral sampling.[13] In this case the data subjects are not randomly selected since they refer others of their acquaintance to participate in the survey. In this manner, the number of subjects grows like a rolling snowball. But this sampling method skews the results. To see how, consider the following scenario: A researcher wants to do a sample of political opinion and uses snowball sampling. She recruits five of her friends, who happen to be of the same political persuasion and thus belong to the same political party. They in turn recruit five other friends who also tend to have similar views because they would like their political preferences to be represented in the survey. The resulting survey could have a statistically significant sample of people but have an inherent political bias and thus not be truly representative of the population. Snowball sampling tends to produce what is known as the Pauline Kael Syndrome, named for the late American film critic. Kael reportedly said after Richard Nixon defeated George McGovern in the U.S. presidential election in 1972: "How could Nixon have won? Nobody I know voted for him."

Fortunately, the NSYR used random sampling rather than a referral sampling technique for choosing their participants.

THE PROBLEM OF OVEROPTIMISM

One problem that comes with evaluating statistics is the so-called Dunning–Kruger effect. This effect, initially analyzed by David Dunning and Justin Kruger,[14] and replicated by others,[15] is the tendency for individuals of low ability to assess their abilities as greater than they are. "Incompetence," they argue, "not only causes poor performance but also the inability to recognize that one's performance is poor." The effect is so pronounced that "participants in the bottom quartile [of whatever skill is being measured] not only overestimated themselves, but thought they were above average."[16] This effect appears in surveys as well. In 2009 the College Senior Survey asked students how they rated their own abilities in various fields. The results perfectly illustrate the Dunning–Kruger effect. If correctly measured, half of the students should be above average (the median) and half of them below average. But the survey asked instead where the students thought they placed. These are the results comparing the percentage of those who thought they were below average compared to those who thought they were above average.[17] For example, 1% of the students thought

> One problem that comes with evaluating statistics is the so-called Dunning–Kruger effect, which has an unexpected twist: the people that are most competent at an ability actually underestimate how well they do compared to others.

they were below average in academic ability while 80% ranked themselves above average.

TABLE 1.1. STUDENTS' SELF-ASSESSMENT OF RANKING ON VARIOUS MEASURES

Subject	Students identifying themselves as below average (%)	Students identifying themselves as above average (%)
Academic ability	1.0	79.6
Computer skills	6.1	45.7
Cooperativeness	1.4	79.4
Creativity	6.0	60.3
Drive to achieve	2.3	79.4
Emotional health	7.7	55.9
Leadership ability	3.5	69.8
Mathematical ability	18.0	44.8
Physical health	7.8	54.2
Self-confidence (intellectual)	4.4	68.2
Self-confidence (social)	10.5	55.2
Self-understanding	2.4	68.8
Understanding of others	1.6	72.7
Writing ability	5.1	65.6

The large disparity between those who thought they were above average and those who thought they were below average demonstrates the tendency of humans to think we are doing better than we actually are.[18] This might explain why the estimates of first-year college students of their academic skills correspond with those of their instructors only 35% of the time. Of course, the students are not the only ones with this problem; 95% of college professors believe that they themselves do above-average work. "People's perceptions of their skills, knowledge, personality, and character often do not mesh with objective reality."[19] Although it has been argued that there is a rational reason for this effect,[20] it exists even when individuals are given direct evidence to the contrary.[21] They appear to be impervious to negative feedback.[22] "We appear to be blissfully gliding along, thinking we understand the world much better than we really do, in effect 'running on empty.'"[23] Individuals not only rate themselves better than they are but also think their friends are more capable and morally superior than is actually the case; conversely, they rate their enemies worse.[24]

The Dunning–Kruger effect also has an unexpected twist. The people that are most competent at an ability actually underestimate how well they do compared to others. "Participants in the top quartile tended to underestimate their ability and test performance relative to their peers. . . . These participants assumed that because they performed so well, their peers must have performed well likewise. This would have led top-quartile participants to underestimate their comparative abilities (i.e., how their general ability and test performance compare with that of their peers), but not their absolute abilities (i.e., their raw score on the test)."[25] This actually gives the competent a trait that looks something like humility.

Since expounded in 1999, the Dunning–Kruger effect has been invoked to explain a multitude of phenomena in a variety of different fields. It has been used to explain why people think they have more friends than they actually do,[26] why incompetent managers surround themselves with incompetent people to the detriment of the organization and the hindering of grassroots improvements,[27] why students overestimate their comprehension of readings,[28] why entrepreneurs overestimate both the potential and actual success of their ventures,[29] why people correctly detect lying less than half the time that they think they do,[30] the overconfidence of individuals in athletic competitions,[31] and the unintentional negative impact of peer reviewers and editors.[32] It has been linked to citizens "making strong political assertions in their social networks and resisting persuasive counterarguments."[33] It has been implicated in undermining the preservation of the environment because "conservationists can be overly confident that we are objective and we know best. Often we are not and we do not."[34] One of the more interesting results is that "people routinely overestimate how well they can communicate" in and understand writing. While people thought that they could accurately detect the tone of a written communication

89% of the time, they correctly did so only 56% of the time,[35] which means that they were only slightly better at doing so than they would have been if they had flipped a coin; essentially, they were guessing, but they thought they were making accurate assessments.

Part of the problem stems from optimism, which is connected with having hope. People are generally optimistic, "When thinking about their future, people are more likely to imagine positive than negative outcomes."[36] We like to think well of ourselves. We are the protagonists of our own stories and thus wish to see ourselves as the good people. "The views that people have of themselves tend to bear the tint of rose-colored glasses, arising from the human desire to think of themselves as capable, moral, and lovable human beings."[37] We need to see things as they really are. The problem with overconfidence is not counting our blessings or thinking on the bright side of things but rather letting our optimism cloud our vision of reality. "Optimism is nice, but not when it reaches delusional limits."[38]

The Dunning–Kruger effect also applies spiritually. A scriptural example of the effect is the attitude of Laman and Lemuel in the Book of Mormon: "We know that the people who were in the land of Jerusalem were a righteous people; for they kept the statutes and judgments of the Lord, and all his commandments, according to the law of Moses; wherefore, we know that they are a righteous people" (1 Nephi 17:22). These are the same people that their father, Lehi, condemned for their "wickedness and abominations" (1 Nephi 1:19) and of which Jeremiah said, "Ye all have transgressed against me, saith the Lord. . . . Your children . . . received no correction: your own sword hath devoured your prophets, like a destroying lion" (Jeremiah 2:29–30). Laman and Lemuel, like those at Jerusalem, overestimated their righteousness and that of their friends and were impervious to correction even when their inadequacy was pointed out to them.

Years before the Dunning–Kruger effect was described, Elder Joseph B. Wirthlin noted:

> Unfortunately, some in the Church may believe sincerely that their testimony is a raging bonfire when it really is little more than the faint flickering of a candle. Their faithfulness has more to do with habit than holiness, and their pursuit of personal righteousness

almost always takes a back seat to their pursuit of personal interests and pleasure. With such a feeble light of testimony for protection, these travelers on life's highways are easy prey for the wolves of the adversary. . . .

Some people are weak in their faith and testimonies but are not even aware of how precarious their situation is. Many of them likely would be offended at the suggestion. They raise their right hand to sustain Church leaders and then murmur and complain when a decision does not square with their way of thinking. They claim to be obedient to God's commandments but do not feel at all uncomfortable about purchasing food at the store on Sunday and then asking the Lord to bless it. Some say they would give their lives for the Lord, yet they refuse to serve in the nursery.

The Savior spoke very explicitly about people who "draw near me with their mouth, and with their lips do honour me, but have removed their heart far from me." (Isa. 29:13.) His words were: "Not every one that saith unto me, Lord, Lord, shall enter into the kingdom of heaven; but he that doeth the will of my Father which is in heaven.

"Many will say to me in that day, Lord, Lord, have we not prophesied in thy name? and in thy name have cast out devils? and in thy name done many wonderful works?

"And then will I profess unto them, I never knew you: depart from me, ye that work iniquity." (Matt. 7:21–23.)

None would want to hear the Lord speak such disappointing words of you. That is why you need to do everything in your power to be absolutely certain that your spiritual bonfire of testimony is burning brightly enough to keep the wolves of darkness away. You can always use more dry kindling.[39]

The Dunning–Kruger effect is alive and well among Latter-day Saints. This is one of the reasons we have interviews with someone else to assess our worthiness and are not allowed just to determine for ourselves if we are worthy. People have a tendency to think their self-assessments are more accurate that than other's assessments are.[40] President Hinckley once shared a story about that: "I recall a bishop telling me of a woman who came to get a recommend. When asked if she observed the Word of Wisdom, she said that she occasionally drank a cup of coffee. She said, 'Now, bishop, you're not going to let that keep me from going to the temple, are you?' To which he replied, 'Sister, surely you will not let a cup of coffee stand between you and the House of the Lord.'"[41]

This woman thought that she was doing better than she actually was and needed an outsider, in this case her bishop, to point it out to her. Since "one of the prerequisites of voluntary self-improvement is actually recognizing the need for improvement,"[42] it follows that no repentance or improvement can be made until the need to do so is not just understood but recognized. Getting a view of reality requires "setting aside storytelling and focusing instead on data."[43] For our purposes, this means looking at the available data rather than at narratives about youth leaving the Church in droves.

How Many in a Drove?

The problem of overoptimism also works the other way, as some are overoptimistic about the Church losing members. Returning to our original question, are youth leaving the Church in droves? Well, that depends. How many youth are in a drove? The English term *drove* referred to animals driven or the path along which they were driven and was metaphorically transferred to any crowd or multitude, especially when moving as a body.[44] Are youth mindless animals herded by adults and institutions or driven about by every wind of doctrine? This seems unlikely. Philology, then, does not tell us much in this case.

It is important to realize that the story about young people leaving the Church in droves is part of a particular narrative,[45] one that is largely untrue. Understanding this narrative is important to understanding what is really going on. The narrative about large numbers leaving the Church is often promoted by people who are somewhere in the process of leaving the Church. They may believe or hope that the narrative is true, but they promote it at least partially as a justification for their own actions. This narrative is also told not just about Latter-day Saints but about members of most faiths. For example, two researchers proclaimed that "however we measure it, every index of interest in, and the power of, religion in the industrial liberal democracies of the West shows decline."[46] There is a widespread belief among Americans that churches are on the way out; 55% of Americans believe churches are "declining" and 42% believe that they are "dying."[47]

A recent longitudinal analysis by the Gallup polling organization trumpeted that church membership in the United States was down over the last two decades but also noted that the general picture was not true of Latter-day Saints, "Membership in a place of worship has been stable among Mormons (near 90% in both time periods) and Jews (in the mid- to low 50% range in both time periods) over the past two decades."[48] The NSYR was actually started because of scare claims rampant in evangelical circles that young people were leaving their churches in droves for alternative religions.[49] The NSYR found that such scaremongering was not justified: "U.S. youth are not flocking in droves to 'alternative' religions and spiritualities such as paganism and Wicca."[50] Another study addressed the issue: *"Young people are leaving the churches in droves! This is so generally believed that nearly everything written about it in periodicals such as Christianity Today is to explain why the exodus is happening and what can be done to reverse the trend."*[51]

The original basis for this claim is supposed to have been a statistic from 1980 showing that people under the age of thirty were almost half as likely to attend church as those who were older, over the age of fifty.[52] Others have pointed to literature from 1971 that made the same argument, noting that only 28% of people in their twenties attended church on Sunday (which compares to 30% now).[53] Data collected later showed the same general pattern but no overall decline. Another longitudinal study that started surveying 18-year-olds in 1965 found that eight years later there was a 30% drop in regular church attendance across the board affecting all denominations, while simultaneously the number of individuals reporting adherence to no religion jumped almost eightfold. Nevertheless, at the next wave of the survey (1982), about half of those who had stopped attending church were regularly attending church again.[54] One researcher explained:

> The truth is that similar results can be found in practically any national survey ever conducted. Younger people, especially those under thirty, have *always been*, and probably will continue to be,

less likely than older Americans to attend church regularly. Why? Because they tend to be unmarried, to stay out late on Saturday night, and to prefer to sleep in on Sunday mornings. But, generation after generation, Americans have greatly increased their church attendance as they get married and have children.[55]

It would appear that the lack of attendance can, to some extent, be attributed to a stage of life that every generation goes through.[56] Thus "declines in religious service attendance among young adults are concentrated entirely among the unmarried."[57] There is more, however, to the leaving-in-droves narrative than that.

There is a "group of Western intellectuals who proclaim the inevitability of a worldwide triumph of *secularization*—the demise of beliefs in the supernatural, these being replaced by entirely material or secular beliefs. For them, secularization is an unshakable matter of faith."[58] Secularization was promoted by the founders of sociology.[59] It is thus not surprising that many social scientists hold these beliefs, and have done so since the end of World War II.[60] During the 1980s and 1990s there were vigorous arguments about secularization, which continue.[61] Social scientists in Europe assumed for many years that modernization promoted secularization.[62] Some, on strictly theoretical grounds, blamed secularization on the "political excommunication of religion," that not being able to bring religion into the public square was deleterious to religious belief.[63] It was part of a particular narrative promoted by social scientists, 61% of whom describe themselves as atheists.[64]

Social sciences, such as sociology, are part of "the modern project of reconstituting society on a rational, universal, secular basis."[65] At its heart, the social sciences had "self-consciously and intentionally displaced western Christianity's integrative and directive role in society." It "represents essentially a secularized version of the Christian gospel and worldview" and is "committed to spreading the 'good news,' as they see it, among those who are lost in darkness."[66] Religion can be replaced by regulation.[67] Some social scientists feel "compelled to fill in the sacred and eschatological void left in Christianity and Judaism's absence by constructing, embracing, and proselytizing the world with a secular salvation gospel of its own making."[68] They thus promote a story about how they think things ought to be, even when the evidence does not support it. They might claim, for example, that secularization is a universal assumption that any serious researcher would take for granted.[69] Others who wish that the narrative were true also support and promote it. Some within the discipline have noticed "the theoretical blinders supplied by secularization theories, blinders that took for granted the growing irrelevance of traditional religious institutions."[70] They argue that if we are to see things as they really are, these blinders need to be removed. Others claim that the secularization hypothesis is "useless"[71] or point out that the lack of confidence in religion is merely a reflection of a lack of confidence in institutions in general.[72] Thus the narrative of inevitable secularization must be more carefully examined.

> The lack of attendance can, to some extent, be attributed to a stage of life that every generation goes through.

Part of the narrative is the rise of the "nones"—those who associate themselves with no religion. The nones are actually not a homogenous group, but a cluster of related groups.[73] They may consider themselves "spiritual but not religious." For example, although almost four out of five graduating college seniors think it is important to integrate spirituality into their lives, only about one in four attended religious services frequently, and almost two in five never did, and fewer attended religious services by the end of their college careers than they did at the beginning.[74] "Though many students . . . profess an interest in 'spirituality,' most have no idea what to do about either spirituality and religion, or where to find the resources for living a more spiritual life."[75] Accordingly, one in fifteen graduating seniors lost their faith while in college.[76] The problem, however, started earlier.

A survey of "3,680 students at 50 colleges at the end of their first year revealed that religious involvement (attendance at religious services, participation in religious clubs, prayer and meditation) had declined noticeably over the course of the school year" while the students "expressed more commitment to integrating spirituality into their own lives," indicating "a disturbing disconnect between students' expectations for their lives and reality." All told, "nearly two-thirds

(63 percent) of the students indicated that their religious or spiritual beliefs had been strengthened during the freshman year, even though more than 90 percent said their religious activity had decreased to some degree."[77] How do we explain the obvious disconnect between the students' claims and their behavior?

The disconnect between claims and behavior has been explained this way: "The world most [people] inhabit is both spiritual and religious at the same time,"[78] but "nonaffiliates and non-attenders . . . often used the language of 'spiritual but not religious' to describe themselves."[79] They borrow this language from certain conservative Protestants for whom "empty 'religion' is rejected in favor of deep personal 'spirituality.'"[80] Conservative Protestants use this language because they believe salvation is a personal affair (marked by spirituality) that is independent of a church (representing religion). Those who neither attend nor affiliate with a church borrow this language to represent "a cultural rhetorical linking religiosity to hypocrisy and empty ritual while claiming that a good and caring life is the best form of spiritual connection."[81]

"What is appealing about 'spirituality' as opposed to 'religion' is precisely that it is undefined—spirituality appears to be a symbolic label adopted to free oneself from the moral obligations and rituals of tradition."[82] This sets up a schism in the use of language: "The irony, of course, is that most of the unaffiliated or nonparticipating people who claim spirituality as a positive alternative to religion are themselves neither. So who really fits the 'spiritual not religious' label? In one case it is used to describe people who are very pious and very active in their churches (conservative Protestants); and in another, it is used to describe a hypothetical distinction between two categories, neither of which apply to the person making the distinction."[83] The NSYR data support this argument. Those most likely to use the term are (in order of likelihood) minority religions, the nonreligious, and Protestants. Latter-day Saints are the least likely by far to apply the phrase "spiritual but not religious" to themselves.[84]

Thus when college students are claiming that their spirituality increased while their actual participation decreased, they "are equating 'religion' to the implausible beliefs and discredited institutions they have rejected. They are claiming 'spirituality' as a reasonably positive and generic category and one that each individual can fill with the content of her own choosing."[85] For them, the term *spiritual* thus becomes a generic positive category with no specific content. For many, "spirituality remains something of an unexamined black box—simply whatever religion isn't."[86] For others the term simply lacks meaning. One study reported that when they asked individuals if they were spiritual, they got responses like, "I haven't given it a thought. What do you mean when you say 'spiritual'?"[87] or, "Actually the word 'spiritual,' I'm not sure. I don't know how to analyze. . . . Well, I don't know. I don't know how to answer that."[88] Scholars are also confused about what the term *spiritual* means.[89] Thus one researcher notes that most young adults who identify "primarily as spiritual often do little more than disassociate themselves from a religious upbringing that they now find oppressive—a way to wash away dogma and doctrine or what they regard as the fictional Santa Claus–like God of their parents, while at the same time retaining some affinity, however vague, with Meaning (whatever that is)."[90]

One facet lost in the discussion of the nones is that those youth who do not leave their religion tend to be more faithful. "Religious young people, even though they may be increasingly in the minority, tend to resist calls for secularist-oriented social relationships and have been crucial to revitalization efforts in many nations. They may have diminished in relative numbers, but these young people have been influential in calling for a return to, or increase in, religion to the public square, in conservative religious political mobilization, and in interfaith conflicts." What the rise of the nones reflects is "a growing divide between younger cohorts who participate in religious organizations and those who do not."[91] Others have argued that the rise of the nones "may result partly from long-term increases in divorce and their impact on intergenerational solidarity and religious formation."[92]

There is some support for the narrative, but its extent is exaggerated. About 27% of Latter-day Saint young adults consider themselves at least somewhat spiritual but not religious, whatever that may mean to them, but only 8% strongly think the label applies to them.[93] This is up from about 3% of Latter-day Saint teenagers.[94] The narrative does not accurately describe the big picture. The facts are also more complicated than the narrative suggests. The faith in secularization exists in spite of the evidence, not because of it. Since this narrative drives some sociological work,[95] it is worth being aware of how it might influence the gathering and analysis of statistics and how it might play into discussions of youth losing faith. One sociologist of religion recommends to churches that "they should listen carefully to the conclusion of scholars that have given time and energy to understanding this situation better, bearing in mind that even the best-intentioned of the latter are not always 'right.' At the same time, such providers—together with the scholars who study them—should do all that they can to correct the distortions that all too often dominate public discussion in this field."[96]

More Good than Bad

The prevalence of a particular narrative about youth leaving the Church obscures a more important and more optimistic story. The truth of the matter is that we do lose some of our youth, certainly more than we would like. If you have lost anyone in your family, then you will feel that this is already too many. But we hold on to more of our youth than anyone else, even the secularists. There actually are a number of things we as a church are doing right, and these things appear when we start sifting through the data.

The results of the National Study of Youth and Religion[97] on how many youth keep their faith may be found in table 1.2. The first column of numbers represents the percentage of youth in high school who belong to the same religion as their parents. The second column represents those who kept their high school religion during their college-age years (whether or not they actually went to college). The third column is a multiplication of those two percentages that gives the number of young adults who were raised in a religion that still belong to that religion in college years. The fourth number represents those in their college years who attend regularly. The fifth column is the number of those belonging to a particular religion that are in the devoted category in their college years. That means they are attending church every week, praying on a regular basis, and reading their scriptures at least once a month. The first, second, and fifth numbers are from the NSYR and the third and fourth numbers are calculated from NSYR data. The various religions are ranked in descending order based on what percentage of young adults were still members in their college-age years (third column).

TABLE 1.2. YOUTH RETENTION IN VARIOUS RELIGIONS OVER TIME

	High school youth in same religion as parents (%)	College-age youth maintaining high school religion (%)	College-age youth keeping faith of childhood (%)	Regular attenders of college age (%)	Devoted college-age members (%)
Latter-day Saint	86	72	62	71	56
Conservative Protestant	86	64	55	34	15
Roman Catholic	83	66	53	21	2
Jewish	75	61	46	11	7
Black Protestant	81	55	43	19	6
Nonreligious	63	68	43	1	0
Other religion	57	72	41	25	15
Mainline Protestant	68	50	34	25	7
Indeterminate	45	10	5	21	5

The bad news is that Latter-day Saints lose one in seven youth in high school and about twice as many in college. All told, we lose just over one-third of the youth by the time they are through with college. This is comparable with the results of the Pew Religious Landscape Survey.[98] Almost half of those are potentially in trouble since they are not devoted.

But the bad news cuts across the board. All religions are losing a substantial portion of their youth and young adults. Only Latter-day Saints, conservative Protestants, and Catholics are managing to retain more than half of them. Even if they keep them on the rolls, no religion other than Latter-day Saints can keep more than a third of their young adults in the pews.

But one should notice that the story is not that all of these young adults are becoming atheists. Even the nonreligious lose more than half of their youth and young adults to some *faith*. The picture is much more complicated than we might simplistically think.

We bring in the other religions mainly as a comparison. I sincerely wish other religions were doing better. Our concern is with Latter-day Saints and our youth and young adult retention, not with how other religions are doing. As one observer reminded her fellow Christians, "Christian teenagers also have these [same] cultural tools at their disposal [as Latter-day Saint teenagers], but the terms for their use are very different," because "at some point, a peculiar God-story must *set the terms* for how teenagers use religion's cultural tools."[99] Our concern is with how we can keep our youth and young adults. We have the same cultural tools at our disposal as other Latter-day Saints in our branches, wards, and stakes. How can we more effectively use them?

The good news is that of those who stay Latter-day Saint, over half are in the devoted category and almost three quarters are regular attenders. We have proportionately almost four times as many devoted young adults as the next closest religion, and over twice as many regular attenders. One NSYR researcher termed Latter-day Saint youth as "the disproportionately devoted."[100] We keep more of our young people than any other religion. Fewer of our college-age young adults are vulnerable than those in other religions. In fact, the authors of the NSYR put it this way: "In general comparisons among major U.S. religious traditions using a variety of sociological measures of religious vitality and salience . . . it is Mormon teenagers who are sociologically faring the best."[101]

Why this is so does not necessarily reduce to a simple formula even if there are a few basic things that explain a great deal; some simplified explanations put forth for Latter-day Saints' success fall short of verification.[102] One evangelical researcher said, "It may be difficult for a 'gentile' or non-Mormon to read Mormon views on God, community, vocation, and eschatology without raising an eyebrow—but it is just as difficult to read the data on Mormon teenagers without feeling a hint of awe."[103] While "the majority of U.S. teens would badly fail a hypothetical short-answer or essay test of the basic beliefs of their religion," Latter-day Saint youth "seem somewhat better able to explain the basic outlook and beliefs of their tradition."[104]

A different study of emerging adults concluded that "Mormons scored higher on [intrinsic religiosity] than did Catholics or non-Catholic Christians."[105] This study concluded that the differences between the groups were a direct result of what was being taught—"people practice what is preached."[106] Another study of students at Latter-day Saint, Catholic, and secular universities found that "Mormons put stronger emphasis on the criteria for adulthood in the areas of interdependence, norm compliance, biological transitions, and family capacities. They also perceived themselves as having achieved the requisite criteria for adulthood to a greater extent than their peers in the areas of independence, interdependence, norm compliance, and family capacities. Furthermore, Mormons rated themselves higher on every variable aimed at assessing spirituality. Finally, Mormons reported engaging in very few behaviors typical of emerging adulthood (i.e., becoming drunk, drug use)." In short, "Mormon emerging adults appear far more likely to become adults who are in greater accordance with their religious doctrine" than their secular or Catholic peers.[107] Any assessment of how the Church is doing on retaining its young people needs to account for the fact that we have been doing some things right—perhaps many things. It is not a matter of things not working—they clearly are; our youth retention statistics are the envy of all the other faiths (one of the NSYR books even has a chapter entitled "Mormon Envy")[108]—but of things not working as well as they might. We are hardly perfect, but we are doing better than we might think.

What we are doing right is easier to see when we recognize where the danger lies, but in order to identify the dangers, we need to dive deeper into the data. It is to that topic that we now turn.

NOTES

1.   The claim has been repeated. For example, Rick Phillips, Ryan T. Cragun, and Barry A. Kosmin, "Increasing Sex Ratio Imbalance among Utah Mormons: Sources and Implications," *Interdisciplinary Journal of Research on Religion* 11, no. 12 (2015): 10.

2. As it happens, the transcript of the remarks shows that he did not say that. Someone else claimed that in a question put to him. There are good reasons for instructions in *Handbook 2: Administering the Church* (Salt Lake City: The Church of Jesus Christ of Latter-day Saints, 2018), §21.1.39, available at churchofjesuschrist.org.

3. Quentin L. Cook, "The Lord Is My Light," *Ensign*, May 2015, 65.

4. I was able to take advantage of the stored data available on the Association of Religion Data Archives (www.thearda.com) to do some analyses of the data that are not available in the publications. Citations to my own analysis of the data are cited as NSYR data, and I note which wave of the data my analysis comes from.

5. Some researchers complain about this. See, for example, Phillips, Cragun, and Kosmin, "Increasing Sex Ratio Imbalance," 6; and William S. Bradshaw Tim B. Heaton, Ellen Decoo, John P. Dehlin, Renee V. Galliher, and Katherine A. Crowell, "Religious Experiences of GBTQ Mormon Males," *Journal for the Scientific Study of Religion* 54, no. 2 (2015): 315. For information on the Church's Correlation Research Division, see *Handbook 2*, §21.1.35.

6. It appears that the total number of Latter-day Saints in the NSYR was 47; see Jonathan P. Hill, "Rejecting Evolution: The Role of Religion, Education, and Social Networks," *Journal for the Scientific Study of Religion* 53, no. 3 (2014): 584.

7. Philip B. Mason, Xiaohe Xu, and John P. Bartkowski, "The Risk of Overweight and Obesity among Latter-Day Saints," *Review of Religious Research* 55, no. 1 (2013): 131–47.

8. Cited in P. Kyle McCarter, *Textual Criticism: Recovering the Text of the Hebrew Bible* (Philadelphia: Fortress, 1986), 19.

9. Christian Smith and Hilary Davidson, *The Paradox of Generosity* (Oxford: Oxford University Press, 2014), 94.

10. Nancy T. Ammerman, "Spiritual but Not Religious: Beyond Binary Choices in the Study of Religion," *Journal for the Scientific Study of Religion* 52, no. 2 (2013): 271.

11. Mark D. Regnerus and Jeremy E. Uecker, "Religious Influences on Sensitive Self-Reported Behaviors: The Product of Social Desirability, Deceit, or Embarrassment?," *Sociology of Religion* 68, no. 2 (2007): 152, 153–55.

12. Regnerus and Uecker, "Religious Influences on Sensitive Self-Reported Behaviors," 158 n. 8; emphasis in original.

13. This problem affects survey data collected by Michael Quinn, John Dehlin, and Jana Riess.

14. Justin Kruger and David Dunning, "Unskilled and Unaware of It: How Difficulties in Recognizing One's Own Incompetence Lead to Inflated Self-Assessments," *Journal of Personality and Social Psychology* 77, no. 6 (1999): 1121–34.

15. Gordon Pennycook, Robert M. Ross, Derek J. Koehler, and Jonathan A. Fugelsang, "Dunning–Kruger Effects in Reasoning: Theoretical Implications of the Failure to Recognize Incompetence," *Psychonomic Bulletin and Review* 24 (2017): 1774–84; Ulrike Malmendier and Timothy Taylor, "On the Verges of Overconfidence," *Journal of Economic Perspectives* 29, no. 4 (2015): 3–4.

16. Kruger and Dunning, "Unskilled and Unaware of It," 1130.

17. Data from Ray Franke, Sylvia Ruiz, Jessica Sharkness, Linda DeAngelo, and John Pryor, *Findings from the 2009 Administration of the College Senior Survey (CSS): National Aggregates* (Los Angeles: Higher Education Research Institute, University of California, Los Angeles, 2010), 97–99. The number of those who thought they were average has been dropped but can be calculated from the table. The important point is the great disparity between those who think they are above average and those who do not.

18. David Dunning, "A Newer Look: Motivated Social Cognition and the Schematic Representation of Social Concepts," *Psychological Inquiry* 10, no. 1 (1999): 1–11; Constantine Sedikides and Aiden P. Gregg, "Self-Enhancement: Food for Thought," *Perspectives on Psychological Science* 3, no. 2 (2008): 102–16; David Dunning, Chip Heath, and Jerry M. Suls, "Flawed Self-Assessment: Implications for Health, Education, and the Workplace," *Psychological Science in the Public Interest* 5, no. 3 (2004): 72.

19. Dunning, Heath, and Suls, "Flawed Self-Assessment," 71, 72, 70.

20. Jean-Pierre Benoît and Juan Dubra, "Apparent Overconfidence," *Econometrica* 79, no. 5 (2011): 1591–625. But note this telling caveat (p. 1606): "Some psychologists and behavioral economists may be uneasy with our approach on the prior grounds that individuals do not use Bayes' rule and, for that matter, may not even understand simple probability."

21. Daniel J. Simons, "Unskilled and Optimistic: Overconfident Predictions Despite Calibrated Knowledge of Relative Skill," *Psychonomic Bulletin and Review* 20 (2013): 601–7.

22. Kruger and Dunning, "Unskilled and Unaware of It," 1130.

23. Frank C. Keil, "Running on Empty? How Folk Science Gets By with Less," *Current Directions in Psychological Science* 21, no. 5 (2012): 329.

24. John R. Chambers, "Why the Parts Are Better (or Worse) Than the Whole: The Unique-Attributes Hypothesis," *Psychological Science* 21, no. 2 (2010): 268–75; Sedikides and Gregg, "Self-Enhancement," 106–7.

25. Kruger and Dunning, "Unskilled and Unaware of It," 1131; Pennycook et al., "Dunning–Kruger Effects in Reasoning," 1774–84.

26. Ezra W. Zuckerman and John T. Jost, "What Makes You Think You're So Popular? Self-Evaluation Maintenance and the Subjective Side of the 'Friendship Paradox,'" *Social Psychology Quarterly* 64, no. 3 (2001): 207–23.

27. Andrew B. Crittenden, Victoria L. Crittenden, and William F. Crittenden, "The Contagion of Trickle-down Incompetence," *Industrial Management* 59, no. 5 (September/October 2017): 12.

28. Dunning, Heath, and Suls, "Flawed Self-Assessment," 87.

29. Gavin Cassar, "Are Individuals Entering Self-Employment Overly Optimistic? An Empirical Test of Plans and Projections on Nascent Entrepreneur Expectations," *Strategic Management Journal* 31, no. 8 (2010): 822–40; Dunning, Heath, and Suls, "Flawed Self-Assessment," 72; Mathew L. A. Hayward, Dean A. Shepherd, and Dale Griffin, "A Hubris Theory of Entrepreneurship," *Management Science* 52, no. 2 (2006): 160–72.

30. Dunning, Heath, and Suls, "Flawed Self-Assessment," 71.

31. Simons, "Unskilled and Optimistic," 601–7; Dunning, Heath, and Suls, "Flawed Self-Assessment," 71.

32. Arthur G. Bedeian, "Peer Review and the Social Construction of Knowledge in the Management Discipline," *Academy of Management Learning & Education* 3, no. 2 (2004): 198–216; compare Dunning, Heath, and Suls, "Flawed Self-Assessment," 90.

33. Ian G. Anson, "Partisanship, Political Knowledge, and the Dunning–Kruger Effect," *Political Psychology* 39, no. 5 (2018): 1174.

34. Douglas Sheil and Erik Meijaard, "Purity and Prejudice: Deluding Ourselves about Biodiversity Conservation," *Biotropica* 42, no. 5 (2010): 566.

35. Justin Kruger, Nicholas Epley, Jason Parker, and Zhi-Wen Ng, "Egocentrism over E-Mail: Can We Communicate as Well as We Think?," *Journal of Personality and Social Psychology* 89, no. 6 (2005): 926, 928.

36. Simons, "Unskilled and Optimistic," 606; Sedikides and Gregg, "Self-Enhancement," 104.

37. Dunning, "Newer Look," 1.

38. Mark Bauerlein, *The Dumbest Generation: How the Digital Age Stupefies Young Americans and Jeopardizes Our Future* (New York: TarcherPerigree, 2009), 195–96.

39. Joseph B. Wirthlin, "Spiritual Bonfires of Testimony," *Ensign*, November 1992, 34–35. My thanks to James Harrop for bringing this talk to my attention.

40. Dunning, Heath, and Suls, "Flawed Self-Assessment," 72; Simine Vazire and Erika N. Carlson, "Others Sometimes Know Us Better Than We Know Ourselves," *Current Directions in Psychological Science* 20, no. 2 (2011): 104–8.

41. Gordon B. Hinckley, "Keeping the Temple Holy," *Ensign*, May 1990, 51.

42. Pennycook et al., "Dunning–Kruger Effects in Reasoning," 1774.

43. David Dunning, Chip Heath, and Jerry M. Suls, "Picture Imperfect," *Scientific American Mind* 16, no. 4 (2005): 20–27.

44. *Oxford English Dictionary*, s.v. "drove."

45. Phillips, Cragun, and Kosmin, "Increasing Sex Ratio Imbalance," 9–12.

46. Marta Trzebiatowska and Steve Bruce, *Why Are Women More Religious Than Men?* (Oxford: Oxford University Press, 2012), 149.

47. *American Views on Church Attendance* (Nashville: LifeWay Research, 2015), 5.

48. Jeffrey M. Jones, "U.S. Church Membership Down Sharply in Past Two Decades," https://news.gallup.com/poll/248837/church-membership -down-sharply-past-two-decades.aspx.

49. Christian Smith and Melinda Lundquist Denton, *Soul Searching: The Religious and Spiritual Lives of American Teenagers* (Oxford: Oxford University Press, 2005), 5, 311–13.

50. Smith and Denton, *Soul Searching*, 31.

51. Rodney Stark, *The Triumph of Faith* (Wilmington, DE: ISI Books, 2015), 188.

52. Stark, *Triumph of Faith*, 188.

53. *Relationships in America Survey* (Austin, TX: The Austin Institute for the Study of Family and Culture, 2014), 10.

54. Michele F. Margolis, *From Politics to the Pews: How Partisanship and the Political Environment Shape Religious Identity* (Chicago: University of Chicago Press, 2018), 67–71, 79–80.

55. Stark, *Triumph of Faith*, 188; *Relationships in America Survey*, 10.

56. Vern L. Bengtson, Merril Silverstein, Norella M. Putney, and Susan C. Harris, "Does Religiousness Increase with Age? Age Changes and Generational Differences over 35 Years," *Journal of the Scientific Study of Religion* 54, no. 2 (2015): 364; Carolyn McNamara Barry and Larry J. Nelson, "The Role of Religion in the Transition to Adulthood for Young Emerging Adults," *Journal of Youth and Adolescence* 34, no. 3 (2005): 247; Phil Davignon, "The Effects of R-Rated Movies on Adolescent and Young Adult Religiosity: Media as Self-Socialization," *Review of Religious Research* 55, no. 4 (2013): 616.

57. Jeremy E. Uecker, Damon Mayrl, and Samuel Stroope, "Family Formation and Returning to Institutional Religion in Young Adulthood," *Journal of the Scientific Study of Religion* 55, no. 2 (2016): 385.

58. Stark, *Triumph of Faith*, 2.

59. Niklas Luhmann, *Die Religion der Gesellschaft* (Frankfurt: Suhrkamp, 2002), 278; Rick Phillips, "Can Rising Rates of Church Participation Be a Consequence of Secularization?," *Sociology of Religion* 65, no. 2 (2004): 140; Emily Sigalow, Michelle Shain, and Meredith R. Bergey, "Religion and Decisions about Marriage, Residence, Occupation, and Children," *Journal for the Scientific Study of Religion* 51, no. 2 (2012): 305.

60. Stark, *Triumph of Faith*, 5; Luhmann, *Die Religion der Gesellschaft*, 278; Neil Gross and Solon Simmons, "The Religiosity of American College and University Professors," *Sociology of Religion* 70, no. 2 (2009): 101–2.

61. John P. Hoffmann, "Declining Religious Authority? Confidence in the Leaders of Religious Organizations, 1973–2010," *Review of Religious Research* 55, no. 1 (2013): 2–3.

62. Grace Davie, "Thinking Sociologically about Religion: Implications for Faith Communities," *Review of Religious Research* 54, no. 3 (2012): 278, 279; Detlef Pollack, "La théorie de la sécularisation au banc d'essai," *Archives de sciences sociales des religions* 167 (2014): 147.

63. Jean-Marc Ferry, "Conviction religieuse et responsabilité politique: La question d'une implication des religions dans nos espaces publics," *Archives de sciences sociales des religions* 169 (2015): 107.

64. Neil Gross and Solon Simmons, "The Religious Convictions of College and University Professors," in *The American University in a Postsecular Age*, ed. Douglas Jacobsen and Rhonda Hustedt Jacobsen (Oxford: Oxford University Press, 2008), 24.

65. Christian Smith, *The Sacred Project of American Sociology* (Oxford: Oxford University Press, 2014), 119–20.

66. Smith, *Sacred Project of American Sociology*, 122, 18, 20.

67. Ferry, "Conviction religieuse et responsabilité politique," 109.

68. Smith, *Sacred Project of American Sociology*, 20.

69. Stark, *Triumph of Faith*, 8.

70. Ammerman, "Spiritual but Not Religious," 276.

71. Luhmann, *Die Religion der Gesellschaft*, 278–79; Pollack, "La théorie de la sécularisation au banc d'essai," 147.

72. Hoffmann, "Declining Religious Authority?," 21–22.

73. *Relationships in America Survey*, 6.

74. Franke et al., *Findings from the 2009 Administration of the College Senior Survey*, 71, 64, 94.

75. Donna Freitas, *Sex and the Soul: Juggling Sexuality, Spirituality, Romance, and Religion on America's College Campuses* (Oxford: Oxford University Press, 2008), 26; page numbers for this book refer to the electronic version.

76. Franke et al., *Findings from the 2009 Administration of the College Senior Survey*, 91.

77. Larry A. Braskamp, "Religious and Spiritual Journeys of College Students," in Jacobsen and Jacobsen, *American University in a Postsecular Age*, 127; Barry and Nelson, "Role of Religion," 246, 128.

78. Nancy T. Ammerman, *Sacred Stories, Spiritual Tribes: Finding Religion in Everyday Life* (Oxford: Oxford University Press, 2014), 49; Ammerman, "Spiritual but Not Religious," 259, 273–74.

79. Ammerman, *Sacred Stories, Spiritual Tribes*, 49.

80. Ammerman, *Sacred Stories, Spiritual Tribes*, 50; Freitas, *Sex and the Soul*, 152.

81. Ammerman, *Sacred Stories, Spiritual Tribes*, 50.

82. Freitas, *Sex and the Soul*, 26.

83. Ammerman, *Sacred Stories, Spiritual Tribes*, 50; Ammerman, "Spiritual but Not Religious," 275; Freitas, *Sex and the Soul*, 43.

84. NSYR wave 3 data.

85. Ammerman, *Sacred Stories, Spiritual Tribes*, 51.

86. Ammerman, "Spiritual but Not Religious," 260; Bengtson et al., "Does Religiousness Increase with Age?," 373.

87. Bengtson et al., "Does Religiousness Increase with Age?," 372; compare Freitas, *Sex and the Soul*, 43–44.

88. Bengtson et al., "Does Religiousness Increase with Age?," 372.

89. Adam B. Cohen, June Gruber, and Dacher Keltner, "Comparing Spiritual Transformations and Experiences of Profound Beauty," *Psychology of Religion and Spirituality* 2, no. 3 (2010): 127.

90. Freitas, *Sex and the Soul*, 36.

91. Hoffmann, "Declining Religious Authority?," 21, 22.

92. Christopher G. Ellison, Anthony B. Walker, Norval D. Glenn, and Elizabeth Marquardt, "The Effects of Parental Marital Discord and Divorce on the Religious and Spiritual Lives of Young Adults," *Social Science Research* 40 (2011): 549.

93. NSYR wave 3 data.

94. NSYR wave 1 data.

95. For example, Jana Riess, *The Next Mormons: How Millennials Are Changing the LDS Church* (Oxford: Oxford University Press, 2019).

96. Davie, "Thinking Sociologically about Religion," 288.

97. From Smith and Denton, *Soul Searching*, 36; and Christian Smith and Patricia Snell, *Souls in Transition: The Religious and Spiritual Lives of Emerging Adults* (Oxford: Oxford University Press, 2009), 109, 304.

98. Stephen Cranney, "Who Is Leaving the Church? Demographic Predictors of Ex–Latter-day Saint Status in the Pew Religious Landscape Survey," *BYU Studies* 58, no. 1 (2019): 100–101.

99. Kenda Creasy Dean, *Almost Christian: What the Faith of Our Teenagers Is Telling the American Church* (Oxford: Oxford University Press, 2010), 60.

100. Dean, *Almost Christian*, 46.

101. Smith and Denton, *Soul Searching*, 261.

102. For example, Joshua Hart and Christopher F. Chabris, "Does a 'Triple Package' of Traits Predict Success?," *Personality and Individual Differences* 94 (2016): 216–22.

103. Dean, *Almost Christian*, 59.

104. Smith and Denton, *Soul Searching*, 137.

105. Kathryn A. Johnson, Adam B. Cohen, and Morris A. Okun, "Intrinsic Religiosity and Volunteering during Emerging Adulthood: A Comparison of Mormons with Catholics and Non-Catholic Christians," *Journal for the Scientific Study of Religion* 52, no. 4 (2013): 848.

106. Johnson, Cohen, and Okun, "Intrinsic Religiosity and Volunteering," 850.

107. Barry and Nelson, "Role of Religion," 253.

108. Dean, *Almost Christian*, 45–60.

2 | **WHITHER THEY WANDER**

PHANTOM MENACES

As with many scientific inquiries, the National Study of Youth and Religion had a number of assumptions and hypotheses when they started out about why youth might keep their faith, many of which turned out to be wrong.

One might suppose, for example, that if the youth simply believe strongly enough, then that belief will carry them through the trials of their faith. What we would need if that were the case are youth who are firm in the faith and as fervent as Nephi. Unfortunately, how fervently youth believed as teenagers seems to have little effect on whether they believed as young adults.[1] This situation has historical precedents. King Benjamin's people said that "the Spirit of the Lord Omnipotent . . . has wrought a mighty change in us, or in our hearts, that we have no more disposition to do evil, but to do good continually" (Mosiah 5:2). There is no question that these people strongly believed. And yet a few years later, many of those who were present as children "did not believe the tradition of their fathers. They did not believe what had been said concerning the resurrection of the dead, neither did they believe concerning the coming of Christ. And now because of their unbelief they could not understand the word of God; and their hearts were hardened. And they would not be bap-

tized; neither would they join the church. And they were a separate people as to their faith, and remained so ever after, even in their carnal and sinful state" (Mosiah 26:1–4).

Perhaps it is simply a matter of socialization. If that were the case, we would need the youth to band together and make friends with those in their classes. Friendship would carry them through.[2] This might not be the case, however. "We should not be too quick to assume that possessing positive illusions about our friends will be beneficial."[3] The Book of Mormon notes the evils that come from "friends in iniquity" (Mosiah 29:22) and that friends can also abandon one who takes a stand for truth (Alma 15:16) or can "combine against all righteousness" (3 Nephi 6:27–28; 7:6). In the Book of Mormon friendship has a rather ambiguous effect when it comes to promoting faithfulness. This ambiguity also appears in sociology. Whether youth liked the other youth in their classes and quorums does not predict commitment as a young adult.[4] This is probably a good thing since only 71% of Latter-day Saint youth like their youth group[5] and only 62% of the friends of Latter-day Saint young adults are themselves Latter-day Saints.[6] These friends may or may not be a good influence.

As the New Testament warns: "Know ye not that the friendship of the world is enmity with God? whosoever therefore will be a friend of the world is the enemy of God" (James 4:4). This is not to say that we cannot make friends with those in the world but rather that it would be a mistake to try to make friends with the world and surrender our faith or our standards to do so. Moroni serves as an example of someone who was faithful in spite of not having "friends nor whither to go" (Mormon 8:5). Other studies have found that having religious friends made absolutely no difference in youth doing things that were against their

Whether youth like the other youth at church does not predict religious commitment later as a young adult. Courtesy of Cheryl Holt/Pixabay.

religion.[7] Still other research suggests that including one bad friend can drag down the entire group of friends and tends to make problems worse,[8] supporting the "friends-in-iniquity" effect. "If an individual's friends would go along in breaking a norm, this strongly increases the chances that the individual in question will break a norm, and vice versa. Social embeddedness per se tells us nothing, it depends on the group the individual is embedded in."[9] The effects can happen quickly; a bad friend, like bad leaders, can be "a poison that can negatively influence behaviors of all those who come into contact with it, and it can spread rather rapidly."[10] Remember also that people tend to think their friends are better than they actually are.[11]

Perhaps immersion in Church activities is the answer. More and better Church activities will keep the youth occupied. There is some partial truth in this. While frequent Church attendance correlated strongly with religiosity, participation in a great number of additional

Church-related activities did not.[12] There is thus no particular reason for Church activities to take up all of one's time.

Perhaps attending a special Latter-day Saint high school with custom curriculum would train youth in such a way that they remain faithful throughout their lives. Faithfulness would simply be a matter of proper indoctrination. This also appears to be an illusion. Attending a religious high school also seemed to make little difference when youth grew up.[13] Seminary attendance, which provides a religious element in an otherwise secular scholastic curriculum, is not the same thing as a religious high school. A study of Latter-day Saints using a nonrepresentative sample concluded that youth who attended four years of seminary and attended Church regularly were 33% more likely to be members in adulthood.[14] Of these two variables, however, Church attendance is more important since in that study seminary attendance alone appeared to make no difference.

> This is not to minimize the importance of fervently believing, having good friends, participating in Church activities, or having religious instruction in school.

This is not to minimize the importance of fervently believing, having good friends, participating in Church activities, or having religious instruction in school. For some youth, one of these things might make all the difference in their life. I know some for whom it has. While any one of these factors might be important for a particular youth, they do not normally predict a youth's faith down the road. Sometimes a youth's faith changes.

APOSTASY AND CONVERSION

According to some studies, about 44% of Americans will adopt a religious affiliation different from that of their parents.[15] They will formally convert from one denomination to another. The process can occur at any stage of life. Even among the elderly about a quarter (27%) will change religious affiliation.[16] The NSYR puts the number of young Americans who convert as higher, with 45–66% of youth and young adults (depending on the denomination) converting to another denomination. Youth would seem to be more likely to change religions than those of older generations. As we saw in the last chapter, Latter-day Saint youth are less likely than that to convert.

We, however, are concerned with Latter-day Saint youth. We are interested in what happens to them if they leave the Church. Among those who leave, we can make a distinction between those who apostatize from the Church and those who convert to another religion. From a relativistic perspective, conversion and apostasy are taken to be different sides of the same coin: conversion to one religion is apostasy from another. But this relativistic viewpoint is actually not the case. In one study looking at sudden changes in the religiosity of youth, the researchers were interested in what happens when youth are converted or lose their faith. They wanted to know the sociologically contributing factors to this process, and they found that the two phenomena, apostasy and conversion, were not the same and that different factors contributed to the different processes. "Thus it may be helpful to think of positive religious transformation and conversions (involving sharp growth in religiosity) and religious apostasy (i.e., losing religion) as two separate entities, each with its own set of mechanisms and patterns. The presence of the one has little in common with the absence of the other."[17] Thus, from a sociological perspective, conversion and apostasy do not look the same either in their causes or their outcomes, even though the relativistic perspective says that they should.

Using data from the first two waves of the National Longitudinal Study of Adolescent to Adult Health (Add Health), the researchers were able to say the following about sudden religious conversions. First of all, "There is no clear religious 'hot spot' during adolescence, although age 18 appears to be the most active or unstable age for both directions of considerable religious change. A larger percentage of these oldest respondents exhibited both considerable growth and decline when compared with other youth of younger ages."[18] (We will return to this point later.)

Apparently, how religious one's peers or parents are does not impact religious conversion. Behavior also does not seem to play much of a role: "Family and behavioral effects tend to receive considerable attention. Yet their effects here are largely absent, save for an association with greater family satisfaction."[19] In this age group, demographic

Age 18 is an active or unstable time of religious change for adolescents. Courtesy of Ernesto Eslava/Pixabay.

factors play a more important role than behavioral factors in conversion. Behavioral factors play a greater role in losing faith than demographic ones. In other words, who one *is* plays a more important role in conversion, but what one *does* plays a bigger role in apostasy. Since the data used in the study were originally gathered as part of a study on factors influencing health, they are fairly blunt instruments; thus the researchers warn that "these data do not capture all aspects of adolescent religious transformation."[20] These studies predict general trends of the masses. They do not dictate the particular path of individuals. Finding faith and losing faith are complex individual processes and these studies simply highlight important factors contributing to the decisions of individual souls.

WHERE ARE THEY GOING?

In the previous chapter I used data from the NSYR to address the issue of how many youth the Church is losing. The NSYR provides data on how many we keep but also on what happens to those we lose.

I will present the data in tabular form. The first column gives, in percentage, the religious affiliation in high school years of those who were raised as Latter-day Saints.[21] The second column represents the religious affiliation of high school Latter-day Saints in the next wave of the study when many of those high school students had moved on to their college years.[22] The third column is the calculated percentage of those who were Latter-day Saints as children and then changed by the time they were in their college years.

TABLE 2.1. RELIGION OF YOUTH GROWING UP IN LATTER-DAY SAINT FAMILIES AT VARIOUS STAGES OF THEIR LIVES

	Religious affiliation in high school (%)	Religious affiliation in college years compared to high school years (%)	Religious affiliation in college years compared to childhood years (%)*
Latter-day Saint	86	72	62
No Religion	13	17	28
Conservative Protestant	1	3	4
Mainline Protestant	0	4	3
Black Protestant	0	3	3
Indeterminate	0	1	1
Roman Catholic	0	0	0
Jewish	0	0	0
Other Religions	0	0	0

* The figures in the third column are calculated by multiplying the number in the second column by the percentage of Latter-day Saints in high school (86%), adding the number from the first column, and rounding. Note that because of rounding errors the percentages in the last column add to 101%.

The Pew Religious Landscape Survey (which surveyed all age groups) came up with similar but slightly different numbers for those who leave the Church.[23] In table 2.2 we will look only at percentages of those who leave (which do not total 100% because of rounding errors).

TABLE 2.2. RELIGIOUS AFFILIATION WHEN LATTER-DAY SAINT YOUNG ADULTS SWITCH RELIGIONS

	According to NSYR data (%)	According to Pew Religious Landscape data (%)
Nonreligious	72	58
Evangelical Protestant	10	18
Mainline Protestant	8	8
Generic Christian	0	10
Black Protestant	8	0
Restorationist Movements	0	4
Buddhists	0	4
Indeterminate	3	0

The big threat to the youth in the Church is not evangelicals but secularists, or nonreligious. The secularists account for more than twice as many losses as those to all other religions combined, and almost three times as many as those lost to other Christian denominations. Ironically, the result of evangelical attempts to bring Latter-day Saints to Christ is that those who do leave the Church do not abandon their faith for Christ but abandon their faith in Christ, because they usually become nonreligious rather than evangelical.[24] Thus evangelical evangelizing can backfire.[25] Latter-day Saints lose more youth to secularism during their college years (and the statistics include those who do not go to college) than in their high school years. Signs of secularization (discussed in a later chapter) during the time that youth are attending college (and before) should be of particular concern to parents and Church leaders.

Latter-day Saints are not the only religion losing youth to the secularists. According to the NSYR, the largest increase in any religious category occurred in the nonreligious group, which includes the atheist, the agnostic, and the apathetic. This group nearly doubled in size, accounting for almost a quarter of all emerging adults.[26] Fifteen percent of emerging adults became nonreligious while in that age group.[27] It is worth comparing the statistics about Latter-day Saints to other religions (see table 2.3).[28]

TABLE 2.3. LOSSES TO SECULARISM ACROSS VARIOUS RELIGIONS

Religion	Youth lost to secularism (%)
Indeterminate	53
Other Religions	52
Jewish	46
Mainline Protestant	33
Roman Catholic	29
Latter-day Saint	28
Black Protestant	26
Conservative Protestant	23

The percentages that various denominations lose to secularism tend to cluster around a quarter, a third, or half of their youth. We are closer to losing about a quarter but are on the high end of that.

About 40% of emerging adults are indifferent to, disconnected from, or even hostile to religion.[29] This is one way in which youth are different from older adults, since older adults tend to leave one denomination for another rather than leaving religion altogether.[30] Since Latter-day Saints lose more than twice as many to secularism as to all other religions combined, those who change to a different Christian sect are a lesser concern and may reflect conversion to another religion rather than apostasy. At least other Christian denominations believe in Christ. We need to recognize the source of the greater threat and arm our youth against that threat.

As a religion, secularism is rarely organized. It is a collection of ideas and assumptions, not all of which are necessarily bad and some of which are mutually incompatible. It is therefore worthwhile to understand which ideas in secularism are most likely to imperil the faith of the youth. It will also be worthwhile to realize that active youth are not a monolithic group but that they fall into a number of smaller categories, each with its own particular challenges and vulnerabilities.

Besides showing a decline in institutional affiliation, the survey indicates a decline in outward measures of religiosity. More than half of emerging adults do not attend church more than a few times a year.[31] (Of graduating college seniors, 37.2% do not attend at all.)[32] One in five never pray alone (almost one in four among Latter-day Saints).[33] Almost three in seven graduating college seniors never pray at all, up from almost three in ten entering freshmen.[34] Half never read scriptures (about one in four among Latter-day Saints).[35] Four in five do not observe a Sabbath (about three in ten among Latter-day Saints).[36] The NSYR notes of religious practices that "emerging adults who as teenagers were LDS engage in all of these religious practices at the highest level, usually significantly higher than all other groups. They also appear to have increased the most (for positive change) or, conversely, decreased the slightest (for negative change) when change over time is evident in these practices. Second, with the exception of the LDS group, in all but one case—conservative Protestants sharing faith, at 51 percent—only minorities of emerging adults in any category engage in any of these religious practices."[37]

Studies have shown that "having strong religious beliefs—having a strong interior commitment to faith—was not a significant predictor of high engagement in religious practices and activities. Thus habits of the hand (i.e., behaviors) were more significant for many students than habits of the heart or head in keeping them connected with spiritual and religious concerns."[38]

NOTES

1. Christian Smith and Patricia Snell, *Souls in Transition: The Religious and Spiritual Lives of Emerging Adults* (Oxford: Oxford University Press, 2009), 219; Larry A. Braskamp, "The Religious and Spiritual Journeys of College Students," in *The American University in a Postsecular Age*, ed. Douglas Jacobsen and Rhonda Hustedt Jacobsen (Oxford: Oxford University Press, 2008), 131.

2. See J. Spencer Fluhman, "Friendship," *Mormon Studies Review* 1 (2014): 6–7.

3. Jason Kawall, "Friendship and Epistemic Norms," *Philosophical Studies: An International Journal for Philosophy in the Analytic Tradition* 165, no. 2 (2013): 354.

4. Smith and Snell, *Souls in Transition*, 219.

5. NSYR wave 1 data.

6. NSYR wave 3 data.

7. Amy Adamczyk and Jacob Felson, "Friends' Religiosity and First Sex," *Social Science Research* 35 (2006): 943, report: "Our findings suggest that the effect of adolescents' own religiosity on first sex does not depend on the religiosity of their friendship group."

8. Thomas J. Dishion, Joan McCord, and François Poulin, "When Interventions Harm: Peer Groups and Problem Behavior," *American Psychologist* 54, no. 9 (1999): 755–64; Murray R. Barrick, Greg L. Stewart, Mitchell J. Neubert, and Michael K. Mount, "Relating Member Ability and Personality to Work-Team Processes and Team Effectiveness," *Journal of Applied Psychology* 83, no. 3 (1998): 387–88; Matthew Bunn and Scott D. Sagan, *A Worst Practices Guide to Insider Threats: Lessons from Past Mistakes* (Cambridge, MA: American Academy of Arts and Sciences, 2014), 9, 10–12, 16–18.

9. Peter Kotzian, "Cosi fan tutte: Information, Beliefs, and Compliance with Norms," *Zeitschrift für Soziologie* 40, no. 4 (2010): 170.

10. Andrew B. Crittenden, Victoria L. Crittenden, and William F. Crittenden, "The Contagion of Trickle-down Incompetence," *Industrial Management* 59, no. 5 (September/October 2017): 11.

11. John R. Chambers, "Why the Parts Are Better (or Worse) Than the Whole: The Unique-Attributes Hypothesis," *Psychological Science* 21, no. 2 (2010): 268–75.

12. Smith and Snell, *Souls in Transition*, 214–15, 218.

13. Smith and Snell, *Souls in Transition*, 216.

14. Jana Riess, *The Next Mormons: How Millennials Are Changing the LDS Church* (Oxford: Oxford University Press, 2019), 26, 257 n. 30.

15. Rodney Stark, *The Triumph of Faith* (Wilmington, DE: ISI Books, 2015), 207.

16. R. David Hayward and Neal Krause, "Changes in Religious Group Affiliation during Older Adulthood: Evidence from an 11-Year Longitudinal Study," *Review of Religious Research* 56, no. 4 (2014): 551.

17. Mark D. Regnerus and Jeremy E. Uecker, "Finding Faith, Losing Faith: The Prevalence and Context of Religious Transformations during Adolescence," *Review of Religious Research* 47, no. 3 (2006): 232.

18. Regnerus and Uecker, "Finding Faith, Losing Faith," 226–27.

19. Regnerus and Uecker, "Finding Faith, Losing Faith," 227.

20. Regnerus and Uecker, "Finding Faith, Losing Faith," 233.

21. From Christian Smith and Melinda Lundquist Denton, *Soul Searching: The Religious and Spiritual Lives of American Teenagers* (Oxford: Oxford University Press, 2005), 36.

22. From Smith and Snell, *Souls in Transition*, 109.

23. Stephen Cranney, "Who Is Leaving the Church? Demographic Predictors of Ex–Latter-day Saint Status in the Pew Religious Landscape Survey," *BYU Studies* 58, no. 1 (2019): 104.

24. Smith and Snell, *Souls in Transition*, 109; Rick Phillips, Ryan T. Cragun, and Barry A. Kosmin, "Increasing Sex Ratio Imbalance among Utah Mormons: Sources and Implications," *Interdisciplinary Journal of Research on Religion* 11, no. 12 (2015): 9.

25. Compare one story of Catholic evangelizing in Donna Freitas, *Sex and the Soul: Juggling Sexuality, Spirituality, Romance, and Religion on America's College Campuses* (Oxford: Oxford University Press, 2008), 47.

26. Smith and Snell, *Souls in Transition*, 105, 106.

27. Calculated from information in Smith and Snell, *Souls in Transition*, 106, 109.

28. Calculated from information in Smith and Denton, *Soul Searching*, 36; and Smith and Snell, *Souls in Transition*, 109.

29. Smith and Snell, *Souls in Transition*, 168.

30. Hayward and Krause, "Changes in Religious Group Affiliation," 551.

31. Smith and Snell, *Souls in Transition*, 112–13.

32. Ray Franke, Sylvia Ruiz, Jessica Sharkness, Linda DeAngelo, and John Pryor, *Findings from the 2009 Administration of the College Senior Survey (CSS): National Aggregates* (Los Angeles: Higher Education Research Institute, University of California, Los Angeles, 2010), 64.

33. Smith and Snell, *Souls in Transition*, 116.

34. Franke et al., *Findings from the 2009 Administration of the College Senior Survey*, 56, 96.

35. Smith and Snell, *Souls in Transition*, 116.

36. Smith and Snell, *Souls in Transition*, 116.

37. Smith and Snell, *Souls in Transition*, 117–18.

38. Braskamp, "Religious and Spiritual Journeys," 131.

3 | CHANGING CATEGORIES

A cursory glance at the statistics presented in the last couple of chapters might give the impression that over time Latter-day Saints lose more and more youth and that inevitably the Church will lose all its members—it is only a matter of time. Since the real threats come from the secularists, not the sectarians, some view secularization as inevitable. Others hypothesize that there are various stages on the way to disbelief and that those with faith simply have not progressed far enough along the process. The data, however, do not support such notions. To understand this better, we need to rethink both the categories into which we classify individuals and how individuals move between various categories.

FIVE CATEGORIES OF FAITHFULNESS

Initially, the National Study of Youth and Religion (NSYR) divided youth into four categories: devoted, regulars, sporadic, and disengaged.[1] Because only 63% of the surveyed youth actually fit into those

The National Study of Youth and Religion originally divided the youth they surveyed into four religious categories: devoted, regulars, sporadic, and disengaged. Courtesy of Intellectual Reserve, Inc.

four categories, the NSYR reexamined its data and took a very different look at the relationship of adolescents to their faith.[2] Because "religiosity is a complex, multidimensional phenomenon," human frailty got in the way of a simple categorization. "Some [individuals] may give responses to survey questions that all reflect 'high' or 'low' religiosity, but many will provide a mix of high and low answers."[3] In other words, although regularly reading scriptures, praying, and attending church tend to go hand in hand with faith in God and giving religion importance, these practices do not always go together. Some individuals may faithfully pray every day but forget to read their scriptures; others may sincerely believe in God and give their faith importance but are irregular in their church attendance. Setting aside their initial analysis for a more comprehensive one, the NSYR divided youth into five classes, regardless of their formal affiliation, based on the content of their faith, their conduct, and the centrality of their faith.[4] Their analysis was based on all American youth and not specifically on Latter-day Saint youth. Their labels for the five classes are Abiders, Adapters, Assenters, Avoiders, and Atheists.[5]

> Although regularly reading scriptures, praying, and attending church tend to go hand in hand with faith in God and giving religion importance, these practices do not always go together.

Abiders

The Abiders (22% of wave one and 20% of wave two) are those who report high levels of practice, belief, and centrality; that is, "high levels of religious service attendance, of personal prayer, and of closeness to God."[6] Abiders tend to believe that God is personally involved in their lives (94%) and that there is life after death (78%). About two-thirds have no doubts about their religion (68%), and about half think that there is more than one true religion (51%). Most (96%) say that their religion is very important to them and that they feel very close to God (82%). They think about the meaning of life at least sometimes (78%)

and do not think of themselves as spiritual but not religious (75%). They usually attend church at least once a week (78%), pray at least once a day (77%), and volunteer at least a few times a year (75%), though less than half help others out on their own (45%).[7] "Youth with an intact family, moderate to high family income, and well-educated parents are more likely to be Abiders than are youth from alternative family arrangements with lower levels of income or parents with lower levels of education." Abiders are more likely to be female than male and younger than older. Latter-day Saints might label those in this category as *faithful*. The NSYR also noted that parents of Abiders tended to have particular traits: "parents of Abiders typically attend church regularly, pray daily for their child, and are more likely to be conservative Protestants than any other religious tradition."[8] The percentage of Latter-day Saints in this category is actually higher than the general population. The NSYR probably identified the parents as more likely to be conservative Protestants because their survey sample included many more identifying with that religion.

Adapters

The Adapters (28% of wave one and 20% of wave two) are basically those who take a smorgasbord approach to religion. They strongly believe in God but are not particularly committed to any denomination and are eclectic in their religious practices. "They typically report high levels of personal religiosity—prayer, importance of faith, closeness to God—but more sporadic involvement in religious practices such as religious service attendance. Responses from their parents indicate similar patterns."[9] "Adapters believe strongly in God but are not exclusivist."[10] Most do not believe that there is only one true religion (92%), about two-thirds of them believe that God is personally involved in their lives (68%), more than half have some doubts about their beliefs (57%), and about half believe in an afterlife (50%). Most (86%) feel at least somewhat close to God, describe themselves as somewhat spiritual but not religious (76%), and think about the meaning of life somewhat often (71%). About half attend church at least once a month (50%) and pray every day (51%); more help others out on their own (60%), and slightly more volunteer at least a few times a year (63%).[11] They are often members of congregations, "The large majority of Adapters are connected to a religious congregation and report relatively positive evaluations of the congregation."[12] They just do not attend that often, although about a quarter of them (26%) attend every week. "Adapters are religious and spiritual but in a very personal and individualistic way."[13] They are "correlated with lower than average levels of family stability and resources; parents of Adapters report the lowest levels of both parental education and income."[14] They are more likely to come from single-parent families or families who experienced a divorce.[15]

> There is no particular category among Latter-day Saints to correlate with this group of people. We might call some Latter-day Saints who show traits consistent with Adapters *smorgasbord* Saints.

There is no particular category among Latter-day Saints to correlate with this group of people. They may or may not be considered active. We might call some Latter-day Saints who show traits consistent with Adapters *smorgasbord* Saints. Among Latter-day Saint young adults, 10% try to include worship practices from Asian religions, 6% from Judaism, and 2% from Wicca or pagan religions.[16] Overall, 12% of Latter-day Saint young adults (about one in eight)—the lowest of any religious group[17] and down from 24% who felt that way as teenagers[18]—think it is acceptable to pick and choose one's religious beliefs. While these are not precisely the same as the criteria for the Adapter category, it is a rough indication of how widespread this category is among Latter-day Saints.

Assenters

The Assenters (30% of wave one and 31% of wave two) are basically those who are involved in a denomination but do not think that religion is particularly important. For them church is something of a social club. So we find that they "are affiliated with religious congregations, but they do not appear to be engaged by these congregations to the same extent as the Abiders." They are average or typical in most respects. They are also "most likely to report that fitting in with what is cool among their peers is important to them."[19] Most (83%) believe that there is not one true religion, but they believe that God is personally involved in their lives (80%); about half (49%) believe that there is life after death; and as many have a few doubts (40%) as have no doubts about their religion (40%). Most feel at least somewhat close to God (85%), that they are somewhat spiritual but not religious (61%), and that their religion is only somewhat important to them (55%).[20] Most (72%) pray at least once a week and might on their own provide some help to others (71%); about two-thirds (67%) attend church at least once a month; and they are almost evenly split on how frequently they volunteer.[21] Latter-day Saints do not seem to have a particular name for this group of individuals though they might be termed *social club* members. They may look like any other faithful, believing Latter-day Saint. Because they are more interested in fitting in with the crowd, Latter-day Saint Assenters will more likely be active in areas where membership in the Church is concentrated and less likely be active in areas where Church membership is less concentrated and where there are other peer groups that that might fill social needs.[22]

Social club members of the Church are vulnerable to manipulation by shame culture. Elder D. Todd Christofferson explains,

Sometimes those who raise a warning voice are dismissed as judgmental. Paradoxically, however, those who claim truth is relative and moral standards are a matter of personal preference are often the same ones who most harshly criticize people who don't accept the current norm of "correct thinking." One writer referred to this as the "shame culture":

"In a guilt culture you know you are good or bad by what your conscience feels. In a shame culture you know you are good or bad by what your community says about you, by whether it honors or excludes you. . . . [In the shame culture,] moral life is not built on the continuum of right and wrong; it's built on the continuum of inclusion and exclusion. . . .

". . . Everybody is perpetually insecure in a moral system based on inclusion and exclusion. There are no permanent standards, just the shifting judgment of the crowd. It is a culture of oversensitivity, overreaction and frequent moral panics, during which everybody feels compelled to go along. . . .

"The guilt culture could be harsh, but at least you could hate the sin and still love the sinner. The modern shame culture allegedly values inclusion and tolerance, but it can be strangely unmerciful to those who disagree and to those who don't fit in."[23]

Because Assenters want to fit in, they are particularly vulnerable to being manipulated by herd mentality. Popularity is important to them (compare 1 Nephi 22:23). They are particularly vulnerable to the mocking fingers of those in the great and spacious building (1 Nephi 8:25–28, 33–34). Lehi warned about those who gave heed to the mocking of the popular, saying "as many as heeded them, had fallen away" (1 Nephi 8:34). Assenters go along and get along but often do not have the spiritual resources to stand independently and do the right thing when it is unpopular.

Avoiders

The Avoiders (17% of wave one and 24% of wave two) are those who vaguely believe but are not really interested in religion. In fact, they are "nearly disengaged from religion." They tend "to be male and at the older end of adolescence" but are rather average otherwise. Their parents tend to be disengaged from religion too: "33 percent of their parents report that they never attend religious services, and the percentage of Avoiders whose parents are unaffiliated with any religious tradition is twice the national average." Nevertheless, "a small proportion of Avoiders claim affiliation with a religious congregation."[24] Latter-day Saints might simplistically think of these individuals as less inactive or disaffected. Most (97%) in this category do not think that there is one true church, most do not think that God is personally involved in their lives (69%), about two-thirds think there might be life after death (66%), and more than half have at least a few doubts about their beliefs (57%). Most feel that God is extremely distant (74%), and they think about the meaning of life at most occasionally (74%); about two-thirds (66%) think of themselves as at least somewhat spiritual but not religious. Faith is not important for many of them (58%).[25] A majority

(83%) pray at most a couple of times a month, attend church a few times a year (77%), rarely volunteer (75%), and helped someone else out a little (66%).

Atheists

The Atheists (3% of wave one and 5% of wave two) consciously choose not to believe in God. Atheists "are predominantly white, male, and at the older end of the age range in our study," and "their family socioeconomic status tends to be above average." Their parents tend to be well educated and "unaffiliated with any particular religious tradition."[26] They do not believe in God (100%), do not believe there is a true religion (98%), and tend not to have doubts about their own beliefs (76%). They are about equally split between believing there is no life after death (40%) and not being sure (44%). For most (84%) faith is not important to them, and they do not think of themselves as spiritual but not religious (61%); many do not think about the meaning of life at all (40%), though a few give the matter some thought (31%). Most never pray (85%) and never go to church (78%); a minority never volunteer (40%) or help others (35%).[27] The few Latter-day Saints who become atheists tend to disaffiliate themselves from the Church.

MOVEMENT BETWEEN CATEGORIES

If we look at only one variable, church attendance, three of the classes of Latter-day Saints (faithful, smorgasbord, and social club members) appear to attend at least somewhat regularly, and two (Avoiders and Atheists) do not. In the Church we used to classify individuals by whether they were active (coming to church) or not. This gave only a partial picture. While 80% of Abiders say they attend religious services more than once a week, only 48% of those who attend religious services once a week are categorized as Abiders.[28] Those who come to church do not necessarily exhibit identical beliefs even though it may seem that way from the perspective of church attendance. Focusing solely on attendance masks significant differences between members. This was expressed in a hymn by John Newton (who also authored "Amazing Grace")[29] that appeared in the Church's first hymnal:

Though in the outward Church below
Both wheat and tares together grow,
Ere long will Jesus weed the crop
And pluck the tares in anger up.

Will it relieve the horror there
To recollect their stations here?
How much they heard, how much they knew?
How much among the wheat they grew?

No; this will aggravate their case;
They perish under means of grace;
To them the word of life and faith
Became an instrument of death.

We seem alike when here we meet;
Strangers may think we all were wheat;
But to the Lord's all-searching eyes,
Each heart appears without disguise.

The tares are spared for various ends,
Some for the sake of praying friends,
Others the Lord against their will,
Employs, his counsels to fulfill.

But though they grow so tall and strong,
His plan will not require them long;
In harvest when he saves his own,
The tares shall into hell be thrown.

O! awful thought, and is it so?
Must all mankind the harvest know?
Is every man a wheat or tare?
Me for the harvest, Lord, prepare.

For soon the reaping time will come,
And angels shout the harvest home,
And angels shout the harvest home.[30]

This poetic recasting of Jesus's parable of the wheat and the tares reminds us that the Church will contain both wheat and tares that

> **Jesus's parable of the wheat and tares reminds us that not everyone will endure to the end or be saved.**

"seem alike" but produce different fruit. Jesus's parable reminds us that not everyone will endure to the end or be saved. The hymn's restatement of the parable reminds us that each individual can choose whether to be wheat or tare. An individual's situation does not have to be static; indeed, it is not.

The various percentages in any given wave of NSYR research imply more stability than actually exists. "Individual religiousness and spirituality are not strongly fixed and stable: they are sensitive to daily experiences and mood."[31] They are accordingly subject to change over time. On the individual level a fair number of individuals changed groups between waves. Table 3.1 shows those changes in percentages.[32]

TABLE 3.1. MOVEMENT OF INDIVIDUALS BETWEEN CATEGORIES IN DIFFERENT WAVES OF THE NSYR

	Ended Abiders (%)	Ended Adapters (%)	Ended Assenters (%)	Ended Avoiders (%)	Ended Atheists (%)
Started Abiders	85	<1	15	0	0
Started Adapters	1	65	28	5	1
Started Assenters	3	4	67	23	3
Started Avoiders	0	5	<1	84	11
Started Atheists	0	2	1	45	52

The table shows both stability and a certain amount of mixing around of the various groups. It might be easier to understand the process by viewing the information as a figure (see next page).

The most stable group is the faithful Abiders, 85% of whom stayed in that category between waves. If Abiders changed groups they were most likely to switch to social-club Assenters. The next most stable group is the inactive Avoiders, 84% of whom stayed in the same category. If Avoiders changed category, they were most likely to become Atheists.

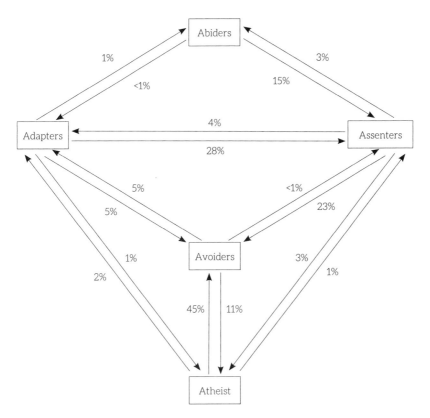

Figure. Movement of individuals between categories in different waves of the NSYR

Two-thirds (67%) of Assenters stayed in their category between waves; if they changed, they were most likely to become Avoiders, though they might become anything. Adapters were almost as stable (65%), and while they might become anything, they were most likely to become Assenters. The least stable category was Atheists, with only 52% remaining in that category across waves; almost half of them became something else, with becoming Avoiders being the most likely change although they could become almost anything. "Being a religious 'none' is not a particularly stable identity."[33] Since about two-thirds of the nonreligious (Atheists and Avoiders) pick and choose elements from different religions,[34] it is not surprising that they are much more likely to become Adapters than any other type of believer.

In general, youth only moved one or two categories between waves but could end up moving almost anywhere. There is an exception to that rule though: Abiders did not become Avoiders or Atheists and vice versa.

To illustrate how these categories work in practice, consider the experience of an acquaintance of mine. "Lucy" was a quiet, kind, thoughtful, and independent young Latter-day Saint woman. She was very intelligent; she was admitted to a top-tier university in a STEM subject. During her first couple of years at the university, she experienced a crisis of faith and became agnostic. She was not certain that there was a God or that she believed anything. After some time, she felt a void in her life and began to attend various churches. She also began praying. After a while she announced in fast and testimony meeting that though there might be many ways back to God, she felt like attending services with members of The Church of Jesus Christ of Latter-day Saints was the right thing for her. She still had problems with some Church programs—for example, she thought that missionary work was evil— but she attended faithfully. Over time, her problems with the Church softened, and the last time I saw her she was stalwart in the Church.

> **During that time, Lucy had a number of tensions with her faith, her Church, and individual members of her Church, but things eventually worked out for her to rekindle her faith.**

Looking at Lucy's faith journey as a transition between categories, she may have started as an Assenter or as an Abider who switched to an Assenter (as about one in seven Abiders do). At college, challenges to her faith shook her, and she switched to an Avoider (as about one in four Assenters do); I do not think that she ever became a full-fledged Atheist, though she may have. Then she changed to an Adapter (as about one in twenty Avoiders do), checking out various religions and denominations. Finally, she transitioned into an Abider, which is rarer but still attested (about 1% of Adapters do so). The process happened over about five or six years. During that time, she had a number of tensions with her faith, her Church, and individual members of her

Church. Things eventually worked out for her to rekindle her faith though.

Lucy's experience reminds us that categories need not be permanent. Some who leave find their way back, though sadly not all do. Her story does falsify certain narratives that circulate in and out of the Church—for example, if the stages of faith were a true concept, then we would expect Atheists to become something of a sink, a black hole that sucked everyone in and never let them leave. In reality, Atheists are more likely to become something else than any other classification.

Lucy's experience also tells us something about conversion. From the NSYR data we would expect it to be rare for individuals to come into the Church as Abiders, firmly committed to the faith from the start. Instead, we would expect them to come in either as smorgasbord members or social-club members, either because they like certain doctrines or practices of the Church or because they are mainly interested in the social aspects of the Church: the activities, the friends, the fellowship. Thus fellowshipping and activities are particularly important for those who are new to the faith and others in the Assenter category. That category is the most likely to transform into a grounded and settled Abider, though it is hard to see how that would happen without the activities providing some content that would ground and settle them, that would help them be "nourished by the good word of God" (Moroni 6:4).

The categories lend themselves to some characterizations that may not be typical of everyone in a particular category. One would expect that those who take a smorgasbord approach would tend to be attracted to certain intellectual ideas in the Church that attract them but would also adopt intellectual ideas from other sources that might not be compatible with the gospel and that might take them away from the Church. This happens in over a third of cases. One would also expect that those who are more interested in the social aspects of the Church would be attracted by friendships but might prize those friendships more than they do the gospel. This happens in just under a third of cases. One expects the Abiders to take their covenants seriously. They keep their covenants, and their covenants will keep them spiritually safe.[35]

CATEGORICAL CONSEQUENCES

The various groups are also characterized by different behaviors and life outcomes. What we are looking at are characteristics of various groups that differ significantly from the average of the entire population.

Looking at measures of health and happiness, youth in the five classes look more or less the same. They tend to be more satisfied with life than sad or depressed, but the variance of scores between these groups tends not to be very great.[36]

About 14% of the youth in the United States smoke tobacco on a daily basis. Avoiders (22%) and Atheists (21%) are much more likely to smoke than average. Abiders, however, are significantly less likely to smoke on a daily basis (5%). Atheists and Avoiders are four times more likely to smoke on a daily basis than Abiders. Adapters and Assenters are about average.[37]

Alcohol consumption is more common than smoking. On average 20% of youth in the United States drink on a weekly basis. Abiders are less than half as likely as average to drink alcohol (9%). Assenters, who tend to do things to fit in, are slightly above average (25%) with a quarter of them drinking on a weekly basis. Avoiders (29%) and Atheists (30%) are even more likely to drink alcohol.[38]

Even more important to Latter-day Saints than the Word of Wisdom is the law of chastity. By about the end of high school, over half the young people in the United States have lost their virginity (54%). Abiders are significantly less likely to have lost their virginity; less than one in three had (31%). Adapters (59%), Assenters (59%), and Avoiders (62%) are all slightly above average. Atheists are significantly above average with more than two-thirds (69%) having lost their virginity. Abiders are half as likely as those in other groups to lose their virginity. Interestingly, Abiders are as likely to be virgins as Atheists are not to be. Furthermore, "although significant proportions of youth transition into sexual activity at some point between the ages of 13 and 21, Atheist youth are likely to make this transition sooner than those from other religious profiles."[39]

Most of the groups tend to have similar educational goals, but Atheists are significantly more likely to want to get postgraduate or professional schooling.[40]

Abiders tended to have the most desirable sociological outcomes. The slightly different devoted category,[41] which makes up just 5% of emerging adults, is composed of those who attend church weekly, pray at least a few times a week, and read their scriptures at least once or twice a month. This is where Latter-day Saints really skew the results. Although they compose just 2.8% of the NSYR's total sample, they account for 21% of the devoted category since 56% of Latter-day Saint youth in the survey are devoted. Latter-day Saint impact is ten times what their proportion of the population is. The devoted (and not just devoted Latter-day Saints) are more likely to get along with their parents,[42] give to charity and volunteer to help others,[43] and interact with others.[44] They are less likely to drink (and particularly less likely to binge drink), smoke, and get into fights.[45] They are less likely to be obese[46] and depressed.[47] They are more likely to get more education, be employed, and have less debt.[48]

Where do Latter-day Saint youth fit into this picture? The NSYR did not separate the different religious traditions in this analysis for a variety of reasons. Since the sample size for Latter-day Saints in this particular study was so small,[49] the results for Latter-day Saints would not be statistically significant.

When we talk about Latter-day Saint youth losing their faith, we seem to be talking about them becoming either Avoiders or Atheists. This study seems to suggest that youth do not just go from being active, committed Latter-day Saints to nonbelievers. Rather they first go through a stage in which the Church and the gospel are either no longer important to them, or they start picking and choosing what parts they will accept. When Latter-day Saints start to see the Church as some sort of social club or take a smorgasbord approach to religion, they are moving off safe ground. While the five categories are helpful in understanding some different stances vis-à-vis faith, they do not get into specific reasons why individuals might shift to the Avoider or Atheist categories. It is to these reasons that we will turn in the next four chapters.

Notes

1. Christian Smith and Patricia Snell, *Souls in Transition: The Religious and Spiritual Lives of Emerging Adults* (Oxford: Oxford University Press, 2009), 259.

2. Lisa D. Pearce and Melinda Lundquist Denton, *A Faith of Their Own* (Oxford: Oxford University Press, 2011). Lisa D. Pearce, Jessica Halliday Hardie, and E. Michael Foster, "A Person-Centered Examination of Adolescent Religiosity Using Latent Class Analysis," *Journal for the Scientific Study of Religion* 52, no. 1 (2013): 60: "This strategy offers an important picture of how a key segment of the adolescent population sorts into clear-cut and consistent profiles of high, moderate, somewhat low, and very low levels of religiosity. However, their classification scheme covers only 63 percent of the youth in the study. They purposefully omit the other 37 percent of cases to not have their analysis of the relationship between religious type and other outcomes 'clouded by more ambiguous cases.'"

3. Pearce, Hardie, and Foster, "Person-Centered Examination," 58.

4. The NSYR did experiment with a six-class model, which basically split the Avoider group into two categories, but did not find that it improved the explanatory power; Pearce, Hardie, and Foster, "Person-Centered Examination," 65–66.

5. When capitalized, *atheist* refers to this particular sociological category. When lowercased, the term has its usual meaning.

6. Pearce and Denton, *Faith of Their Own*, 70.

7. Pearce, Hardie, and Foster, "Person-Centered Examination," 67–68.

8. Pearce and Denton, *Faith of Their Own*, 71, 70.

9. Pearce and Denton, *Faith of Their Own*, 74.

10. Pearce, Hardie, and Foster, "Person-Centered Examination," 69.

11. Pearce, Hardie, and Foster, "Person-Centered Examination," 67–68.

12. Pearce and Denton, *Faith of Their Own*, 74.

13. Pearce, Hardie, and Foster, "Person-Centered Examination," 68–69.

14. Pearce and Denton, *Faith of Their Own*, 75.

15. Melinda Lundquist Denton, "Family Structure, Family Disruption, and Profiles of Adolescent Religiosity," *Journal for the Scientific Study of Religion* 51, no. 1 (2012): 52, 53.

16. NSYR wave 3 data.

17. NSYR wave 3 data. Catholics, Jews, and the nonreligious are the most likely to take this approach; in each case about two-thirds of them do.

18. NSYR wave 1 data.

19. Pearce and Denton, *Faith of Their Own*, 72–73.

20. Pearce, Hardie, and Foster, "Person-Centered Examination," 67. A healthy minority (42%) feel that their religion is very important to them.

21. Pearce, Hardie, and Foster, "Person-Centered Examination," 68.

22. One wonders if the tendency for Abiders to attend because it is the popular thing to do might explain the rise in activity rates in locations where the Church predominates as opposed to places where the concentration of Latter-day Saints is not as great; see Rick Phillips, "Religious Market Share and Mormon Church Activity," *Sociology of Religion* 59, no. 2 (1998): 120–21.

23. D. Todd Christofferson, "The Voice of Warning," *Ensign*, May 2017, 110.

24. Pearce and Denton, *Faith of Their Own*, 73–74.

25. Pearce, Hardie, and Foster, "Person-Centered Examination," 67.

26. Pearce and Denton, *Faith of Their Own*, 71–72.

27. Pearce, Hardie, and Foster, "Person-Centered Examination," 67–68.

28. Pearce, Hardie, and Foster, "Person-Centered Examination," 70.

29. Karen Lynn Davidson, *Our Latter-Day Hymns* (Salt Lake City: Bookcraft, 1988), 418.

30. John Newton, "Though in the Outward Church Below," *Hymns* (Salt Lake City: The Church of Jesus Christ of Latter-day Saints, 1948), no. 102.

31. Carolin Rigo, Filip Uzarevic, and Vassilis Saroglou, "Make Love and Lose Your Religion and Virtue: Recalling Sexual Experiences Undermines Spiritual Intentions and Moral Behavior," *Journal for the Scientific Study of Religion* 55, no. 1 (2016): 34–35.

32. Pearce and Denton, *Faith of Their Own*, 101.

33. Jeremy E. Uecker, Damon Mayrl, and Samuel Stroope, "Family Formation and Returning to Institutional Religion in Young Adulthood," *Journal of the Scientific Study of Religion* 55, no. 2 (2016): 403; Mark D. Regnerus and Jeremy E. Uecker, "Finding Faith, Losing Faith: The Prevalence and Context of Religious Transformations during Adolescence," *Review of Religious Research* 47, no. 3 (2006): 221–22.

34. NSYR wave 3 data.

35. Neal A. Maxwell, "'Overcome . . . Even As I Also Overcame,'" *Ensign*, May 1987, 71.

36. Pearce and Denton, *Faith of Their Own*, 80.

37. Pearce and Denton, *Faith of Their Own*, 78; Adam R. Fisher, "A Review and Conceptual Model of the Research on Doubt, Disaffiliation, and Related Religious Changes," *Psychology of Religion and Spirituality* 9, no. 4 (2017): 362.

38. Pearce and Denton, *Faith of Their Own*, 78; Fisher, "Review and Conceptual Model," 362.

39. Pearce and Denton, *Faith of Their Own*, 78–79.

40. Pearce and Denton, *Faith of Their Own*, 80.

41. Because at the end of wave three 56% of Latter-day Saints were in the devoted category, I would guess that at least that many would be in the Abiders category.

42. Smith and Snell, *Souls in Transition*, 259, 104, 304, 261–62.

43. Smith and Snell, *Souls in Transition*, 262–63; Joanna Blogowska, Vassilis Saroglou, and Catherine Lambert, "Religious Prosociality and Aggression: It's Real," *Journal for the Scientific Study of Religion* 52, no. 3 (2013): 528–29.

44. Smith and Snell, *Souls in Transition*, 263–64.

45. Smith and Snell, *Souls in Transition*, 265–66.

46. Smith and Snell, *Souls in Transition*, 266–67. This may not be true of Latter-day Saints; see Philip B. Mason, Xiaohe Xu, and John P. Bartkowski, "The Risk of Overweight and Obesity among Latter-Day Saints," *Review of Religious Research* 55, no. 1 (2013): 131–47.

47. Smith and Snell, *Souls in Transition*, 267–68.

48. Smith and Snell, *Souls in Transition*, 270–71.

49. Pearce and Denton, *Faith of Their Own*, 197. The study was based on those who were personally interviewed in depth, and only six Latter-day Saints were so interviewed. A bishop in a typical ward has a larger, more statistically significant sample size.

4 | DELVING INTO DOUBT

The reasons why youth abandon faith have been much debated. The debate has largely been fueled by anecdote rather than data. Most of us know individuals who have lost their faith. We may know them well enough to have heard their particular reasons. If we have heard the reasons for more than one individual's departure, we may have started to look for patterns and generalize from the examples we personally know. Suppose, for example, that doubt figures into all the anecdotes we have heard. We might then conclude: people lose their faith because of doubt. This is true if we understand that *some* people lose their faith because of doubt. It is not true if we believe that *all* people lose their faith because of doubt. The truth of the matter is that there are many reasons why individuals lose their faith, and there is often not one single reason. The major reasons will be discussed in the next four chapters. We will start with the one that often appears in narratives about individuals leaving the Church: doubt.

Does Doubt Drive Disaffiliation?

There is a tendency in the extant literature and in many narratives to overemphasize the role of doubt in the process of losing faith or ceasing to participate.[1] The NSYR provided data on why youth ceased to attend church or believe the tenets of their church. While youth who drop out of participation may look the same on the surface, the NSYR found a difference between those who stop

> It turns out that most youth cannot really identify why they lost their faith or stopped coming.

coming to church and those who stop believing. The reasons, under their categorizations, are summarized in table 4.1.[2]

TABLE 4.1. REASONS WHY INDIVIDUALS CEASED PARTICIPATING IN THEIR CHURCH

Reason	Those who stopped attending (Avoiders) (%)	Those who stopped believing (Atheists) (%)
Intellectual skepticism and disbelief	11	32
Vague or no reason	41	24
Lack of interest	17	13
Just stopped attending	0	12
Life disruptions	13	10
Dislikes religion / bad experience	6	7
Lacked parental support	5	1
Availability problem	4	0
Felt no religious need	3	0

It turns out that most youth cannot really identify why they lost their faith or stopped coming. When the NSYR asked teenagers who stopped attending religious services why they stopped attending, a full 41% responded that they did not know, and another 17% said they lost interest.[3] Of those that stopped believing, 24% could give no reason,

13% just lost interest, and 12% just stopped coming; that accounts for half of those who stopped believing.

The table suggests that doubts and intellectual skepticism are almost three times as likely to take someone into the Atheist category as the Avoider category, but that interpretation is deceptive. It ignores the fact that the percentage who stopped believing amounts to only 2% of the total number of youth, while the number who stopped attending amounts to about eight times as many. It is also worth noting that almost one in four who stopped believing and more than four out of ten who stopped attending could not identify a reason why they changed to the category that they did. Even though someone who becomes a nonbeliever is more likely to do so because of doubts than someone who becomes a nonattender, doubts turn three times as many into nonattenders as nonbelievers. Furthermore while less than half (48.5%) of adolescents in high school had a lack of doubts,[4] only 28% of the most highly religious in their young adult years had a lack of doubts.[5] Among Latter-day Saint young adults, one in three (33%) had at least a few doubts, but only 4% had many doubts.[6] Doubts can arise from a variety of sources[7] and are part of the mortal condition of living by faith. But doubts alone do not cause unbelief. The picture turns out to be much more complicated than that.

BY DOUBT ALONE?

When the NSYR used qualitative comparative analysis to look at "combinations of causal factors most likely shifting the more highly religious teenagers into the least religious emerging adult religious groups within five years,"[8] they found that doubts played a role generally when other factors were present:

- the teen's parents give faith low importance and don't frequently attend religious services
- the teen gives faith low importance
- the teen does not pray or read scriptures frequently
- the teen has some doubts about their faith
- the teen has few adults in the congregation to whom he or she can turn for help

The NSYR did note that the analysis did not account for all the cases (not all of which involved doubt), but it did account for a majority.[9] Doubts come into play when religious faith has not been important in the home—or consequently in the youth's life—and where there are few in his congregation to whom the youth (more often male than female) can turn to answer his doubts or defend his faith.[10] Since faith has been less important to his parents, it is unlikely that they will be in a position to defend his faith.

An anecdote might illustrate the importance of having those who can and will defend faith. A number of years ago, I had the chance to talk to a senior scholar, whom I admire, of a different denomination about how he had kept his faith even though he had studied under a professor who was particularly hostile to both the Bible and his beliefs. He replied that he had encountered the works of another scholar who defended the Bible in his work. This gave him a concrete example of how to deal with the doubts and arguments against the Bible and religion in a way that was both good scholarship and faith promoting. Some, like my friend, may come across such exemplars from afar, but youth are more likely to find such exemplars among the people that they meet in their own congregations.

> **Doubt is most devastating when the youth's defenses are down by not reading scriptures or praying regularly and by being casual in his or her faith.**

Doubt is most devastating when the youth's defenses are down (by not reading scriptures or praying regularly and by being casual in his or her faith) and when parents and others in the congregation cannot or will not defend the faith. (As Elder Jeffrey R. Holland put it, "In matters of faith and conviction, it helps to direct your inquiry toward those who actually have some!")[11] These factors actually weaken the youth's safety net. Doubts play a role only when the individual's safety net is weakened or missing altogether.

Ultimately, youth are responsible and accountable for their own faith. When youth encounter doubts, the first line of defense is knowing for themselves the truthfulness of the gospel through faithfulness

When parents can be articulate defenders of faith, they can bolster the faith of struggling youth. Courtesy of Kris/Pixabay.

and diligence, personal study, prayer, and revelation—practices that have often been compared to providing oil in the parable of the ten virgins. When these factors are absent, doubt encounters little resistance. In the parable of the ten virgins, the virgins get up to trim their lamps (and lamps in Jesus's day were not very big and did not hold that much oil),[12] and the five foolish virgins complain that "our lamps are going out."[13] Their lack of personal preparation meant that they did not have the crucial reserves when they needed them.

How Do We Defend against Doubt?

When youth's faith falters, ideally parents serve as the first external line of defense. When parents can be articulate defenders of faith, they can bolster the faith of struggling youth. But those who leave because of doubts say that faith was not that important to their parents. One researcher noted that young adults who do not consider themselves religious "often spoke of parents who had grown up in strict religious households, who felt a lot of resentment toward religion, and who believed they must shield their kids from the experience of forced church or synagogue attendance that they had endured as children. Many of these students chalked up their lack of religiosity and undeveloped spiritual life to their parents' desire to avoid influencing them about faith and belief, which translated into having no religious background to draw on or even reject in their young adult lives."[14]

Other adults that the youth can trust form the next line of defense. These could be Sunday School teachers, youth leaders, quorum or class advisers, ministering brothers or sisters, members of the bishopric, seminary or institute instructors, or even others who can defend the youth's faith or be able to provide a reason for the hope that is within them (1 Peter 3:15). One study showed that individuals are most likely to get useful help and advice from those with whom they discussed religion or spirituality.[15] Of youth in general who have doubts, 60% of them end up in the highest religious category as young adults if they have adults in the congregations who can help them through their doubts.[16] To this end, Elder M. Russell Ballard recently told seminary and institute instructors to know the content of the Gospel Topics essays on the Church website "like you know the back of your hand."[17] Becoming familiar with those topics is also not bad advice for bishops, stake presidents, youth leaders, and parents.

Unfortunately, there are many ways in which doubting youth may not receive the help they need. Sometimes there is no response to the issue that concerns them, although this situation is actually fairly rare. In most cases, there are careful and thoughtful responses to those issues. More frequently, those who need the answers do not know where to find them (see Doctrine and Covenants 123:12) as they fail to learn about the information that is available. Sadly, this sometimes occurs because those who should have been in a position to know about the answers have thought them to be unimportant and have neglected or even deliberately hidden them, like hiding a candle under a bushel. Whatever the cause, when parents and other adults in the congregation whom the youth trust have failed to inform themselves concerning the intellectual issues about which the youth have doubts, they cannot defend the youth's faith.

Placing a candle under a bushel basket obscures and snuffs out light. Courtesy of Myriam Zilles/Pixabay.

Can We Delay Our Doubts?

Timing in such situations is crucial. The safety net needs to be in place before there is a crisis of faith. When the crisis hits, there is only a limited window of opportunity to assuage the doubts. Though the crisis of faith can last for years, it can sometimes destroy faith in only a couple of weeks.[18] Often others do not detect the crisis of faith until the window of opportunity is past. The responses are then too little and too late. Most who work seriously in apologetics (defending the faith) have had the sad experience of being called in too late. This gives rise to stories of apologetics being ineffective, but it might be analogous to contacting the oncologist after the patient already has stage IV cancer.

One of Jesus's parables is applicable to the situation: "Neither do men light a candle, and put it under a bushel" (Matthew 5:15). What would have been obvious to Jesus's audience is opaque to those who read the scriptures in English. That is because to us a *bushel* is a wooden basket for carrying apples or other large fruit. Placing a candle (or lamp, which is the term that Jesus used) under a bushel basket obscures the light. In Jesus's day a *modion* (the word translated as "bushel") was used for measuring grain or oil and was made of metal.[19] Putting a lamp under a *modion* did not just obscure the light but cut it off altogether and, if not removed fairly quickly, put it out. Doubts function like the *modion*, cutting off the flame of faith and, if allowed to remain, snuffing it out. The safety net needs to be in place before faith fails.

As Elder Neal A. Maxwell noted, "We have heard and rejoiced in the stories of gallant members who have been rescued 'downstream' by the various organizational 'fish out' parties; what we have not heard about are how many men who might have been bishops were swept beyond our reach by youthful habits or attitudes which hardened under the full gaze of some of us who might have intervened intelligently while there was still time."[20] The key point is to intervene intelligently in a timely fashion. Intelligent intervention is more than just simply listening to their doubts—it needs to supply answers and provide "a reason of the hope that is in you" (1 Peter 3:15).

One of the problems with such intervention is that doubters often are not open about their doubts until they are at an advanced stage. A number of things may cause this reticence: the inability to articulate the doubts, not knowing where to go for help, not wanting help, wanting to resolve the problem without outside assistance— and the list goes on and on. "At whatever point one articulates one's doubts, one may appear to have been dissembling or hiding one's ideas, raising questions

> The point of study and seeking learning and reading the best books is to find resources that can be used to build faith because not everyone has it.

about one's truthfulness in both the past and the present."[21] Doubters may be aware that they accuse believers of the same deception that they themselves are practicing. "The doubter who is a member of a religious community falls easily into a position of hypocrisy or false pretense. . . . To feel that one is deceiving others about one's religious beliefs may be equally painful for a person who has lost faith in God. By continuing within the religious community, the doubter may feel that he or she is playing a part, pretending, acting as though in possession of a belief or conviction not there. Such a person may experience troubling uncertainty about how far to comply with the public forms of assent required by a faith community."[22]

From a scriptural perspective, when the safety net fails, there are usually two scriptural injunctions that have not been heeded. It is common in the Church to quote Doctrine and Covenants 88:118: "Seek ye diligently and teach one another words of wisdom; yea, seek ye out of the best books words of wisdom; seek learning, even by study and also by faith." But in truncating the scripture at this point, we often leave out the explicit purpose of doing so. We seek out of the best books because "all have not faith" (Doctrine and Covenants 88:118). The point of study and seeking learning and reading the best books is to find resources that can be used to build faith because not everyone has it.

The second scriptural injunction that has often been ignored is the duty "to gather up the libelous publications that are afloat; and all that are in the magazines, and in the encyclopedias, and all the libelous histories that are published, and are writing, and by whom, and present the whole concatenation of diabolical rascality and nefarious and murderous impositions that have been practiced upon this people—that we may not only publish to all the world, but present them to the heads of government in all their dark and hellish hue" (Doctrine and Covenants 123:4–6). Joseph Smith repeatedly emphasized the importance of this work:

> It is an imperative duty that we owe to God, to angels, with whom we shall be brought to stand, and also to ourselves, to our wives and children, . . . to all the rising generation, and to all the pure in heart— . . . Therefore, that we should waste and wear out our lives in bringing to light all the hidden things of darkness, wherein we know them; and they are truly manifest from heaven—These should then be attended to with great earnestness. Let no man count them as small things; for there is much which lieth in futurity, pertaining to the saints, which depends upon these things. (Doctrine and Covenants 123:7, 9–15)

This does not mean that everyone needs to do this work or that other good things should be left undone in order to do it, but it is a work that needs to be done. Someone has to do it, and everyone needs to be able to access the fruits of those labors (see Doctrine and Covenants

123:13). Otherwise we risk being "blinded by the subtle craftiness of men, whereby they lie in wait to deceive" and being "only kept from the truth because they know not where to find it" (Doctrine and Covenants 123:12).

Not knowing the truth because of not knowing where to find it is a problem that was already identified in 1839 and unfortunately is still with us today. Because the youth do not know where to find the truth, approximately 1.5% of them are hit with doubts without a local apologetic safety net. More could and should be done for these individuals.

Should We Encourage Doubt?

Above all, we should not introduce or celebrate doubt.[23] President Thomas S. Monson warned (quoting J. Reuben Clark): "He wounds, maims, and cripples a soul who raises doubts about or destroys faith in the ultimate truths. God will hold such a one strictly accountable; and who can measure the depths to which one shall fall who willfully shatters in another the opportunity for celestial glory."[24]

"A destroyer of faith—particularly one within the Church, and more particularly one who is employed specifically to build faith," according to Elder Boyd K. Packer, "places himself in great spiritual jeopardy. He is serving the wrong master, and unless he repents, he will not be among the faithful in the eternities."[25] He went on to say:

> The idea that we must be neutral and argue quite as much in favor of the adversary as we do in favor of righteousness is neither reasonable nor safe. In the Church we are not neutral. We are one-sided. There is a war going on, and we are engaged in it. It is the war between good and evil, and we are belligerents defending the good. We are therefore obliged to give preference to and protect all that is represented in the gospel of Jesus Christ, and we have made covenants to do it.[26]

Elder Maxwell also cautioned: "Students will assume that what we do not defend we do not think worth defending. Also, by even appearing to throw in with the world, we throw off those who may just be making their first tentative moves toward faith and spiritual stability. ... If we let go, we are not only accountable for our own fall, but also for those we knock loose from their faith and for those who let go when they see us let go."[27]

More recently, Elder Holland stated: "To lead a child (or anyone else!), even inadvertently, away from faithfulness, away from loyalty and bedrock belief simply because we want to be clever or independent is license no parent nor any other person has ever been given. In matters of religion a skeptical mind is not a higher manifestation of virtue than is a believing heart, and analytical deconstruction in the field of, say, literary fiction can be just plain old-fashioned destruction when transferred to families yearning for faith at home."[28]

But doubts are not the major reasons that individuals fall away or fall through the cracks. Another study of those of all ages who do not attend church found that of Christians who stopped attending, only 6% actively doubted their Christian faith. Over five times as many stopped attending because they were not practicing their faith and about an equal number just did not consider it that important.[29] Doubt, it turns out, plays a much smaller role than way of life.

The smaller role of doubt turned up in a recent unrepresentative survey of adults who had left the Church. The survey asked the reasons why these former members had left the Church. Only one historical or doctrinal issue even appeared in the top ten reasons why they left the Church: the historical authenticity of the Book of Mormon and the Book of Abraham.[30] Those who would save the faith of others need to be able to articulate why the events described in these books really happened. They also need to respond to other intellectual issues, but the doubts and the intellectual issues are not the main reasons why individuals leave their faith. How they live their life plays a greater role. It is to those other factors that we now turn.

NOTES

1. For example, Adam R. Fisher, "A Review and Conceptual Model of the Research on Doubt, Disaffiliation, and Related Religious Changes," *Psychology of Religion and Spirituality* 9, no. 4 (2017): 358.
2. This is a compilation of Christian Smith and Melinda Lundquist Denton, *Soul Searching: The Religious and Spiritual Lives of American Teenagers* (Oxford: Oxford University Press, 2005), 89, 105.

3.	Smith and Denton, *Soul Searching*, 105.

4.	Lisa D. Pearce, Jessica Halliday Hardie, and E. Michael Foster, "A Person-Centered Examination of Adolescent Religiosity Using Latent Class Analysis," *Journal for the Scientific Study of Religion* 52, no. 1 (2013): 64.

5.	Christian Smith and Patricia Snell, *Souls in Transition: The Religious and Spiritual Lives of Emerging Adults* (Oxford: Oxford University Press, 2009), 221.

6.	NSYR wave 3 data. Among Protestants, Catholics, and Jews, the number is near or over one-half. Even among the nonreligious, 37% have doubts about being nonreligious and 5% have many doubts.

7.	Fisher, "Review and Conceptual Model," 359.

8.	Smith and Snell, *Souls in Transition*, 230.

9.	Smith and Snell, *Souls in Transition*, 230.

10.	Social science often lumps different types of support together into "social support," which can be "emotional support, informational support, and instrumental or tangible support," the latter consisting of material support; Stephen M. Merino, "Social Support and the Religious Dimensions of Close Ties," *Journal for the Scientific Study of Religion* 53, no. 3 (2014): 596.

11.	Jeffrey R. Holland, "The Message, the Meaning, and the Multitude," *Ensign*, November 2019, 6.

12.	For example, Jewish Museum JM 14-69 is 3 cm in height and 9.1 cm long; Andrews S. Ackerman and Susan L. Braunstein, *Israel in Antiquity* (New York: The Jewish Museum, 1982), 110. Another example is Jewish Museum T11 which is 3.5 cm high and 7.1 cm in diameter, in Ackerman and Braunstein, *Israel in Antiquity*, 93. This indicates a maximum capacity of about 115 ml. At most one could expect sixteen hours of illumination from a large full lamp. See also Marti Lu Allen, "The Virgin's Lamps: *Shine Beautiful!*," in *Masada and the World of the New Testament*, ed. John F. Hall and John W. Welch (Provo, UT: BYU Studies, 1997), 170–95.

13.	Matthew 25:8; my translation.

14.	Donna Freitas, *Sex and the Soul: Juggling Sexuality, Spirituality, Romance, and Religion on America's College Campuses* (Oxford: Oxford University Press, 2008), 36.

15.	Merino, "Social Support," 606–8.

16. Smith and Snell, *Souls in Transition*, 221.

17. https://www.lds.org/broadcasts/article/evening-with-a-general
-authority/2016/02/the-opportunities-and-responsibilities-of-ces
-teachers-in-the-21st-century: "The efforts to inoculate our young people will often fall to you CES teachers. With those thoughts in mind,
find time to think about your opportunities and your responsibilities.
Church leaders today are fully conscious of the unlimited access to
information, and we are making extraordinary efforts to provide accurate context and understanding of the teachings of the Restoration.
A prime example of this effort is the 11 Gospel Topics essays on LDS.org
that provide balanced and reliable interpretations of the facts for con-
troversial and unfamiliar Church-related subjects. It is important that
you know the content in these essays like you know the back of your
hand. If you have questions about them, then please ask someone who
has studied them and understands them. In other words, 'seek learning, even by study and also by faith' as you master the content of these
essays."

18. Fisher, "Review and Conceptual Model," 362.

19. R. P. Duncan-Jones, "The Size of the Modius Castrensis," *Zeitschrift für
Papyrologie und Epigraphik* 21 (1976): 59–60.

20. Neal A. Maxwell, *A More Excellent Way: Essays on Leadership for Latter-
day Saints* (Salt Lake City: Deseret Book, 1967), 53.

21. John D. Barbour, *Versions of Deconversion: Autobiography and the Loss
of Faith* (Charlottesville: University Press of Virginia, 1994), 106.

22. Barbour, *Versions of Deconversion*, 107.

23. For example, Patrick Q. Mason, *Planted: Belief and Belonging in an Age of
Doubt* (Provo, UT: Neal A. Maxwell Institute for Religious Scholarship;
Salt Lake City: Deseret Book, 2015), 32–34, 43–44.

24. Thomas S. Monson, *Pathways to Perfection* (Salt Lake City: Deseret
Book, 1973), 186.

25. Boyd K. Packer, "The Mantle Is Far, Far Greater Than the Intellect," *BYU
Studies* 21, no. 3 (1981): 7.

26. Packer, "Mantle Is Far, Far Greater Than the Intellect," 8.

27. Neal A. Maxwell, *Deposition of a Disciple* (Salt Lake City: Bookcraft,
1975), 24–25.

28. Jeffrey R. Holland, "A Prayer for the Children," *Ensign*, May 2003, 86.

29. LifeWay Research, *Unchurched Report* (LifeWay Research, 2017), 10.
30. Jana Riess, *The Next Mormons: How Millennials Are Changing the LDS Church* (Oxford: Oxford University Press, 2019), 223–24.

5 | **REASONS FOR LEAVING**

A number of factors other than doubt can influence the decline in the faith of youth. Not only did the NSYR track thousands of youth for a decade, but they also engaged in in-depth interviews with a significant number of the youth at various stages. These interviews let the youth explain their reasoning behind the decisions they made and why they answered some of the survey questions the way they did. This provides richer data than simple statistics.

Although the data published by the NSYR does not directly address the issue of why some Latter-day Saint youth become atheist, agnostic, or apathetic, it does delve into the reasons why youth in general choose that path. For the sake of discussion, we assume here that reasons why Latter-day Saint youth choose that path are similar to reasons that youth in general choose that path. The NSYR cataloged a number of different reasons why youth lose their religion, and doubt by itself actually did not make the list. The reasons that did make a difference, however, are worth noting: disruptions to routine, distractions, differentiation, postponed family formation, honoring diversity, keeping options open, self-confident self-sufficiency, partying, politics, pornography, and loss of trust.

DISRUPTIONS TO ROUTINE

At their best, the positive virtues of religion become so ingrained that they become second nature. At a step removed from that is religion as a habit. Disruptions to routine can interrupt habits. "Many life transitions and disturbances of diverse sorts—divorce, death of a family member, leaving home, job loss" make people "less likely to attend religious services."[1] About one in eight teenagers (13%) in high school who once attended religious services but stopped did so because of some disruption to their life.[2] This lowers slightly to one in ten (10%) who actively became nonreligious.[3] While it is true that "in certain cases, hardship and poor family environments can enhance religiosity,"[4] the opposite is also true (compare Alma 62:41).

Leaving home

One major disruption to routine is leaving home, which many youth do after graduating from high school, typically around age eighteen. Thus, as noted in a previous chapter, "age 18 appears to be the most active or unstable age for both directions of considerable religious change."[5] The most unstable age for religious change correlates with one of the biggest disruptions to routine; it is tempting to see this as more than just coincidence.

Should young adults then stay home and not go to college? Not necessarily. Not attending college is associated with both a decrease in church attendance and an increased likelihood of disaffiliation.[6] College, in and of itself, does not promote disaffiliation or decline in importance of religion, although there is a decline in religious service attendance. There is an exception to this observation: "Those who do major in these fields [those whose classes might challenge religious faith]—the social sciences and the humanities—are the most likely to diminish their religiosity."[7]

The most unstable age for religious change, age 18, correlates with one of the biggest disruptions to routine. Courtesy of Maura Barbulescu/Pixabay.

Some of this erosion of emerging adults' faith can be attributed to the attitudes of their professors: "College and university professors on the whole are indeed less religious than other Americans."[8] Some claim that 23.4% of college professors are atheist or agnostic compared to 6.9% of the American population as a whole.[9] And at "elite doctoral-granting universities," the percentage of atheists and agnostics among professors rises to more than a third (36.6%).[10] While such percentages are for the university as a whole, certain disciplines have higher concentrations: "Psychology and biology have the highest proportion of atheists and agnostics, at about 61 percent. Not far behind is mechanical engineering, where 50 percent of professors are atheists or agnostics. Next in line come economics, political science, and computer science, where about 40 percent of the professors fall into the category of nonbelief."[11] Nevertheless, surveys find that "faculty tend to be very tolerant of most religious groups. . . . There are two exceptions to this tolerance: Mormons and Evangelicals."[12] Thus faculty members tend to have negative feelings toward Latter-day Saints; a third of all faculty members dislike Latter-day Saints,[13] but that increases to 42%

among the humanities faculty.[14] This negative opinion persists despite Latter-day Saints being slightly overrepresented in faculty compared to their presence among the general population.[15] "While believers can indeed be found in the upper echelons of academe, those campuses appear to be places where there is either less interest in or less space for more fervent forms of religiosity."[16] The biases of faculty tend to spread to their students in other attitudes:

> The proportion of students who believe that marijuana should be legalized (32.3% at college entry vs. 53.4% at the end of senior year), that same-sex couples should have the right to legal marital status (59.3% vs. 72.8%), and/or that abortion should be legal (51.6% vs. 63.8%) all increased by more than ten percentage points between freshman and senior year. Correspondingly, a decrease of nine percentage points was seen among the proportion of students believing that it is important to have laws prohibiting homosexual relationships (23.8% vs. 14.9%).[17]

It is not just the faculty who erode the faith and practice of youth. "In classes and discussions, a small coterie of antiorthodox skeptics, however, always manages to remain unconvinced, and they often have great difficulty concealing their disdain for any expression of uncompromising orthodox belief."[18] While these students trumpet their tolerance, they will not tolerate orthodoxy. For example, Anatoly Brekhman, a former freshman counselor at Yale, relates, "I had a freshman who came in and said, 'I'm the most pure girl in the entire world. I don't have sex, I don't drink, I don't smoke, I don't do drugs, and I don't eat meat.' And out of those five things, probably four were not true by the end of the first term."[19] Brekhman sees this as a good thing. Whether the parents who are paying through the nose for a student's Ivy League experience appreciate the corruption of their child seems to be irrelevant. Brekhman's "expectation is that you come here and you drop all your limits and you experiment because that's the nature of college."[20] For many on college campuses, orthodoxy, or rather orthopraxy, with its strict limitations on behavior, is a threat to such experimentation and cannot be tolerated.

Again, we are dealing with generalities, and the college experience can be quite complex and individual. One study out of the NSYR looked at changes between creationist and evolutionist stances (neither of which was further defined) among members of various religious groups from high school to college. It found that during college, 11% of Latter-day Saints switched from a creationist to an evolutionist stance, and 13% switched from an evolutionist stance to a creationist one, making Latter-day Saints the only religious category that was more likely to become creationist than evolutionist with education.[21] The researcher concluded his study noting, "There is no evidence that attending college (including attending a religiously affiliated institution) and graduating from college has any influence on whether a young person changes his or her beliefs. Although not statistically significant, adolescent creationists who have attended any type of college are actually slightly *less* likely to accept evolution. Moreover, there is no evidence that attending college prevents those adolescents who accept the possibility of evolution to later reject it. This finding should be troubling for those subscribing to the idea that a lack of accurate information is the primary reason people reject evolution."[22] This suggests that students do not necessarily find their professors' and fellow students' ardent attempts at converting them to an intellectual position persuasive.

Divorce

Another major disruption to routine is divorce. Even Jesus recognized that divorce may be necessary in some cases (Matthew 19:7–9). The reason he gave—spousal infidelity—is the top reason given for divorce in the United States, cited by 37% of those who divorced, though neglect, emotional abuse, and substance abuse also rank highly.[23] Even where divorce is the best-case scenario, there are still consequences, which are often negative. While it is well established that "biological two-parent families produce the most religious offspring,"[24] some recent research looks at the effects of a parent's divorce on teenage religiosity.[25] The research does not look directly at Latter-day Saints because some researchers actually threw out all their data on Latter-day Saints. The general picture seems to work with the religions they did look at, with some differences between religions in degree but not of kind. They conclude that "the children of divorce are disproportionately likely to reject any faith they were raised in, or adopt religion if they grew up without one."[26]

How big a difference does divorce make? "Coming from a divorced family doubles the likelihood that Protestants, liberal or conservative, will become apostates." Additionally, "parental divorce approximately doubles the likelihood that people who grow up as Catholics will become apostates as adults." For these researchers an apostate is someone who loses all their faith and becomes irreligious. Another effect of divorce is that "respondents from divorced single-parent families are more than twice as likely to change to another religion."[27] A separate study confirmed that "adults who lived with a single parent during their formative years have more than twice the odds of disaffiliating as those who lived with continuously married parents." On the other hand, the study found "no statistically significant effect of divorce on religious disaffiliation for those who were living with a stepparent at age 16 compared to those with married parents." But that presumes that one or both of the originally married parents were not regular in their attendance. If a child's biological parents were religiously active and subsequently divorced, the child is three times more likely to switch religions when living in a stepfamily than a child raised in a family that did not divorce.[28]

> **Children of divorced parents also may not be able to reconcile religious teachings that emphasize the sanctity of marriage with their own family experience.**

This study did not find any significant decrease in attendance associated with divorce, although one might suppose that apostatizing would have some effect on attendance. If it did not, then the individuals were not attending church before the divorce, and the divorce simply formalized the break. Other studies claim that "the offspring of divorce report significantly lower levels of adult religious attendance than their counterparts from intact families."[29] Adults who were raised in a married family with two active parents are more than twice as likely to actively attend church as an adult (44%) than those who were raised in a religiously active single-parent home (21%).[30]

One thing that divorce did not seem to influence as much was private behaviors like prayer. While public devotion (for example, going to church) lessened, private devotions like prayer seem not to have.[31]

One of the factors impacting children of divorce is that "the offspring of divorce express less admiration for the morality and the spirituality of their parents than do their counterparts from intact families," particularly when the divorce was acrimonious.[32] In other words, "divorce may disqualify parents as spiritual models or spiritual exemplars. Children of divorced parents also may not be able to reconcile religious teachings that emphasize the sanctity of marriage with their own family experience and may devalue their religion as a means of resolving such cognitive dissonance, a process referred to as sacred loss or desecration."[33] The situation might be slightly more complicated:

> Briefly, offspring may be unmotivated to emulate the religious practices or spiritual orientations of parents who engage in high levels of discord and fail to provide a calm, loving environment for their upbringing. Children may also be unable to learn about religious or spiritual matters from parents who are preoccupied with their own issues or physically absent due to post-divorce custodial arrangements. . . . Young people who observe self-centered or mean-spirited interactions among their parents may quickly recognize the inconsistency of such conduct with spiritual teachings of love, forgiveness, and trust. The cognitive dissonance that may result among offspring can be resolved by rejecting parents' religious teachings, and perhaps other traditional institutions as well.[34]

Children of divorce are also "more likely to have been raised without religion, than children from intact families,"[35] because "divorce is one of the strongest and most robust predictors of having left the Church."[36] Children whose parents are in unhappy, high-conflict marriages fare about the same as children of divorced parents in terms of religiosity.[37]

Parental divorce can provoke a change in religiosity both ways; it can make some children less religious and some children more religious. After a parental divorce, Abiders are three times more likely to shift to an Assenter or an Adapter and Adapters three times more likely to shift to an Assenter than those whose families stayed intact.

For those groups religion becomes less important. After a divorce, Assenters are two and a half times as likely to become Abiders and four times as likely to become Adapters. For them, religion becomes more important. Avoiders and Atheists seem to experience no significant change in their religiosity. Thus for those for whom religion was important, the divorce serves to decrease the importance and outward practice of religion, but it can serve to increase both among those for whom it was not previously that important.[38]

Death

A third factor disrupting routine is death. One study concluded that "the death of a parent while growing up increases the likelihood of denominational change. This is a surprising result given that many studies have concluded that parental death has negligible long-term effects on offspring."[39]

All these factors do not change the reality that the individual makes his or her own choices. It does suggest that family dynamics can play a role. Studies like this one underscore the importance of families. Parents need to be careful and intentional about the example they set for their children, as a bad example undermines what they may be teaching: "when they saw your conduct they would not believe in my words" (Alma 39:11).

The flip side of this study is that we can expect that many who join the Church will come from a background of broken homes without much of a religious background. This brings its own challenges and falls outside the scope of our discussion here.

Apostasy

A final major life disruption peculiar to Latter-day Saints but not covered in studies that I have encountered, though I do not know its prevalence, is apostasy or transgression that results in the Church discipline of a parent. This can have a devastating effect on children and their faith, although I am unaware of any formal study of the matter.

Students feel that social media sites that require them to use their own names have to be carefully managed so that they always appear to be positive and happy. This illusion can be exhausting to maintain. Courtesy of Erik Lucatero/Pixabay.

DISTRACTIONS

In the parable of the seeds, Jesus notes that some gospel seeds do not grow because they are choked by the cares of the world (Matthew 13:7, 22). Such cares distract us from pursuing the gospel. The sociological research shows that after two thousand years, the cares of the world are still with us as much as ever.

> Emerging adults engage in a number of other issues and activities that often distract them from possible religious and spiritual interests and involvements. To begin with, the central task of emerging adult life itself—learning to stand on one's own two feet—is in some sense one big, macro distraction from religious devotion. . . . Outside of work and possibly school, emerging adults spend a good amount of time attending to various errands associated with living on their own. . . . Fun-related distractions in many emerging adults' lives include . . . any other number of recreational and social activities that take time, energy, and sometimes money and planning. On top of all that is time spent on gadgets. . . . Social life can be distracting and draining in other ways as well. . . . More generally, there is simply too much else going on at the time to go to church, synagogue, temple, or mosque.[40]

Spending time on social media means that young adults are not spending that time elsewhere. A different study noted that "the tendency of [younger adults] to set aside religion when life gets in the way seems more likely due to their current life stage—many are in school, or the parents of young children—than because of their membership in" a particular generational cohort.[41] While being so distracted that one has no time to go to church at all definitely seems to be a key indicator in taking individuals away from faith, even irregular attendance because of distraction can cause problems.

Social media can take an inordinate amount of time. College "students are checking their accounts compulsively throughout the day, with approximately 31 percent of students checking at minimum twenty-five times and potentially up to a hundred."[42] Students feel that social media sites like Facebook that require them to use their own names have to be carefully managed, even curated, so that they always appear to be positive and happy—this illusion can be exhausting to maintain.[43] Looking at others' depictions of their happy lives makes them feel judgmental about others and bad about themselves.[44] Ironically, students feel that they can be truer to themselves when they appear under a fake name, and then they can be as nasty as they want to be.[45] This also makes them prone to bullying, which is also distracting.[46]

One particular distraction—materialism and the pursuit of wealth—also tends to decrease religiosity.[47] That wealth in general tends to lessen religiosity is noted not only in the Book of Mormon but also in social science research.[48]

DIFFERENTIATION

Children inherit half of their genetic material from each parent. Consequently, they share a number of physical traits in common with their parents. When raised by their parents, they will pick up some of the same mannerisms as their parents and, in many things, the same tastes as their parents. Yet each individual is also different from their parents. Children are not their parents, even though they may look and act much like them. A number of years ago, the teenage and young adult boys in a family I know all sounded the same as their father on the phone. The father was a physician in a small town, and so the boys would not infrequently have the experience of hearing all sorts of unpleasant symptoms gushed forth on the phone all while they were trying desperately to bring to the caller's attention that they were not their father. They wanted to be distinguished from their father if only so they did not have to hear about someone's symptoms. How do children show their uniqueness? "Part of emerging adults' central life task of standing on their own is establishing identity differentiation. . . . Religion, particularly public religious practice, is one arena that effectively offers emerging adults an opportunity to achieve clear identity differentiation. . . . Religion also seems to many to be of less consequence than matters of education, finances, love interests, childbearing, and other more pressing areas, as a possible place to slack off, drop out, or otherwise become quite different from one's parents."[49]

If religion is not that big a thing, then losing it is no great loss. This, of course, assumes that religion is not that big a thing to the youth. That, in itself, is a warning sign that we have explored in a previous chapter. But the desire to be different encompasses more than not considering religion that important. Sometimes the desire to be different drives youth to rebel against something they know is considered important to their parents. Differentiation can encompass a multitude of variations, which we will not explore further.

Postponed Family Formation and Childbearing

We have already noted that a general pattern repeated over generations is for youth to be less religious until they settle down and get married.[50] The demographic tendency is to postpone settling down, unintentionally producing a reduction in the religious involvement of young adults.[51] Settling down thus is connected with being "grounded and settled" in the gospel (Colossians 1:23). American youth, even Latter-day Saint youth, are getting married at a later age than they used to. In 1998 the mean age of marriage for Latter-day Saint women in the United States was 21,[52] in 2010 it was up to 23.[53] This is still significantly younger than the national average. According to the Baylor Religion Survey, 75% of Latter-day Saints were married by the age of 26,[54] while the national average (mean) in 2019 was 29.8 years for men and 27.8 years for women.[55] This means young adults are spending more time as singles, a situation that makes it likely for them to lose faith and thus increase the risk that they will not return to faith when they do marry.

There are some reasons for the postponement of marriage. Until about the twentieth century, the average lifespan was about half of what it is now,[56] although even then there were cases in which people lived as long as we do today (the Coptic clergyman Shenoute lived to be more than one hundred). But those cases were the exception and not the rule. If the average life expectancy at birth was between twenty-two and twenty-five years, then there was a big incentive not to wait until twenty-eight to get married. This even shows up in classic fiction: In *Pride and Prejudice*, Lydia Bennett runs off to live with a man outside of marriage at age fifteen. Her living with someone outside of marriage is the scandal, not her age—today the reverse would be true. In premodern times, a married couple in their twenties had a one in four chance that one or both partners would die within ten years,[57] and given the hazards of childbearing before modern medicine, it was more likely to be the wife. There is a demographic fact behind all the stepmothers in fairy tales. Historically, youth were married off soon after puberty. Doing so maximized the length of time they might spend within a family, and thus settled in the gospel. Now, with probably many more years of life ahead, the impetus to marry and settle down has lessened. Consequently, the amount of time youth spend being single and risking loss of faith has increased. Latter-day Saint young adults, however, are the least likely of any religious group to postpone marriage.[58]

HONORING DIVERSITY

One of the fashionable intellectual buzzwords today is *diversity*. The current fad of seeking diversity originates in Supreme Court Justice Lewis F. Powell's 1978 opinion in *Regents of the University of California v. Bakke*, wherein racial quotas were forbidden but affirmative action was permitted because Justice Powell claimed that diversity in the classroom was a compelling state interest. While it is not clear that efforts to increase appreciation of diversity have been successful, and if so why,[59] it is usually seen as a very good thing. But it is not necessarily so.

> For most of their lives, from preschool on, most emerging adults have been taught by multiple institutions to celebrate diversity, to be inclusive of difference, to overcome racial divides, to embrace multiculturalism, to avoid being narrowly judgmental towards others who are out of the ordinary. . . . Despite the value of such inclusiveness and acceptance generally . . . this general orientation when brought to questions of religious life tends to undermine the effectiveness of particularities of faith traditions and practices. . . . As a result, most emerging adults are happy with religion so long as it is general and accepting of diversity but are uncomfortable if it is anything else.[60]

In this nebulous view, diversity has become a real problem.[61]

Biological diversity is arguably a good thing for a species. The idea is that a wide variety of genetic traits means a greater chance that the species will have a particular trait that makes it fit to survive. While this is good for a species, it is not necessarily good for an individual of that species because significant divergence from the trait that makes the species fit for survival ensures that the individual with divergence will not survive. In a similar way, diverging from the

Diversity for diversity's sake creates problems and may be chosen over the gospel.

gospel can produce catastrophic consequences. The Church is a defined group of individuals who have specific things (covenants) in common. While on some issues a wide variance can exist within the Church, covered by such phrases as "individual circumstances" or "adapting to local needs," on other issues, variance is simply not possible. It is important to recognize in what areas diversity may be permitted and even desirable and where it may not. It is also worth noting that diversity in organizations brings both positive and negative consequences.[62]

Diversity for diversity's sake creates problems. Diversity provides "competing definitions of what is true and good from which to choose, beyond those prescribed by various church doctrines."[63] In such a case, diversity may be chosen over the gospel. A famous quotation attributed to the Anglican priest William Law (1686–1761) comes to mind: "If you have not chosen the Kingdom of God first, it will in the end make no difference what you have chosen instead." Even diversity.

One pair of researchers noted that interacting with religiously diverse groups either "results in dilution of traditional religious commitments or production of stronger boundaries."[64] Thus individuals tended either to shed their own religious commitments[65] or to emphasize the distinctive traits of their religion. They interviewed one progressive activist who claimed that he often had "very little in common" with those of his own denomination and did not feel accountable to them:

> I feel my real community to be among progressive minded people.
> . . . Really I would say the biggest defining issue among religion now
> is not Jew, Catholic, Protestant: it's fundamentalist religion or, what
> I would say, a status quo, hierarchical vision of religion versus progressive, non-hierarchical, non-fundamentalist. The differences
> are the most profound between those two camps, not between Jews
> and Muslims or Muslims and Christians. I can sit in a room with
> progressive religionists from whatever faith and feel like I'm perfectly at home with them because we share that common view of
> what religion should be.[66]

While the particular progressive political views might be an issue and run counter to the gospel, the researchers noted that "for many progressive religious people, policing religious distinctiveness is not of particular concern."[67] A nonrepresentative survey of Latter-day Saints showed that uncritical acceptance of ill-considered notions of diversity has a tendency to lead people out of the Church and recounts how it was one individual's "openness to diversity that led to doubts about her faith."[68] Other researchers see the embrace of diversity as destroying religious distinctiveness, noting the "enigma of inclusiveness: that a moral system valuing diversity that begins by valuing everyone's particular differences somehow ends up devaluing any given particular difference."[69] Diversity is celebrated as long as it doesn't make you different.

KEEPING OPTIONS OPEN

Youth have incredible potential. A baby could grow to be a concert pianist, a phlebotomist, or a plumber. For years teachers and parents have encouraged children and youth to maximize their potential by keeping their options open. As a result, "Emerging adults are generally loath to close doors or burn bridges. Instead, they want to keep as many options open as possible. . . . If religion means being sober, settled, and steadfast, and if emerging adulthood means postponing those things, then it means not being particularly concerned about religion."[70]

One problem with keeping our options open is that opportunities are not necessarily available indefinitely. Every choice that we make opens doors to certain opportunities just as it closes other doors. Part of wisdom is being able to see which opportunities are worth taking advantage of and which are worth letting go. Wisdom consists, at least in part, in being able to see where potential paths might lead.

The mentality of keeping one's options open can spill into other areas. Some youth (about 30%) want to have more of a cafeteria approach to religion, picking and choosing the beliefs that they want. They are picky "about what they are willing to adopt of their religious tradition's beliefs and practices, some of which they think are 'outdated.' They often hold certain 'different opinions' and desires from what their religion allows, so they pick and choose what they want to accept. [They] disagree, neglect, or ignore the official teachings of their faiths most often on the following religious issues: sex before marriage, the need for regular religious service attendance, belief in the existence of hell, drinking alcohol, taking drugs, and use of birth control."[71] As one emerging adult put it, religion provides "something to fall back on. If this isn't enough, then tweak your religion a bit to fit your needs, or find another religion. It's really pretty simple."[72] This is usually not a particularly fruitful way of enhancing religion: "Potpourri religion is usually not very deep and sustaining; digging shallow wells in a field usually will not produce water."[73]

In the Church we often teach that individuals have agency and that they are "free to choose" (2 Nephi 2:27). But by taking that phrase out of context, we undermine the scripture. Yes, we are "free to choose"—we are "free to choose liberty and eternal life, through the great Mediator of all men, or to choose captivity and death, according to the captivity and power of the devil" (2 Nephi 2:27). In this scripture, Lehi points out that we can choose the consequences, but we do so by choosing those actions that will lead to those consequences. He is not claiming that we are free to choose what to do and then pick our own consequences regardless of what we do. We cannot choose to put our hand on a hot stove and then choose not to be burned. The action leads to the consequence. Thus, we do not have "free agency"—we have "moral agency." God explained that "every man may act in doctrine and principle pertaining to futurity, according to the moral agency which I have given unto him, that every man may be accountable for his own sins in the day of judgment" (Doctrine and Covenants 101:78). The right to choose is inextricably connected with accountability for those choices.

> **We do not get to pick and choose what parts of the gospel we will obey.**

We do not get to pick and choose what parts of the gospel we will obey. As Elder Neal A. Maxwell observed, "Our relationship to living prophets is not one in which their sayings are a smorgasbord from which we may take only that which pleases us. We are to partake of all that is placed before us, including the spinach, and to leave a clean plate!"[74] President Russell M. Nelson has instructed parents to "warn [their children] that they will encounter people who pick which commandments they will keep and ignore others that they choose to break. I call this the cafeteria approach to obedience. This practice of picking and choosing will not work. It will lead to misery. To prepare to meet God, one keeps *all* of His commandments."[75]

SELF-CONFIDENT SELF-SUFFICIENCY

The confusion about our moral agency can be taken even further. Instead of thinking that we can choose to follow what is right and what is wrong, some think that we can choose what is right and what is wrong. The NSYR found this to be a problem among youth. "They were authorized as individuals to know and choose what is right, at least for themselves. It was difficult for them to imagine an objective reference point beyond their own individual selves by which to evaluate themselves, their lives, and those of others. They could decide what to believe about ultimate reality based on what feels right to them, whatever fits their personal experience. . . . Why would an emerging adult want or need religious faith?"[76]

If someone thinks that they can determine right or wrong for themselves, then scriptures, prophets, or a church saying otherwise become an inconvenience at best. As a result, the freedom to choose and the wide variety of choices combine with "the value American society places on freedom and choice to prompt many youth to follow spiritual directions they know from personal experience rather than church teachings they hear from pastors and priests."[77]

The scriptures, however, "have enlarged the memory of this people, yea, and convinced many of the error of their ways" (Alma 37:8). They were written "that ye may learn to be more wise than we have been" (Mormon 9:31). Rejecting them usually condemns us to learn for ourselves "by sad experience" (Doctrine and Covenants 121:39) what we could have learned from them.

Partying

When then does religion become inconvenient? When it interferes with what we want to do.

> One of the other reasons why many, though not all, emerging adults may want to distance themselves from religion is that religion in their minds conflicts with certain other lifestyle options that are higher priorities. Most of them want to party, to hook up, to have sex in relationships, and to cohabit; or if they do not do these things now, many at least want to keep them as options for the future. . . . Many want to have sex with a boyfriend or girlfriend, or to at least be free to do so if the occasion arises, and many want to be able to hook up with someone they meet to whom they may feel attracted. Many also want to cohabit with current or future serious partners or fiancés before getting married. And all of this, emerging adults are aware, contradicts the teachings of most religions. So they simply avoid religion and thereby resolve the conflict. . . .

Framed as a social-psychological causal mechanism, most emerging adults reduce a certain cognitive dissonance they feel—arising from the conflict of religious teachings against partying and sex before marriage versus their wanting to engage in those behaviors—by mentally discounting the religious teachings and socially distancing themselves from the source of those teachings. In this simple way, the role of sex, drinking, and sometimes drugs is often important in forming emerging adults' frequent lack of interest in religious faith and practice.[78]

Sin and the desire to sin, or at least keeping the option open, are a powerful motivation to silence those voices that might suggest otherwise. While actual sin may not figure in all cases of youth (or adults) losing their religion, it plays its role in many cases and must be considered in the complete picture. "Behavior that does not conform to religious norms may also lead to change in religious attachment. For example, 42 percent of Mormons who had stopped attending church reported a 'lifestyle as no longer compatible with participation in the church.'"[79] According to one study, five times as many people stopped going to church because their lifestyle was incompatible with the teachings of their church than because they had doubts about it.[80]

Among emerging adults (18- to 23-year-olds) in America, 84% have engaged in sexual relations and 66% have done so with more than one partner.[81] Thus about five-sixths of emerging adults may potentially fall under those whose sex lives conflict with their religion and, if they give it much thought, will fall under the temptation to make their beliefs conform to their practice. For teenagers, the NSYR has published data about sexual activity that better distinguishes between American teens in general and Latter-day Saint teens. Among Americans 37.2% of teenagers have been sexually active and another 24.5% wish they were. Among Latter-day Saints 12.6% of teenagers have been sexually active and another 14.9% wish they were.[82] So while Latter-day Saints have less of a problem than most of the nation, it is still a problem.

Partying often includes alcohol or substance abuse. Alcohol use plays a smaller role than other factors in decreased religiosity,[83] perhaps because many other religions do not have religious barriers against

Partying often includes alcohol or substance abuse. Courtesy of Lecheniye Nar-komanii/Pixabay.

alcohol use. The NSYR noted that "there is less of a difference between those who increased their drinking and those who did not, although respondents who drank more at Wave III than at Wave I diminish their religious service attendance at noticeably higher rates."[84] Surveying prospective college graduates, the Higher Education Research Institute reports that "about a third of all respondents indicate that they 'frequently' drank beer (33.4%) and/or wine/liquor (31.5%) in the past year. In terms of heavy episodic drinking, slightly less than half the students report they had not had more than five drinks in a row in the past two weeks (44.7%), though the majority did at least once (55.3%)."[85] The use of alcohol increases with time in college, as does partying in general.[86] When compared to the NSYR's research, these results indicate that college students are slightly less likely to drink than emerging adults generally but are more likely to binge drink.[87]

Others see the problem as more severe: "Among college students, about 80 percent drink alcohol, about 40 percent binge drink, and about 20 percent binge drink three or more times within a 2-week period."[88] Binge drinking may be more prevalent among adolescents than older adults: "Because human adolescents may be less sensitive than adults to certain aversive effects of alcohol, they may be at higher risk for consuming more drinks per drinking occasion." Adults tend to suffer more of the immediate adverse effects of binge drinking than adolescents do.[89] This does not mean that adolescents and emerging adults do not suffer negative consequences: "These consequences include risky sexual behavior; physical and sexual assaults; potential effects on the developing brain; problems in school, at work, and with the legal system; various types of injury; car crashes; homicide and suicide; and death from alcohol poisoning."[90] Over half of college-age youth who binge drink suffer from blackouts.[91] Those who habitually binge drink also suffer brain damage that reduces their brain's capacity 10% (like going from an A to a B).[92] One might also note that while religion in general dampens aggression, alcohol makes religious people more aggressive than nonreligious people.[93]

The relationship of alcohol to sexual activity is somewhat obscured by the focus of social scientists. Social scientists have focused on the relationship of alcohol to what they term as risky sexual behavior, by which they mean behavior during sex that is likely to permit the transmission of a sexual disease, a relationship that is by no means clear[94]—in part because social desirability bias skews correct reporting (only about half of those engaging in the behavior will admit to it).[95] But "if engaging in casual sex is itself construed as risky, then at least at first glance the high simultaneous frequency of these behaviors would seem to support previous studies that found alcohol and risky sex to be correlated at the global level."[96] It is clear that many individuals drink alcohol as a means to prepare themselves for sexual contact, especially casual contact with someone new.[97] For some, "alcohol had become such an integral part of their sexual scripts [that they] questioned if they would ever have sex if they did not drink."[98]

Using drugs (the study looked only at marijuana use) is associated with both decreased church attendance and increased likelihood of disaffiliation. Since marijuana has been illegal in most places, using it may be a form of taking risks, which is frequently associated with decreased church attendance.[99]

Two related facets of partying can alter an individual's faith. While the substance abuse facet of partying is clearly related to losing faith, sexual activity likewise correlates to the loss of faith; however, we defer discussion of this aspect to a later chapter.

POLITICS

While parties and pursuant promiscuity pose problems for faith, another sort of party can as well—political parties.

The Church is politically neutral. It does not endorse political parties, political platforms, or political candidates. It may, however, take political stands on moral and social issues.[100] The Church wants its members to be politically informed and involved, but only as private individuals: "As citizens, Church members are encouraged to participate in political and governmental affairs, including involvement in the political party of their choice. Members are also urged to be actively engaged in worthy causes to improve their communities and make them wholesome places in which to live and rear families."[101]

The guidance that the Church gives its members in choosing political candidates is that "honest men [and women] and wise men [and women] should be sought for diligently, and good men [and women] and wise men [and women] ye should observe to uphold; otherwise whatsoever is less than these cometh of evil" (Doctrine and Covenants 98:10). The fact that honest individuals and wise individuals are listed separately implies that both qualities might not exist in a given candidate—obviously someone who is both wise and honest is preferable but might not be available—and so one should choose the candidate who is either wise or honest, though sometimes the choice might be between individuals who embody neither characteristic. Nevertheless, all political parties contain individuals who are good and honest.

In general, youth and young adults are disengaged and disinterested in civic and political life.[102] "Adolescents and emerging adults today tend to be less involved in various forms of overt political activity and are less reliably and consistently involved in politics than previous cohorts of young citizens." Over a quarter (27%) are completely disinterested in politics. About one in eight (13%) were uninformed and said they did not know enough to be engaged in the process. About one in five (19%) distrusted either the political process or the politicians. They think "politics was inherently about manipulation and deceit."[103] About one in ten (10%) are not engaged because they feel helpless to change anything. Just over a quarter (27%) are marginally political. But 4% of emerging adults are politically engaged, in fact extremely engaged. "They see opportunities for having an impact on society for the better and believe they are obliged to take on those challenges. They strive for economic and educational opportunity, grassroots urban renewal, racial justice, the end of human trafficking, and

> Political platforms usually contain elements that are compatible with the gospel, but no political party or platform completely aligns with the gospel.

other causes through creative communication, community organizing, and social movement activism. They view anything less as a selfish indifference that is morally intolerable."[104]

Political platforms usually contain elements that are compatible with the gospel, but no political party or platform completely aligns with the gospel. (And just because a politician is elected on a particular platform is no guarantee that he or she will pursue that platform after the election.) Therefore, no political party should be unequivocally endorsed. Because political platforms have elements that overlap with the gospel of Jesus Christ, there is a danger that one can transfer the locus of loyalty from Jesus Christ and his gospel to a secular political cause.

While "scholars have long presumed that religion is independent of the political attributes with which it is correlated," recent research has shown that "people are willing to leave what may be long-term relationships with a religious organization because of the political presence of an unpopular group in the political environment." Scholars had noticed that in recent years "Democrats have reduced their attendance at religious services,"[105] and they decided to investigate that phenomenon. (Others have found that both conservatives and liberals believe in fairness and caring for others, but conservatives also tend to prioritize respect for authority, loyalty to one's group, and purity or sanctity, while these values tend to be unimportant to liberals.[106] Since some of these moral traits are related to religiosity, not valuing these points might estrange some from religion. This was not examined by the researchers.) The researchers found that political disagreements among members of local congregations might cause individuals first to disaffiliate with the congregation and later—when the church continued to allow the offending individuals to attend or if the attitudes were perceived to be widespread throughout the denomination—to cease to identify with the denomination. While this phenomenon is better known among the political left, it occurs on both sides of the aisle and does not happen to all those who are politically involved; instead, "political disagreement tends to drive the decision making of those marginally attached to a congregation."[107] It is more likely that those who put politics above the gospel will find a political reason to leave.

Another danger in putting politics above the gospel is that some individuals begin to think of everything in terms of politics, including the gospel. They think of the Church as just another political organization, capable of being manipulated by political means. An unspoken assumption behind this thinking is that Church leaders are just men, that they are not inspired and do not receive revelation, and that mortals, rather than Jesus Christ, are at the head of the Church. So they participate in candlelight vigils and protests and send out press releases trying to put political pressure on the Church to encourage, or even demand, it to conform to their own ideal rather than Christ's.

Politics can affect religion in another way. Young adults who stop attending church tend to do so before their political views crystalize. The political viewpoints adopted while they are not attending changes their chances of returning to faith when they start raising their own families. Young adults who join political parties that are more religiously oriented are more likely to return to attending church as young parents than if they join parties that are less religiously oriented.[108]

Pornography

The prevalence of pornography has had a devastating impact on faith that is often unacknowledged. This is somewhat surprising considering that pornography led to King David's downfall (2 Samuel 11:2–4).

The Bible makes a point that David was not doing what he was supposed to be doing—leading the army (2 Samuel 11:1)—and instead was looking at a woman bathing from the roof of his palace (2 Samuel 11:2). David's involvement in pornography marks a turning point in his life. Before that incident he had been a shepherd, the defeater of Goliath, a successful military leader, the Psalmist, and the proposed builder of the temple. After that point, the Bible depicts him as spending the rest of his life dealing with the consequences of his actions:

- David's viewing of pornography led to adultery with Bathsheba (2 Samuel 11:4).
- After she became pregnant and her husband Uriah refused to be complicit in the cover-up, David arranged Uriah's death (2 Samuel 11:14–17) and then married Bathsheba (2 Samuel 11:27).
- Following after his father's example, Amnon, David's son, raped his half-sister Tamar (2 Samuel 13:1–18). Although David was angry, he did nothing (2 Samuel 13:21).
- Tamar's full brother, Absalom, on the other hand, killed Amnon (2 Samuel 13:28–29), resulting in Absalom's estrangement from David's family (2 Samuel 13:34–14:27).
- Absalom later revolted against David (2 Samuel 15:1–12) and during the revolt publicly raped all of David's concubines (2 Samuel 16:21–22).

While David's case is extreme, it provides a useful historical example of the consequences of viewing pornography. It illustrates the words of Jesus: "whosoever looketh on a woman to lust after her hath committed adultery with her already in his heart" (Matthew 5:28).

Many subjects are unprepared to discuss the topic of pornography. One researcher noted that his "research team found men consistently inarticulate about the subject."[109] "Just like the psychiatrists debating the matter, these men are seldom prepared to label it a problem, but they also clearly display enough halting conversation about it that neither are they prepared to suggest that nothing is wrong or off-kilter."[110] "The therapy community has been largely dismissive of alleged problems connected with pornography use and associated deception."[111] Pornography is more common among men than women,[112] although "when female adolescents watched more pornography, they became more strongly involved with the material than male adolescents did."[113]

Even adolescent girls are more articulate on the subject than most men; as one put it, "I feel betrayed by it really. Because a lot of it is watched by guys really, and I feel like I'm being stripped bare even if it's not my body. And it bothers me."[114]

Reliable and accurate data on pornography use is hard to get. Although pornography is a multibillion-dollar industry,[115] "reliable data on and analyses of pornography use are exceptionally rare. Academics are in no hurry to collect such data. And if studies of adult pornography use are unusual, research on adolescent usage is even more unique."[116] Estimates on youth pornography use vary from 7 to 98%.[117] Part of the reason for the paucity of data is ethical: "experimental research on adolescents' use of pornography is ethically not possible—it is usually illegal to show pornography to minors."[118] Finding a control group is also a problem. Researchers bemoan the fact that "finding a control group with no exposure to sexually explicit material seems increasingly less possible."[119] Avoiding pornography takes a concerted effort. "Unlike in the past, those who wish to avoid pornography have to go out of their way to do so."[120] Research on pornography also poses another ethical dilemma: how does a researcher investigate pornography without being exposed to it?

Researchers are also concerned that social desirability bias distorts the information gathered. The NSYR determined that among adolescent boys, 70% claim that they never use pornography, but the study also found reasons to suggest considerable social desirability bias in the numbers since they also found during the in-person interviews that "a majority of adolescent boys do not think there is a problem with viewing pornography, and they admit to doing this very thing ('infrequently,' of course)."[121] Because social desirability bias is so frequently assumed in studies on pornography,[122] that factor itself has been studied.[123] But the results of that study did not go as anticipated. There is "a statistically reliable social desirability bias against reporting the consumption of pornography, but, among those who admit such consumption, there is no additional bias against reporting the amount of pornography consumed on a daily basis."[124] Religious people tend to be more open about reporting their pornography exposure and consumption, but "less religious people are actually more hesitant to report recent pornography consumption than are those who are more religious."[125] The "results [of the study] suggest that we can place about as much confidence in the self-reports of religious individuals as we do in the self-reports of the irreligious when it comes to pornography-related measures."[126] Thus, "religious individuals really do watch less pornography than the less religious," despite studies to the contrary.[127] If anything, "social desirability concerns might motivate religious consumers to underreport pornography's negative consequences rather than overreport them."[128] Men who use pornography perceive their use as uniformly positive[129] and tend not to see the negative effects.

Even with the social desirability bias, a number of interesting results come from the data. First, it does appear that over an almost forty-year span (1973–2010), pornography use by men has been gradually increasing.[130] Second, the data show "a nearly linear association" between pornography use among adolescents and lack of religiosity.[131] Third, pornography use and religious attendance do not correlate. Fourth, the importance of religion for daily life, however, correlates with avoiding pornography.[132] Data from other surveys show that the use of pornography "deadens religious impulses."[133]

Latter-day Saints are among the groups that "display the lowest stated rates of pornography use here, though these numbers may be artificially low due to stronger than average social desirability bias." Latter-day Saints showed the lowest pornography use among adolescents (6.2%).[134] Among young adult Latter-day Saint males, the numbers are higher, with 26.3% reporting having viewed a pornographic movie in the last year; among females this was 12.5%.[135] The Relationships in America survey similarly recorded Latter-day Saint men as the group of religious men with the lowest use of pornography, with 14% using it in the previous week. Latter-day Saint women's use, however, while significantly lower than the men's at 3%, was tied for fifth lowest.[136]

In an attempt to avoid the tendency to regress toward a lower mean, to avoid recall bias, and to alleviate social desirability bias, the Relationships in America survey asked, "When did you last intentionally look at pornography?"[137] In general, "43 percent of men and 9 percent of women report watching pornography in the last week,"[138] with 24% of men reporting that it was either today or yesterday. Thus "men's porn use clusters around the most recent options, hinting at possible compulsive behavior." Over an entire lifespan, women's use declines with age (perhaps a generational effect), but men's use declines only slightly with age.[139] Church activity makes a difference too[140]—"weekly church attenders are the least likely to report pornography use in the past week, while those who rarely or never attend do so at double the rate."[141]

> Attempts to categorize pornography users according to demographic factors are often contradictory. Basically anyone is susceptible.

Attempts to categorize pornography users according to demographic factors are often contradictory. Basically anyone is susceptible.[142] "Higher parent education, higher socioeconomic status, greater attachment to school, healthier family relationships, and more frequent family religious practices are predictive of less exposure to pornography for adolescents."[143] Parental disapproval is a deterrent[144] since boys are more likely to view it when they have private computers in their rooms[145] or when they are at friends' houses.[146] When viewing pornography is seen as socially acceptable among peers, its use also increases.[147]

Teenagers tend to fall into one of four categories of pornography use. The most common category (which may be subject to social desirability bias) is nonusers or infrequent users (34.5%). The next most common category is occasional users (23.3%). This is closely followed by increasingly frequent users (21.8%). The least common is heavy users whose involvement in sexual behavior is decreasing their use of pornography (20.4%).[148] For teenage females, the most frequent category is stable nonusers or infrequent users (91.6%). The next most common trajectory is increasingly frequent users (5.1%). This is closely followed by stable occasional users (3.3%).[149] For most teenage males, pornography use increased over time if only slightly[150] and became more coarse.[151] Among young women, those who used pornography tended to be more interested in sexual matters and were more likely to think what was depicted was realistic.[152] Involvement in sexual behavior decreases pornography use in young women but not young men.[153]

The survey's results for young adults were similar but not directly comparable because different categories were used.[154]

The effects are far worse than many of us likely imagine and are unfortunately too numerous to detail here. Though the effects of pornography are negative in social, spiritual, and other ways, we only have space here to discuss the negative effects on general spirituality. One study showed that "excessive pornography use may have a negative impact on one's spirituality such as preventing the establishment of spiritual connections in the first place."[155] Another study showed that "the use of pornography interfered with or disrupted one's relationship with God,"[156] an effect that 43% of users recognized.[157] A third study found that "more frequent porn consumption, especially for religious persons, is associated with guilt and embarrassment, and hurts one's relationship with God or interest in spiritual things, while also potentially creating feelings of scrupulosity that may influence individuals to withdraw from family."[158] Another study found that "persons who viewed pornography reported more frequent religious doubts, lower levels of religious salience, and lower prayer frequency" six years after they viewed the pornography even if church attendance only decreased slightly.[159] Longitudinal studies using NSYR data showed that viewing pornography in the teenage years decreased service attendance, frequency of prayer, the importance of faith, and closeness to God in the emerging adult years, while increasing religious doubts.[160] Religious doubts are linearly correlated to earlier pornography use. While prayer, church attendance, and the importance of religion generally decrease with pornography use, these same practices actually increase slightly in frequency once pornography use is more frequent than once a week, suggesting either that some users turn to religion as a means of escape or that they have completely rationalized their pornography use and disassociated their practice from the teachings of their religion.[161]

Pornography use undermines religion, but religion also protects against pornography use. Yet "religious/spiritual beliefs and practices are effective deterrents of pornography use only insofar as they are practiced for their intrinsic value or meaning rather than their extrinsic or social value."[162] In other words, if one believes religion is true, one is less likely to use pornography; if one believes religion is merely socially useful, all bets are off.

LOSS OF TRUST

About one in sixteen youth who either stop attending or stop believing do so because they had a bad experience and consequently distrust religion.[163] One reason for this is that "most massive violations of trust are violations of integrity."[164] Integrity includes more than just honesty; it also includes congruence between one's action and beliefs.[165] For some people, "spirituality is about integrity."[166] Along with integrity, intent is important. The intent needs to be "honorable and clear" and beneficial.[167] Lehi tells his sons, "I have none other object save it be the everlasting welfare of your souls" (2 Nephi 2:30). Even suspected hidden agendas undermine trust,[168] as does incompetence and a track record of failure.[169] "If we don't accomplish what we are expected to do, it diminishes our credibility."[170]

> In the context of the Church, loss of trust is usually a result of individuals in the Church not acting as they are supposed to act, not staying true to their integrity, or not keeping their intent in line with gospel principles.

Trust and faith are closely related—almost synonymous—and destruction of trust can destroy faith. Even children know that not everyone can be trusted, and "young children are less likely than adults to give people who make incorrect statements in their own favor the benefit of the doubt, assuming instead that these kinds of inaccuracies arise from a malicious intent to deceive."[171] In the context of the Church, this loss of trust is usually a result of individuals in the Church not acting as they are supposed to act, not staying true to their integrity, or not keeping their intent in line with gospel principles. If youth confuse their loss of trust in a specific individual or set of individuals with their trust in God, then the loss of trust leads to a loss of faith.

"When people trust and that trust is exploited, they become more cynical."[172] Although cynicism has been given a variety of definitions,[173] in regard to the Church cynicism is a "disillusionment resulting from the failure of specific institutions . . . to meet the high expectations."[174] Cynicism is not a personality trait per se, but an attitude or philosophy about human nature.[175] Common to most definitions of cynicism "is the belief that others lack integrity and cannot be trusted."[176] In the workplace cynics "distrust the motives of their leaders and believe that their employers, when presented with the opportunity, will exploit their contributions."[177] In the Church, cynics may believe that Church leaders will exploit them given the chance. Cynicism is caused, in part, by the observation of "self-interested behavior" on the part of leaders, which leads to a "sense of betrayal."[178] It is also caused when someone "perceives that the organization has failed to meet its obligations," such as the violation of organizational procedures, leading to "reactions such as anger, outrage, distrust, and resentment."[179] It can also be caused by an individual's holding "unrealistically high expectations" that are subsequently unmet.[180]

One of the factors linked to cynicism is the manner of communication. "Honest and frequent communication generates perceptions of fairness and trust. . . . Failure to communicate important information, in contrast, particularly during times of organizational unrest, violates the contract, resulting in unmet expectations, fear, distrust, and, ultimately, cynicism. . . . Moreover, attempts by management to deny well-crafted rumors serve only to exacerbate [individuals'] contempt and distrust toward management."[181] Those who have lost trust in the Church or its leaders often accuse the Church of failing to communicate or of hiding important information. In most cases, however, it is not a matter of the Church failing to communicate but rather of the individuals failing to pay attention.

Taking offense, however, is a more frequent reason for members of the Church to lose trust. "Individuals consider the nature of their treatment . . . as a criterion of fairness. Honesty, ethicality, politeness, and respect in interpersonal dealings are prominent factors in . . . perceptions of justice. . . . When these standards are not honored, perceptions of interactional injustice will result, thus leading to negative attitudes such as dislike and distrust toward the purveyors of the discourteous treatment."[182] Members of the Church and especially local leaders who give offense by being dishonest or failing to live the teachings of the

Honest and frequent communication generates perceptions of fairness and trust. Courtesy of Julita/Pixabay.

Church demonstrate a lack of integrity in their behavior and invite cynicism. The Lord has warned that those who wish to exercise "power or influence" must be "without hypocrisy, and without guile" (Doctrine and Covenants 121:41–42). One Church leader noted of another's lack of integrity, "When they saw your conduct they would not believe in my words" (Alma 39:11).

Loss of trust and the resultant cynicism make an individual increasingly reluctant to be identified with an offending organization and less committed to the organization[183]—which in this case would be the Church. Some theorize that organizations, such as churches, "endure because the various stakeholders continue to have their needs met through their association with the organization."[184] Thus when the need to have one's true faith affirmed is betrayed by a lack of integrity, then the betrayed individual will not desire to associate with or commit to an organization. Those who have demonstrated a lack of integrity often attribute the lack of commitment by the offended person to "obstinacy or some irrational resistance to change," even though no "compelling case to [change] had been presented to them."[185] Presenting a compelling case is what the scriptures call "persuasion" (Doctrine and Covenants 121:41).

When leaders employ "the use of assertive tactics, such as social pressure and coercion," it increases cynicism[186] because one "characteristic of cynicism is a clear-sighted impatience with fraudulence and hypocrisy."[187] Because "the goal of management techniques continues to be control and manipulation,"[188] management techniques are ineffective against cynicism. We have been warned that attempts "to exercise control or dominion or compulsion upon the souls of the children of men, in any degree of unrighteousness" are counterproductive (Doctrine and Covenants 121:37) and can result in the "belief that others are deceitful, self-serving, untrustworthy, and malevolent."[189]

Research on cynicism suggests that there is a way to reach cynical individuals and bring them back into faith because "cynics care deeply about their organization." After all, "cynicism is a malleable attitude, shaped greatly by the . . . context."[190] Just as the self-interested violation of trust leads to cynicism, learning about selfless examples of trustworthiness lessens cynicism.[191] "Integrity (adherence to an acceptable set of principles) and benevolence (concern for the individual's well-being), in particular, might correlate negatively with cynicism."[192] Cynics are thought to be more likely to change under the influence of those who are "generally well-liked, seen as knowledgeable about the subject matter, possessed of high power and status in the organization, and trustworthy."[193] The road back is not easy because "a brother offended is harder to be won than a strong city" (Proverbs 18:19).

Looking Back

What is interesting about this list of factors that influence youth to lose their faith is that for the most part, the factors are behaviorally or event driven rather than philosophically or intellectually driven. On the other hand, having doubts about religious beliefs was only weakly correlated with retaining or losing faith and did not show up on the list as a major factor. Doubts play a role in loss of belief and commitment but only in combination with other factors: faith did not play a big role in the teen's parents' lives, the parents were lax in their church attendance, faith already played less of a role in the teen's life (usually accompanied by less frequent religious devotion like prayer, church attendance, and scripture reading), and the youth did not know other individuals who could defend their faith. All told, "half of American nonreligious teens who were raised in a religion apparently lost their faith or dropped out of religion for fairly passive reasons: for lack of interest, for reasons unknown or vague," and so forth.[194]

The factors discussed throughout this chapter should not be thought of as mutually exclusive reasons for abandoning faith. If 84% of youth have sex lives that are incompatible with their faith and 30% want to pick and choose their beliefs,[195] there has to be some overlap. We are looking at a list of prominent factors, not of separate causes. Different individuals can have a different set of factors influencing their individual decisions and still end up with the same results.

While intellectual issues may not play the largest role in loss of faith, they still play a role, and it is to that role that we now turn.

NOTES

1. Christian Smith and Patricia Snell, *Souls in Transition: The Religious and Spiritual Lives of Emerging Adults* (Oxford: Oxford University Press, 2009), 75; Nicolette D. Manglos, "Faith Pinnacle Moments: Stress, Miraculous Experiences, and Life Satisfaction in Young Adulthood," *Sociology of Religion* 74, no. 2 (2013): 176, 179; R. David Hayward and Neal Krause, "Changes in Religious Group Affiliation during Older Adulthood: Evidence from an 11-Year Longitudinal Study," *Review of Religious Research* 56, no. 4 (2014): 550.
2. Christian Smith and Melinda Lundquist Denton, *Soul Searching: The Religious and Spiritual Lives of American Teenagers* (Oxford: Oxford University Press, 2005), 105.
3. Smith and Denton, *Soul Searching*, 89.
4. Manglos, "Faith Pinnacle Moments," 177.
5. Mark D. Regnerus and Jeremy E. Uecker, "Finding Faith, Losing Faith: The Prevalence and Context of Religious Transformations during Adolescence," *Review of Religious Research* 47, no. 3 (2006): 226–27.
6. Jeremy E. Uecker, Mark D. Regnerus, and Margaret L. Vaaler, "Losing My Religion: The Social Sources of Religious Decline in Early Adult Years," *Social Sources* 85, no. 4 (2007): 1678–81.

7.   Uecker, Regnerus, and Vaaler, "Losing My Religion," 1669.

8.   Neil Gross and Solon Simmons, "The Religious Convictions of College and University Professors," in *The American University in a Postsecular Age*, ed. Douglas Jacobsen and Rhonda Hustedt Jacobsen (Oxford: Oxford University Press, 2008), 20.

9.   Gross and Simmons, "Religious Convictions," 22–23.

10. Gross and Simmons, "Religious Convictions," 23.

11. Gross and Simmons, "Religious Convictions," 24.

12. Gary A. Tobin and Aryeh K. Weinberg, *Religious Beliefs and Behavior of College Faculty* (San Francisco: Institute for Jewish and Community Research, 2007), 16.

13. Tobin and Weinberg, *Religious Beliefs and Behavior*, 12, 81.

14. Tobin and Weinberg, *Religious Beliefs and Behavior*, 82.

15. Tobin and Weinberg, *Religious Beliefs and Behavior*, 3, 19–20.

16. Gross and Simmons, "Religious Convictions," 26.

17. Ray Franke, Sylvia Ruiz, Jessica Sharkness, Linda DeAngelo, and John Pryor, *Findings from the 2009 Administration of the College Senior Survey (CSS): National Aggregates* (Los Angeles: Higher Education Research Institute, University of California, Los Angeles, 2010), 32–33.

18. Robert J. Nash and DeMethra LaSha Bradley, "The Different Spiritualities of the Students We Teach," in Jacobsen and Jacobsen, *American University in a Postsecular Age*, 138.

19. "Are You Charlotte Simmons?," *Yale Alumni Magazine*, March/April 2005, http://www.yalealumnimagazine.com/issues/2005_03/charlotte.html.

20. "Are You Charlotte Simmons?"

21. Jonathan P. Hill, "Rejecting Evolution: The Role of Religion, Education, and Social Networks," *Journal for the Scientific Study of Religion* 53, no. 3 (2014): 584, 589–90.

22. Hill, "Rejecting Evolution," 591.

23. *Relationships in America Survey* (Austin, TX: The Austin Institute for the Study of Family and Culture, 2014), 43. People often give more than one reason for divorce. Adding the top seven responses, for example, gives 205%.

24. Jeremy E. Uecker and Christopher G. Ellison, "Parental Divorce, Parental Religious Characteristics, and Religious Outcomes in Adulthood," *Journal of the Scientific Study of Religion* 51, no. 4 (2012): 777–78.

25. Hsien-Hsein Lau and Nicholas H. Wolfinger, "Parental Divorce and Adult Religiosity: Evidence from the General Social Survey," *Review of Religious Research* 53, no. 1 (September 2011): 85–103; Uecker and Ellison, "Parental Divorce," 777–94.

26. Lau and Wolfinger, "Parental Divorce and Adult Religiosity," 98–99; Regnerus and Uecker, "Finding Faith, Losing Faith," 221; and Adam R. Fisher, "A Review and Conceptual Model of the Research on Doubt, Disaffiliation, and Related Religious Changes," *Psychology of Religion and Spirituality* 9, no. 4 (2017): 362.

27. Lau and Wolfinger, "Parental Divorce and Adult Religiosity," 95, 93, 92.

28. Uecker and Ellison, "Parental Divorce," 786–88.

29. Jiexia Elisa Zhai, Christopher G. Ellison, Norval D. Glenn, and Elizabeth Marquardt, "Parental Divorce and Religious Involvement among Young Adults," *Sociology of Religion* 68, no. 2 (2007): 135, 139.

30. Uecker and Ellison, "Parental Divorce," 790.

31. Uecker and Ellison, "Parental Divorce," 790–91.

32. Zhai et al., "Parental Divorce and Religious Involvement," 135; Christopher G. Ellison, Anthony B. Walker, Norval D. Glenn, and Elizabeth Marquardt, "The Effects of Parental Marital Discord and Divorce on the Religious and Spiritual Lives of Young Adults," *Social Science Research* 40 (2011): 548.

33. Uecker and Ellison, "Parental Divorce," 779.

34. Ellison et al., "Effects of Parental Marital Discord," 549.

35. Zhai et al., "Parental Divorce and Religious Involvement," 136.

36. Stephen Cranney, "Who Is Leaving the Church? Demographic Predictors of Ex–Latter-day Saint Status in the Pew Religious Landscape Survey," *BYU Studies* 58, no. 1 (2019): 106.

37. Ellison et al., "Effects of Parental Marital Discord," 548.

38. Melinda Lundquist Denton, "Family Structure, Family Disruption, and Profiles of Adolescent Religiosity," *Journal for the Scientific Study of Religion* 51, no. 1 (2012): 54–60.

39. Lau and Wolfinger, "Parental Divorce and Adult Religiosity," 99.

40. Smith and Snell, *Souls in Transition*, 76–77.

41. Vern L. Bengtson, Merril Silverstein, Norella M. Putney, and Susan C. Harris, "Does Religiousness Increase with Age? Age Changes and Generational Differences over 35 Years," *Journal of the Scientific Study of Religion* 54, no. 2 (2015): 373.

42. Donna Freitas, *The Happiness Effect: How Social Media Is Driving a Generation to Appear Perfect at Any Cost* (Oxford: Oxford University Press, 2017), 13–14.

43. Freitas, *Happiness Effect*, 43–80.

44. Freitas, *Happiness Effect*, 239.

45. Freitas, *Happiness Effect*, 124–42.

46. Freitas, *Happiness Effect*, 143–71.

47. Manglos, "Faith Pinnacle Moments," 180.

48. Gregory S. Longo and Jungmeen Kim-Spoon, "What Drives Apostates and Converters? The Social and Familial Antecedents of Religious Change among Adolescents," *Psychology of Religion and Spirituality* 6, no. 4 (2014): 285.

49. Smith and Snell, *Souls in Transition*, 78.

50. Rodney Stark, *The Triumph of Faith* (Wilmington, DE: ISI Books, 2015), 188.

51. Smith and Snell, *Souls in Transition*, 79; Bengtson et al., "Does Religiousness Increase with Age?," 365.

52. Tim B. Heaton, "Religious Influences on Mormon Fertility: Cross-National Comparisons," in *Latter-day Saint Social Life: Social Research on the LDS Church and Its Members* (Provo, UT: Religious Studies Center, Brigham Young University, 1998), 425–40, table 14.2.

53. Naomi Schaefer Riley, *Got Religion? How Churches, Mosques, and Synagogues Can Bring Young People Back* (West Conshohocken, PA: Templeton, 2014), 92.

54. Baylor Religion Survey, wave 4 data, data courtesy of Association of Religion Data Archives.

55. https://www.census.gov/data/tables/time-series/demo/families/marital.html. By comparison the mean age of first marriage has been:

	Men	Women
2010	28.2	26.1
2000	26.8	25.1
1990	26.1	23.9
1980	24.7	22.0
1970	23.2	20.8
1960	22.8	20.3
1950	22.8	20.3

56. Roger S. Bagnall and Bruce W. Frier, *The Demography of Roman Egypt* (Cambridge: Cambridge University Press, 1994), 109–10.

57. Bagnall and Frier, *Demography of Roman Egypt*, 123.

58. NSYR wave 3 data.

59. Carol T. Kulik and Loriann Roberson, "Common Goals and Golden Opportunities: Evaluations of Diversity Education in Academic and Organizational Settings," *Academy of Management Learning & Education* 7, no. 3 (2008): 313–14, 316–17.

60. Smith and Snell, *Souls in Transition*, 80–81.

61. Fisher, "Review and Conceptual Model," 362.

62. Antje Buche, Monika Jungbauer-Gans, Annekatrin Niebuhr, and Cornelius Peters, "Diversität und Erfolg von Organisationen," *Zeitschrift für Soziologie* 42, no. 6 (2013): 483–501.

63. Bengtson et al., "Does Religiousness Increase with Age?," 366.

64. Grace Yukich and Ruth Braunstein, "Encounters at the Religious Edge: Variation in Religious Expression across Interfaith Advocacy and Social Movement Settings," *Journal for the Scientific Study of Religion* 53, no. 4 (2014): 791.

65. Compare Fisher, "Review and Conceptual Model," 362–63.

66. Yukich and Braunstein, "Encounters at the Religious Edge," 801; ellipses in original.

67. Yukich and Braunstein, "Encounters at the Religious Edge," 795.

68. Jana Riess, *The Next Mormons: How Millennials Are Changing the LDS Church* (Oxford: Oxford University Press, 2019), 43.

69. Smith and Snell, *Souls in Transition*, 81.

70. Smith and Snell, *Souls in Transition*, 80.

71. Smith and Snell, *Souls in Transition*, 167.

72. Quoted in Nash and Bradley, "Different Spiritualities of the Students We Teach," 140.

73. Scotty McLennan, quoted in Larry A. Braskamp, "Religious and Spiritual Journeys of College Students," in Jacobsen and Jacobsen, *American University in a Postsecular Age*, 133.

74. Neal A. Maxwell, *Things As They Really Are* (Salt Lake City: Deseret Book, 1978), 50.

75. Russell M. Nelson, "Face the Future with Faith," *Ensign*, May 2011, 34.

76. Smith and Snell, *Souls in Transition*, 82.

77. Bengtson et al., "Does Religiousness Increase with Age?," 366.

78. Smith and Snell, *Souls in Transition*, 83–84.

79. William S. Bradshaw, Tim B. Heaton, Ellen Decoo, John P. Dehlin, Renee V. Galliher, and Katherine A. Crowell, "Religious Experiences of GBTQ Mormon Males," *Journal for the Scientific Study of Religion* 54, no. 2 (2015): 313.

80. *Unchurched Report* (Nashville: LifeWay Research, 2017), 10; Fisher, "Review and Conceptual Model," 362.

81. Mark D. Regnerus and Jeremy E. Uecker, *Premarital Sex in America: How Young Americans Meet, Mate, and Think about Marrying* (Oxford: Oxford University Press, 2011), 25.

82. Mark D. Regnerus, *Forbidden Fruit: Sex and Religion in the Lives of American Teenagers* (Oxford: Oxford University Press, 2007), 132–33.

83. Uecker, Regnerus, and Vaaler, "Losing My Religion," 1678–81.

84. Uecker, Regnerus, and Vaaler, "Losing My Religion," 1677.

85. Franke et al., *College Senior Survey*, 22–23. Similar figures (though smaller and slightly older) are reported in National Institutes of Health, "Screening for Alcohol Use and Alcohol-Related Problems," *Alcohol Alert* 65 (April 2005): 6. This suggests that the problem is getting worse.

86. Franke et al., *College Senior Survey*, 94–95.

87. Smith and Snell, *Souls in Transition*, 265.

88. National Institutes of Health, "Underage Drinking—Highlights from the Surgeon General's Call to Action to Prevent and Reduce Underage Drinking," *Alcohol Alert* 73 (October 2007): 2.

89. National Institutes of Health, "A Developmental Perspective on Underage Alcohol Use," *Alcohol Alert* 78 (July 2009): 2.

90. National Institutes of Health, "Underage Drinking."

91. National Institutes of Health, "Alcohol's Damaging Effect on the Brain," *Alcohol Alert* 63 (October 2004): 1–2.

92. According to Susan Tapert, cited in Michelle Trudeau, "Teen Drinking May Cause Irreversible Brain Damage," NPR, January 25, 2010, http://www.npr.org/templates/story/story.php?storyId=122765890.

93. Aaron A. Duke and Peter R. Giancola, "Alcohol Reverses Religion's Prosocial Influence on Aggression," *Journal for the Scientific Study of Religion* 52, no. 2 (2013): 279–92.

94. Arguing that it does are Harrell Chesson, Paul Harrison, and William J. Kassler, "Sex under the Influence: The Effect of Alcohol Policy on Sexually Transmitted Disease Rates in the United States," *Journal*

of Law & Economics 43, no. 1 (2000): 215–38; Jeffrey T. Parsons, Kalil J. Vicioso, Joseph C. Punzalan, Perry N. Halkitis, Alexandra Kutnick, and Mary M. Velasquez, "The Impact of Alcohol Use on the Sexual Scripts of HIV-Positive Men Who Have Sex with Men," *Journal of Sex Research* 41, no. 2 (2004): 160–72. Arguing that it does not are Barbara Critchlow Leigh, "The Relationship of Substance Use during Sex to High-Risk Sexual Behavior," *Journal of Sex Research* 27, no. 2 (1990): 199–213; Diane M. Morrison, Mary Rogers Gillmore, Marilyn J. Hoppe, Jan Gaylord, Barbara C. Leigh, and Damien Rainey, "Adolescent Drinking and Sex: Findings from a Daily Diary Study," *Perspectives on Sexual and Reproductive Health* 35, no. 4 (2003): 162–68; Carlos J. Vélez-Blasini, "Evidence against Alcohol as a Proximal Cause of Sexual Risk Taking among College Students," *Journal of Sex Research* 45, no. 2 (2008): 118–28; Erin W. Moore, Jannette Y. Berkley-Patton, and Starlyn M. Hawes, "Religiosity, Alcohol Use, and Sex Behaviors among College Student-Athletes," *Journal of Religion and Health* 52, no. 3 (2013): 930–40; Sandra D. Reid, "Time for a Regional Alcohol Policy—A Literature Review of the Burden of Normative Alcohol Use in the Caribbean," *Journal of Public Health Policy* 36, no. 4 (2015): 469–83. Arguing that the evidence is unclear is M. Lynne Cooper, "Does Drinking Promote Risky Sexual Behavior? A Complex Answer to a Simple Question," *Current Directions in Psychological Science* 15, no. 1 (2006): 19–23.

95. Joseph W. LaBrie and Mitchell Earleywine, "Sexual Risk Behaviors and Alcohol: Higher Base Rates Revealed Using the Unmatched-Count Technique," *Journal of Sex Research* 37, no. 4 (2000): 321–26.

96. Vélez-Blasini, "Evidence against Alcohol," 125.

97. Mark T. Temple and Barbara C. Leigh, "Alcohol Consumption and Unsafe Sexual Behavior in Discrete Events," *Journal of Sex Research* 29, no. 2 (1992): 207–19; Vélez-Blasini, "Evidence against Alcohol," 123.

98. Parsons et al., "Impact of Alcohol Use," 164.

99. Uecker, Regnerus, and Vaaler, "Losing My Religion," 1678–81.

100. *Handbook 2: Administering the Church* (Salt Lake City: The Church of Jesus Christ of Latter-day Saints, 2018), §21.1.29, available at churchof jesuschrist.org. For an interesting historical perspective on the issue, see Davis Bitton, *George Q. Cannon: A Biography* (Salt Lake City: Deseret Book, 1999), 203–4, 258–59, 306–9, 328–30, 360–63.

101. *Handbook 2*, §21.1.29.

102. Christian Smith, Karl Christoffersen, Hilary Davidson, and Patricia Snell Herzog, *Lost in Transition: The Dark Side of Emerging Adulthood* (Oxford: Oxford University Press, 2011), 195–225, 232.

103. Smith et al., *Lost in Transition*, 195, 197, 199, 201, 203.

104. Smith et al., *Lost in Transition*, 204, 208, 70 n. 5.

105. Paul A. Djupe, Jacob R. Neiheisel, and Anand E. Sokhey, "Reconsidering the Role of Politics in Leaving Religion: The Importance of Affiliation," *American Journal of Political Science* 62, no. 1 (2018): 162, 161.

106. Arthur C. Brooks, *Love Your Enemies* (New York: HarperCollins, 2019), 90–98.

107. Djupe, Neiheisel, and Sokhey, "Reconsidering the Role of Politics," 162–63, 173, 162.

108. Michele F. Margolis, *From Politics to the Pews: How Partisanship and the Political Environment Shape Religious Identity* (Chicago: University of Chicago Press, 2018).

109. Mark D. Regnerus, *Cheap Sex: The Transformation of Men, Marriage, and Monogamy* (Oxford: Oxford University Press, 2017), 127.

110. Regnerus, *Cheap Sex*, 127; compare 113; Jochen Peter and Patti M. Valkenburg, "Adolescents and Pornography: A Review of 20 Years of Research," *Journal of Sex Research* 53, nos. 4–5 (2016): 524–25.

111. Spencer T. Zitzman and Mark H. Butler, "Wives' Experience of Husbands' Pornography Use and Concomitant Deception as an Attachment Threat in the Adult Pair-Bond Relationship," *Sexual Addiction & Compulsivity* 16 (2009): 236; Myles Chisholm and Terry Lynn Gall, "Shame and the X-rated Addiction: The Role of Spirituality in Treating Male Pornography Addiction," *Sexual Addiction & Compulsivity* 22 (2015): 265.

112. *Relationships in America Survey*, 27; Dawn M. Szymanski, Chandra E. Feltman, and Trevor L. Dunn, "Male Partners' Perceived Pornography Use and Women's Relational and Psychological Health: The Roles of Trust, Attitudes, and Investment," *Sex Roles* 73 (2015): 187; Peter and Valkenburg, "Adolescents and Pornography," 515; Suzan M. Doornwaard, Regina J. J. M. van den Eijnden, Geertjan Overbeek, and Tom F. M. ter Bogt, "Differential Developmental Profiles of Adolescents Using Sexually Explicit Internet Material," *Journal of Sex Research* 52, no. 3 (2015): 270; Aaron M. Frutos and Ray M. Merrill, "Explicit Sexual Movie Viewing in the United States according to Selected Marriage and Lifestyle, Work and Financial, Religion and Political Factors," *Sexual-*

ity & Culture 21 (2017): 1066, 1076; Nicholas P. Newstrom and Steven M. Harris, "Pornography and Couples: What Does the Research Tell Us?," *Contemporary Family Therapy* 38 (2016): 417; Cameron C. Brown, Jared A. Durtschi, Jason S. Carroll, and Brian J. Willoughby, "Understanding and Predicting Classes of College Students Who Use Pornography," *Computers in Human Behavior* 66 (2017): 115; Elizabeth M. Morgan, "Associations between Young Adults' Use of Sexually Explicit Materials and Their Sexual Preferences, Behaviors, and Satisfaction," *Journal of Sex Research* 48, no. 6 (2011): 521.

113. Peter and Valkenburg, "Adolescents and Pornography," 521.

114. Quoted in Regnerus, *Forbidden Fruit*, 176; compare Szymanski, Feltman, and Dunn, "Male Partners' Perceived Pornography Use," 188.

115. Brown et al., "Understanding and Predicting Classes," 114. For example, in 2006 it grossed at least seven billion dollars; see Paul J. Wright, "U.S. Males and Pornography, 1973–2010: Consumption, Predictors, Correlates," *Journal of Sex Research* 50, no. 1 (2013): 60. See also Norman Doidge, *The Brain That Changes Itself* (New York: Viking, 2007), 103.

116. Regnerus, *Forbidden Fruit*, 174; Samuel L. Perry, "Pornography Consumption as a Threat to Religious Socialization," *Sociology of Religion* 76, no. 4 (2015): 436–37; Peter and Valkenburg, "Adolescents and Pornography," 509–31.

117. Rates for unintentional exposure to pornography among adolescent males range from 19 to 84%; Peter and Valkenburg, "Adolescents and Pornography," 514. Rates of intentional viewing of adolescent males range from 7 to 59%; Peter and Valkenburg, "Adolescents and Pornography," 514–15; compare Samuel L. Perry and George M. Hayward, "Seeing Is (Not) Believing: How Viewing Pornography Shapes the Religious Lives of Young Americans," *Social Forces* 95, no. 4 (2017): 1757–59. The rates from studies that do not consider intentionality range from 7 to 98%; Peter and Valkenburg, "Adolescents and Pornography," 515.

118. Peter and Valkenburg, "Adolescents and Pornography," 510; Goran Koletić, "Longitudinal Associations between the Use of Sexually Explicit Material and Adolescents' Attitudes and Behaviors: A Narrative Review of Studies," *Journal of Adolescence* 57 (2017): 120.

119. Koletić, "Longitudinal Associations," 120.

120. Regnerus, *Forbidden Fruit*, 173.

121. Regnerus, *Forbidden Fruit*, 174–75. Compare Regnerus, *Cheap Sex*, 114; Perry and Hayward, "Seeing Is (Not) Believing," 1759.

122. Peter and Valkenburg, "Adolescents and Pornography," 510.

123. Kyler R. Rasmussen, Joshua B. Grubbs, Kenneth I. Pargament, and Julie J. Exline, "Social Desirability Bias in Pornography-Related Self-Reports: The Role of Religion," *Journal of Sex Research* 55, no. 3 (2018): 381–82.

124. Rasmussen et al., "Social Desirability Bias," 385–86.

125. Rasmussen et al., "Social Desirability Bias," 387, 389.

126. Rasmussen et al., "Social Desirability Bias," 390.

127. Rasmussen et al., "Social Desirability Bias," 390; Perry, "Pornography Consumption," 438; Peter and Valkenburg, "Adolescents and Pornography," 518; Samuel L. Perry, "Does Viewing Pornography Diminish Religiosity over Time? Evidence from Two-Wave Panel Data," *Journal of Sex Research* 54, no. 2 (2017): 214–15. Rasmussen et al., "Social Desirability Bias," 390–92, discuss the flaws in the studies that suggest that people in more religious states consume more pornography than those in less religious states. Those studies are actually measuring the amount of neophyte pornography use rather than that of experienced pornography users.

128. Rasmussen et al., "Social Desirability Bias," 389.

129. Dan J. Miller, Gert Martin Hald, and Garry Kidd, "Self-Perceived Effects of Pornography Consumption among Heterosexual Men," *Psychology of Men & Masculinity* 19, no. 3 (2018): 469–76.

130. Wright, "U.S. Males and Pornography," 64–65.

131. Regnerus, *Forbidden Fruit*, 175–76.

132. Regnerus, *Forbidden Fruit*, 175; Sam A. Hardy, Michael A. Steelman, Sarah M. Coyne, and Robert D. Ridge, "Adolescent Religiousness as a Protective Factor against Pornography Use," *Journal of Applied Developmental Psychology* 34 (2013): 138.

133. Regnerus, *Cheap Sex*, 127; Perry, "Pornography Consumption," 438.

134. Regnerus, *Forbidden Fruit*, 175–76.

135. NSYR wave 3 data. Given that most of those who say that they viewed a pornographic movie in the previous year said that they viewed more than one and 2% said that they viewed more than one a week, it is unclear how much social desirability bias should be expected here.

136. *Relationships in America Survey*, 28.

137. Regnerus, *Cheap Sex*, 114.

138. Regnerus, *Cheap Sex*, 114; *Relationships in America Survey*, 27; Lorne Campbell and Taylor Kohut, "The Use and Effects of Pornography in Romantic Relationships," *Current Opinion in Psychology* 13 (2017): 7. Compare this to the 35% for men and 3% for women cited in Chisholm and Gall, "Shame and the X-rated Addiction," 260.

139. Regnerus, *Cheap Sex*, 115–16; Wright, "U.S. Males and Pornography," 65; Frutos and Merrill, "Explicit Sexual Movie Viewing," 1076.

140. Peter and Valkenburg, "Adolescents and Pornography," 518; Doornwaard et al., "Differential Developmental Profiles," 270; Brown et al., "Understanding and Predicting Classes," 115.

141. *Relationships in America Survey*, 28; Wright, "U.S. Males and Pornography," 65–66, 69; Perry, "Pornography Consumption," 438; Perry, "Does Viewing Pornography Diminish Religiosity?," 215.

142. Peter and Valkenburg, "Adolescents and Pornography," 518–19; Frutos and Merrill, "Explicit Sexual Movie Viewing," 1073. See Alin C. Cotigă and Sorina D. Dumitrache, "Men's Sexual Life and Repeated Exposure to Pornography: A New Issue?," *Journal of Experiential Psychotherapy* 18, no. 4 (2015): 43, for some of these factors involved in pornography use by adults. Koletić, "Longitudinal Associations," 122, 126, 128; Hardy et al., "Adolescent Religiousness," 133, 138; Brown et al., "Understanding and Predicting Classes," 115; Doornwaard et al., "Differential Developmental Profiles," 270.

143. Hardy et al., "Adolescent Religiousness," 131.

144. Eric E. Rasmussen, Nancy Rhodes, Rebecca R. Ortiz, and Shawna R. White, "The Relation between Norm Accessibility, Pornography Use, and Parental Mediation among Emerging Adults," *Media Psychology* 19 (2016): 431–54.

145. Doornwaard et al., "Differential Developmental Profiles," 275–76; Koletić, "Longitudinal Associations," 122.

146. Peter and Valkenburg, "Adolescents and Pornography," 519.

147. Rasmussen et al., "Norm Accessibility, Pornography Use, and Parental Mediation," 431–54.

148. Doornwaard et al., "Differential Developmental Profiles," 274, 277; Koletić, "Longitudinal Associations," 122.

149. Doornwaard et al., "Differential Developmental Profiles," 274; Koletić, "Longitudinal Associations," 122.

150. Doornwaard et al., "Differential Developmental Profiles," 275.
151. Peter and Valkenburg, "Adolescents and Pornography," 518.
152. Doornwaard et al., "Differential Developmental Profiles," 276; Koletić, "Longitudinal Associations," 122.
153. Peter and Valkenburg, "Adolescents and Pornography," 518.
154. Brown et al., "Understanding and Predicting Classes," 118. Porn Abstainers (62.4% of the sample) claim not to use it often. Auto-Erotic Porn Users (18.6% of the sample) use pornography once to a few times per month mainly for sexual arousal and masturbation, though they are the group most likely to be in a romantic relationship. Complex Porn Users (19% of the sample) use pornography once or twice a week for a wide variety of reasons but mainly for sexual arousal and masturbation and to expand their knowledge of sexual practices; they are the least religious of the categories and tend to have the least self-esteem.
155. Chisholm and Gall, "Shame and the X-rated Addiction," 263.
156. Chisholm and Gall, "Shame and the X-rated Addiction," 263; Perry, "Does Viewing Pornography Diminish Religiosity?," 215.
157. Perry, "Does Viewing Pornography Diminish Religiosity?," 215.
158. Perry, "Pornography Consumption," 439.
159. Perry, "Does Viewing Pornography Diminish Religiosity?," 220–21. This was also found in a different cross-sectional study; Frutos and Merrill, "Explicit Sexual Movie Viewing," 1075.
160. Perry and Hayward, "Seeing Is (Not) Believing," 1757–88.
161. Perry, "Does Viewing Pornography Diminish Religiosity?," 220–24.
162. Chisholm and Gall, "Shame and the X-rated Addiction," 263.
163. Smith and Denton, *Soul Searching*, 89, 105.
164. Stephen M. R. Covey and Rebecca R. Merrill, *The Speed of Trust: The One Thing That Changes Everything* (New York: Free Press, 2006), 54; Austin F. R. Smith and Vincent J. Fortunato, "Factors Influencing Employee Intentions to Provide Honest Upward Feedback Ratings," *Journal of Business and Psychology* 22, no. 3 (2008): 192.
165. Covey and Merrill, *Speed of Trust*, 54, 62–63; Joel E. Urbany, "Inspiration and Cynicism in Values Statements," *Journal of Business Ethics* 62, no. 2 (2005): 179, 180.
166. Donna Freitas, *Sex and the Soul: Juggling Sexuality, Spirituality, Romance, and Religion on America's College Campuses* (Oxford: Oxford University Press, 2008), 44.

167. Covey and Merrill, *Speed of Trust*, 77.

168. Covey and Merrill, *Speed of Trust*, 54–55.

169. Covey and Merrill, *Speed of Trust*, 55; Lynne M. Andersson, "Employee Cynicism: An Examination Using a Contract Violation Framework," *Human Relations* 49, no. 11 (1996): 1411.

170. Covey and Merrill, *Speed of Trust*, 55.

171. Candice M. Mills and Frank C. Keil, "The Development of Cynicism," *Psychological Science* 16, no. 5 (2005): 389.

172. Detlef Fetchenhauer and David Dunning, "Why So Cynical? Asymmetric Feedback Underlies Misguided Skepticism regarding the Trustworthiness of Others," *Psychological Science* 21, no. 2 (2010): 190; David J. Stanley, John P. Meyer, and Laryssa Topolnytsky, "Employee Cynicism and Resistance to Organizational Change," *Journal of Business and Psychology* 19, no. 4 (2005): 437, argue, "It is unlikely that one would willingly make oneself vulnerable to the actions of another if his/her motives were in question, or the action was expected to fail."

173. Stanley, Meyer, and Topolnytsky, "Employee Cynicism and Resistance," 430–35.

174. Andersson, "Employee Cynicism," 1396.

175. Andersson, "Employee Cynicism," 1397–98; Fuli Li, Fan Zhou, and Kwok Leung, "Expecting the Worst: Moderating Effects of Social Cynicism on the Relationships between Relationship Conflict and Negative Affective Reactions," *Journal of Business and Psychology* 26, no. 3 (2011): 340.

176. Stanley, Meyer and Topolnytsky, "Employee Cynicism and Resistance," 435–36.

177. Andersson, "Employee Cynicism," 1396.

178. Andersson, "Employee Cynicism," 1400.

179. Andersson, "Employee Cynicism," 1403; Stanley, Meyer and Topolnytsky, "Employee Cynicism and Resistance," 437.

180. Andersson, "Employee Cynicism," 1404.

181. Andersson, "Employee Cynicism," 1410; parenthetical references deleted throughout. Arthur G. Bedeian, "Even If the Tower Is 'Ivory,' It Isn't 'White': Understanding the Consequences of Faculty Cynicism," *Academy of Management Learning & Education* 6, no. 1 (2007): 26; Urbany, "Inspiration and Cynicism," 179; William H. Bommer, Gregory A. Rich, and Robert S. Rubin, "Changing Attitudes about Change: Longitudinal Effects of Transformational Leader Behavior on Employee Cynicism

about Organizational Change," *Journal of Organizational Behavior* 26, no. 7 (2005): 736.

182. Andersson, "Employee Cynicism," 1411.

183. Bedeian, "Consequences of Faculty Cynicism," 18–19.

184. James H. Turner and Sean R. Valentine, "Cynicism as a Fundamental Dimension of Moral Decision-Making: A Scale Development," *Journal of Business Ethics* 34, no. 2 (2001): 125.

185. Bommer, Rich, and Rubin, "Changing Attitudes about Change," 736, 735.

186. Li, Zhou, and Leung, "Expecting the Worst," 341.

187. Samantha Vice, "Cynicism and Morality," *Ethical Theory and Moral Practice* 14, no. 2 (2011): 175.

188. Andersson, "Employee Cynicism," 1412.

189. Andersson, "Employee Cynicism," 1397.

190. Bommer, Rich, and Rubin, "Changing Attitudes about Change," 748, 736.

191. Fetchenhauer and Dunning, "Why So Cynical?," 192.

192. Stanley, Meyer, and Topolnytsky, "Employee Cynicism and Resistance," 437; Janie Harden Fritz, Naomi Bell O'Neil, Ann Marie Popp, Cory Williams, and Ronald C. Arnett, "The Influence of Supervisory Behavioral Integrity on Intent to Comply with Organizational Ethical Standards and Organizational Commitment," *Journal of Business Ethics* 114, no. 2 (2013): 260.

193. Bommer, Rich, and Rubin, "Changing Attitudes about Change," 737.

194. Smith and Denton, *Soul Searching*, 216, 229–31, 90.

195. Smith and Snell, *Souls in Transition*, 167.

6 | INTELLECTUAL ISSUES

Although youth are less likely to leave the Church for intellectual reasons, some youth still lose their faith because of them. Usually the intellectual reasons they cite are those covered in the Gospel Topics essays available on the Church's website. Intellectual theories, unarticulated assumptions, and the consequences of different theories loom larger in the sociological data.

The English word *theory* comes from Greek *theōria*, related to the verb *theōrō*, which means "to see." A theory is a way of seeing things. Thus it is a way of looking at the world, a particular way to view facts and other evidence. A theory even dictates what constitutes evidence. For example, members of the Church know that Joseph Smith translated the Book of Mormon by looking into the Urim and Thummim. What is the Urim and Thummim? It is whatever instrument Joseph Smith used to translate the Book of Mormon. There seems to have been more than one of these objects. All were made of stone. Some were apparently indistinguishable from normal rocks. Apparently in order to see the translation, Joseph needed to block out the light and so would put the stone inside a hat and look into it, using his face and the hat to make things dark enough to see. This *image* contradicts the *picture* of what some artists have *imagined* it must have been like and the *image* that we *see* in our mind's eye. The additional details contradict our *theory*, our way of looking at things. We may think that what we picture in our mind's eye matches reality, but we may need to disabuse ourselves of that notion: "Eye hath not seen, nor ear heard, neither have entered into the heart of man, the things which God hath prepared for them that love him" (1 Corinthians 2:9).

In this chapter, we will examine some of the theories and unarticulated assumptions that the National Study of Youth and Religion (NSYR) identified as undermining the faith of youth. This specific set of intellectual ideas was common among youth of all denominations. We should remember that the NSYR initially came into being to test ideas circulating in evangelical scare literature that U.S. teenagers were leaving in droves to become pagans and Wiccans. The study was actually designed to detect if youth are leaving and what their reasons for doing so might be. They found that "U.S. youth are not flocking in droves to 'alternative' religions and spiritualities such as paganism and Wicca."[1]

In the first wave of the NSYR, 267 youth of the 3,290 surveyed had in-depth interviews lasting from one and a half to three hours; this included 21 Latter-day Saint youth. These in-depth interviews provide a window into the thinking of the youth studied and thus enable us to see some of the intellectual issues involved in loss of faith. We will also show how commonly accepted intellectual theories differ from the gospel and what difference that makes.

MORALISTIC THERAPEUTIC DEISM

The NSYR found a common view of religion that cut across denominational lines (and I have heard it expressed by many Latter-day Saints).

> We suggest that the de facto dominant religion among contemporary U.S. teenagers is what we might call "Moralistic Therapeutic Deism." The creed of this religion, as codified from what emerged from our interviews, sounds something like this:

The NSYR found a common view of religion that cuts across denominational lines and includes certain beliefs about God. Courtesy of marinas32/Pixabay.

A God exists who created and orders the world and watches over human life on earth.

God wants people to be good, nice, and fair to each other, as taught in the Bible and by most world religions.

The central goal of life is to be happy and to feel good about oneself.

God does not need to be particularly involved in one's life except when God is needed to resolve a problem.

Good people go to heaven when they die.

Such a de facto creed is particularly evident among mainline Protestant and Catholic youth, but is also visible among black and conservative Protestants, Jewish teens, other religious types of teenagers, and even many non-religious teenagers in the United States.[2]

One of the interviews that the NSYR cited as an example of Moralistic Therapeutic Deism was a "17-year old white Mormon boy from Utah."[3] So we know that at least some Latter-day Saint youth are affected by this view.

Others have also noticed this tendency,[4] though they used other terms, like "fuzzy fidelity,"[5] "believing without belonging,"[6] or "Golden Rule Christians,"[7] while at the same time noting that "synagogue members fit this profile, as well, and some of those least connected to religious communities opined that this is what *should* count." They see it as "America's mainstream form of religiosity, with a focus on living one's faith every day and a relative disinterest in doctrinal orthodoxy."[8]

Moralistic Therapeutic Deism has a few basic premises: First, it "is about inculcating a moralistic approach to life. It teaches that central to living a good and happy life is being a good, moral person. That means being nice, kind, pleasant, respectful, responsible, at work on self-improvement, taking care of one's health, and doing one's best to be successful."[9] On the surface this sounds a lot like "being honest, true, chaste, benevolent, virtuous, and in doing good to all men" (Articles of Faith 1:13), except that being honest, true, and chaste are not actually listed.

> We might talk, for example, about God's unconditional love, when the scriptures never say that God's love is unconditional.

Second, Moralistic Therapeutic Deism is "about providing therapeutic benefits to its adherents. This is not a religion of repentance from sin, of keeping the Sabbath, of living as a servant of a sovereign divine, of steadfastly saying one's prayers, . . . et cetera. Rather, what appears to be the actual dominant religion among U.S. teenagers is centrally about feeling good, happy, secure, at peace. It is about attaining subjective well-being, being able to resolve problems, and getting along amiably with other people."[10] God is supposed to make us feel better about ourselves through no effort on our part.

Finally, Moralistic Therapeutic Deism "is about belief in a particular kind of God: one who exists, created the world, and defines our general moral order, but not one who is particularly personally involved in one's affairs—especially affairs in which one would prefer not to have God involved. Most of the time, the God of this faith keeps a safe distance."[11] In this way "God is something like a combination Divine Butler and Cosmic Therapist: he is always on call, takes care of problems that arise, professionally helps his people to feel better about themselves, and does not become too personally involved in the process."[12] Religion is reduced to being nice: "If it's not nice, it's not religion."[13]

Moralistic Therapeutic Deism often hides among religious people: "We are not suggesting that Moralistic Therapeutic Deism is a religion that teenagers (and adults) either adopt and practice wholesale or not at all. Instead, the elements of its creed are normally assimilated by degrees, in parts, admixed with elements of more traditional religious faiths. Indeed, this religious creed appears to operate as a parasitic faith. It cannot sustain its own integral, independent life; rather it must attach itself like an incubus to established historical religious traditions, feeding on their doctrines and sensibilities, and expanding by mutating their theological substance to resemble its own distinctive image."[14] Moralistic Therapeutic Deism takes elements of the gospel and distorts them into something that sounds the same but is really different. We might talk, for example, about God's unconditional love, when the scriptures never say that God's love is unconditional.[15] Indeed, Jesus said, "Greater love hath no man than this, that a man lay down his life for his friends. Ye are my friends, if ye do whatsoever I command you" (John 15:13–14). We tend to quote the first verse, which mentions that Jesus loved us enough to lay down his life, but omit the second, which puts conditions on whether one manifestation of that love, his atoning sacrifice, applies to us.

Various measures of Moralistic Therepeutic Deism appeared in the surveyed youth. Thus 42% of them said that religion should make them happy, 37% of them said that religion should make them feel good about themselves, and 34% said that religion should make them feel better about themselves. By comparison, repentance was mentioned as a theme in only 4% of the teenage population, and obeying God in only 5%.[16]

The NSYR found that teenagers learn Moralistic Therapeutic Deism not only from their peers but also from their parents. Parents, for example, might teach their children that they ought to be kind to each other regardless of who started a quarrel. But if they fail to recognize that sometimes one of the children really did start the dispute, the parents can inadvertently signal that they do not care about justice, only about niceness—therefore, iniquity is no big deal as long as one is nice.

What happens to teenagers who subscribe to Moralistic Therapeutic Deism? Later waves of the NSYR study looked into the issue:

> What has become of the MTD five years later, now that those teens have become emerging adults?
>
> The latest wave of research reveals that MTD is still alive and well among 18- to 23-year-old American youth. . . . The concentration of MTD talk among emerging adults has been somewhat diluted, but that is not to say that MTD has disintegrated as a de facto believed and practiced faith. It has not. . . .
>
> Emerging adults have a lot more personal, real-life experience than teenagers do. And as the teenage faith of MTD has had to confront and address life's realities during the transition to emerging adulthood—the five years studied here—MTD itself has been put to the test. For some, MTD seems to have sufficed for managing life. For others, it seems MTD has simply proved too thin or weak to deal with life's challenges. Confronted with real existential or material difficulties, some emerging adults appear to have backed away from the simple verities of MTD or perhaps have moved forward into somewhat more complex, grounded, or traditional versions of religious faith. In short, there seem to be certain tests in life through which some youth find that MTD proves an unrealistic account or an unhelpful way to respond.[17]

One of the first points to notice is the time lag between what is taught (and practiced) and the challenge to the faith. What the youth learned as children and teenagers was put to the test when they were emerging adults. What was reaped as a young adult was sown much earlier. I will illustrate this with an unscientific anecdote. A number of years ago I lived in a ward with a large Primary but without a single active young man. The bishop studied the problem and found that all of the teenagers had become less active between the ages of 8 and 12. While there were a number of different causes for the inactivity, there was also a gap of a number of years between the cause and the effect. Longitudinal studies like the NSYR can help us see that relationship.

Youth who as children and teenagers learn Moralistic Therapeutic Deism as the content of their religious faith will not find it sufficient to sustain them through the challenges of life. Some of them, as noted by the NSYR, leave their faith. When it comes to the intellectual content of what we are teaching youth, we should be teaching the gospel rather than Moralistic Therapeutic Deism. Let us contrast what the scriptures teach to the points of Moralistic Therapeutic Deism to see why it is not the gospel.

The first point of the de facto creed of Moralistic Therapeutic Deism is that "a God exists who created and orders the world and watches over human life on earth."[18] The scriptures teach that God created the world as a place of testing where he could prove us to see if we would do all things that the Lord our God commands us (see Abraham 3:25). Sometimes he intervenes on our behalf, but other times he tries our patience and our faith (see Mosiah 23:21). God allows mortals to do evil to others "according to the hardness of their hearts, that the judgments which he shall exercise upon them in his wrath may be just" (Alma 14:11).

The second point is that "God wants people to be good, nice, and fair to each other, as taught in the Bible and by most world religions."[19] In multiple passages God enjoins us to "do good" (for example, Matthew 5:44; Mark 14:7; Luke 6:35; John 5:29; 2 Nephi 26:33), and he set the example for us because he "went about doing good" (Acts 10:38). The term *nice* is never used in the scriptures. (It originally comes from Latin *nescius* "ignorant"; in the thirteenth through sixteenth centuries it usually meant "stupid"; in the fourteenth through seventeenth centuries it also often meant "wanton" or "immoral"; somehow in the sixteenth through nineteenth centuries it meant "refined" or "finicky"; and only in the eighteenth century did it acquire the additional current meaning of "agreeable."[20] In the twenty-first century "'nice' is often a polite euphemism for 'needy, weak, predictable, boring, inexperienced, and unattractive.'")[21] The term *fair* is usually used in the scriptures in the sense of *beautiful* and only once in the sense of *equal:* In the war chapters of the Book of Mormon, Moroni sees that the Lamanites are ensconced in what used to be Nephite strongholds, and "having no hopes of meeting them upon *fair* grounds, therefore, he resolved upon a plan that he might decoy the Lamanites out of their strongholds" (Alma 52:21).

What the scriptures ask us to be is not *fair* or *nice* but *just*, which is not entirely the same thing. The good that God wants us to do is to keep his commandments (Matthew 19:16–19), which we may not consider nice or fair and which we may not even think of as good (2 Nephi 15:20). True, those who keep the commandments are often good, nice, and fair to others, but we should not confuse what it is that God is actually asking of us. Jesus acknowledged that the gospel he taught would not necessarily make one get along amiably with other people:

> Whosoever therefore shall confess me before men, him will I confess also before my Father which is in heaven. But whosoever shall deny me before men, him will I also deny before my Father which is in heaven. Think not that I am come to send peace on earth: I came not to send peace, but a sword. For I am come to set a man at variance against his father, and the daughter against her mother, and the daughter in law against her mother in law. And a man's foes shall be they of his own household. He that loveth father or mother more than me is not worthy of me: and he that loveth son or daughter more than me is not worthy of me. And he that taketh not his cross, and followeth after me, is not worthy of me. He that findeth his life shall lose it: and he that loseth his life for my sake shall find it. (Matthew 10:32–39)

The Greek term translated as "shall confess" is *homologēsei*, the same term that was used at the beginning of contracts to indicate that one party accepted the terms of the other party. It is covenantal language. Agreeing with Jesus and accepting his terms and covenants can put us at odds with those around us. Thinking we can gain peace by agreeing with those around us can put us at odds with Jesus and make us unworthy of him.

Focusing on niceness may be counterproductive. There is essentially no correlation between morality and niceness/nastiness, but there is some correlation showing that people who are moral and nasty (or at least not nice) tend to be highly religious while those who are nice and not moral tend not to be religious.[22] Thus focusing on being nice distracts us from behaving morally and may inadvertently encourage immoral behavior.

The third point of Moralistic Therapeutic Deism is that "the central goal of life is to be happy and to feel good about oneself."[23] This is simply not true. According to the scriptures this life is a test to prove whether we will be obedient to God's commandments (Abraham 3:25). We sometimes rip the phrase "men are, that they might have joy" out of its proper context: "Behold, all things have been done in the wisdom of him who knoweth all things. Adam fell that men might be; and men are, that they might have joy. And the Messiah cometh in the fulness of time, that he may redeem the children of men from the fall" (2 Nephi 2:24–26). Having joy comes in the context of Christ redeeming us from our sins. We are also wont to quote the first part of a statement attributed to Joseph Smith but leave off the last part: "Happiness is the object and design of our existence, and will be the end thereof, if we pursue the path that leads to it; and this path is virtue, uprightness, faithfulness, holiness, and keeping all the commandments of God."[24] If we do not pursue the correct path, we will not achieve the happiness that we seek. As Brigham Young noted, "What principal object have human beings in view? Happiness. Give me glory, give me power, give me wealth, give me a good name, give me influence with my fellow-men, give me all these, and it does not follow that I am thereby made happy; that depends altogether upon what principle those acquisitions were gained."[25] Feeling good about ourselves may prevent us from repenting when we need to. Ironically, in the pursuit of feeling good about ourselves, we may inadvertently cut ourselves off from the process that will truly make us happy.

> Having joy comes in the context of Christ redeeming us from our sins.

The fourth point of Moralistic Therapeutic Deism is that "God does not need to be particularly involved in one's life except when God is needed to resolve a problem."[26] God stated the same sentiment in a slightly different way: "In the day of their peace they esteemed lightly my counsel; but, in the day of their trouble, of necessity they feel after me" (Doctrine and Covenants 101:8). He knows well that this is the attitude of the natural man. In some of the statements surrounding this sentence, God sets the record straight: "They were slow to hearken unto the voice of the Lord their God; therefore, the Lord their God is slow to hearken unto their prayers, to answer them in the day of their trouble" (Doctrine and Covenants 101:7). From God's perspective we "must needs be chastened and tried, even as Abraham, who was commanded to offer up his only son. For all those who will not endure chastening, but deny me, cannot be sanctified" (Doctrine and Covenants 101:4–5). The former Oxford and Cambridge professor C. S. Lewis put it another way:

> Imagine yourself as a living house. God comes in to rebuild that house. At first, perhaps, you can understand what He is doing. He is getting the drains right and stopping the leaks in the roof and so on: you knew that those jobs needed doing and so you are not surprised. But presently, He starts knocking the house about in a way that hurts abominably and does not seem to make sense. What on earth is He up to? The explanation is that He is building quite a different house from the one you thought of—throwing out a new wing here, putting on an extra floor there, running up towers, making courtyards. You thought you were going to be made into a decent little cottage: but He is building a palace.[27]

We may want God to leave us alone to do our own thing, unless we want him to intervene, but that is not the way that God sees it. The God of the scriptures loves us enough to chasten us[28] as well as to try our patience and faith (Mosiah 23:21).

The final point is that "good people go to heaven when they die."[29] Latter-day Saints have a more nuanced view of rewards in the next life (see Doctrine and Covenants 76), even if we sometimes have a tendency to reduce it to a somewhat simplistic view.

Of the five points of the de facto creed, the first two points and the last point would have to be nuanced and the other two rejected. The restored gospel of Jesus Christ is simply not compatible with Moralistic Therapeutic Deism.

If we want to help the youth keep their faith, equipping them with the tools to combat Moralistic Therapeutic Deism is one place to start.

Other Intellectual Issues

Thus far, in our examination of the data from the NSYR we have looked at some of the scattered clues in the NSYR analysis. The NSYR actually devoted an entire book to the subject of youth losing their religion and their way.[30] We have already noted that intellectual reasons play a smaller role in youth losing their faith than behaviors or events. Here

"The undeniable reality is that emerging adult problems are ultimately problems of our entire culture and society."

we are interested only in those intellectual reasons that the NSYR found for people losing their faith.

The first thing to notice is that "most of the problems in the lives of youth have their origins in the larger adult world into which the youth are being socialized. . . . One way or another, adults and the adult world are almost always complicit in the troubles, suffering, and misguided living of youth, if not the direct source of them. The more adults can recognize and admit that fact, we think, the sooner we will be able to address some of young people's problems more constructively. . . . The undeniable reality . . . is that emerging adult problems are ultimately problems of our entire culture and society."[31]

Since the problems among the youth usually come from the adults, it is our responsibility to do something about them.

"You Took No Thought"

Many who work with youth and young adults have noticed the moral drift among them. (Moral here has to do with the larger issue of discerning right and wrong and not just the narrower understanding of sexual morality.) This presents something of a challenge to researchers. "Emerging adult thinking about morality (as with most of the rest of adult Americans) is not particularly consistent, coherent, or articulate." It is not that young adults have been thinking about how to be degenerate or anything of the sort. "Not many of them have previously given much or any thought to many of the kinds of questions about morality that we asked."[32] One manifestation of this situation is that people who have doubts complain that they have never heard about a particular issue before. This often does not mean that those issues have not been discussed in public or even in church. Often it means that the individual has never paid much attention, or sometimes any attention. I remember things like the failure of the Kirtland Safety Society, polygamy, and the Mountain Meadows Massacre all being taught in seminary. I wonder when I hear accounts of those being surprised by something like that why they have not heard of those things. I have taught enough to know that not all students pay attention and that not all that pay attention understand what is being taught even if it is taught plainly. The fact that most young adults (or adults for that matter) have not given much if any thought to moral issues is a disappointment but not a surprise. Nevertheless, the lack of giving thought beforehand to these issues can and does have disastrous consequences.

> **The lack of giving thought beforehand to these issues can and does have disastrous consequences.**

Not only can it be a problem when young adults have given no thought to these moral issues, but it can also be a problem if parents or local church leaders have not either. After all, "without awareness of moral issues, ethical decisions are compromised."[33] Thus failure to give thought to issues can create a situation where actions are unintentionally misaligned with words. A breach in integrity ripples out into breaches in the trust and faith of others.

Problems with moral reasoning are prevalent among young adults, and these problems were summarized under the following headings: moral individualism, moral relativism, moral sources, moral instincts and happiness, moral dilemmas, and moral compromises.

MORAL INDIVIDUALISM

The NSYR noted that "six out of ten (60 percent) of the emerging adults we interviewed . . . said that morality is a personal choice, entirely a matter of individual decision. Moral rights and wrongs are essentially matters of individual opinion, in their view. Furthermore, the general approach associated with this outlook is not to judge anyone else on moral matters, since they are entitled to their own personal opinions."[34]

Such young adults see "not 'immoral' people but people who make moral judgments of others as society's real problem." From this point of view, "to express one's own moral view is thus synonymous with dominating and controlling others, a kind of pathology that violates other people's dignity and rights."[35] Such young adults

> have not been taught well how to differentiate between strong moral and religious claims that should be tolerated, if not respected, and those that deserve to be refuted, rejected, and opposed. Very few have been given the reasoning tools and skills to discern such important differences. As a result, many emerging adults [I would include adults as well] simply end up trying to completely avoid making strong moral claims themselves, as well as avoiding criticizing the moral views of others. . . . But what few of them seem to realize is that such a position makes it impossible to rationally evaluate or criticize any moral wrong, including the horrific destruction and violence that helped drive them to this tolerant position in the first place. That is a problem.[36]

Even well-meaning Latter-day Saints can display or advocate these viewpoints.

Judging others

One way to spot a moral individualist is the repeated expression "Who am I to judge?"[37] Moral individualists do not like to be judged or challenged on their moral positions. The Book of Mormon gives examples of one individual and two groups that objected to being judged, and these are instructive and relevant to the moral individualism of the present day.

First, Laman and Lemuel objected to their father, "We know that the people who were in the land of Jerusalem were a righteous people; for they kept the statutes and judgments of the Lord, and all his commandments, according to the law of Moses; wherefore, we know that they are a righteous people; and *our father hath judged them*" (1 Nephi 17:22).

Arnold Friberg, *Nephi Rebuking His Rebellious Brothers*. Courtesy of churchofjesuschrist.org. Nephi describes Laman and Lemuel's talk by saying, "After this manner of language did my brethren murmur and complain against us" (1 Nephi 17:22).

Judging the inhabitants of Jerusalem was apparently a bad thing to have done because Laman and Lemuel thought them to be righteous. Lehi had in fact judged them, and quite harshly, saying things like "Wo, wo, unto Jerusalem, for I have seen thine abominations!" (1 Nephi 1:13). Abominations is a much harsher word than sins, transgressions, or mistakes. This made Lehi quite unpopular with the supposedly righteous people of Jerusalem. "The Jews did mock him because of the things which he testified of them; for he truly testified of their wickedness and their abominations" (1 Nephi 1:19). (There are those awful words again.) Consequently, "when the Jews heard these things they were angry with him; yea, even as with the prophets of old, whom they had cast out, and stoned, and slain; and they also sought his life, that they might take it away" (1 Nephi 1:20). Lehi might have sent his sons back (twice), but once he left Jerusalem, he never went back; it was too dangerous—and all because he was so judgmental. Nephi describes Laman and Lemuel's talk by saying, "After this manner of language did my brethren murmur and complain against us" (1 Nephi 17:22).

A second example is King Noah. Abinadi, essentially a nobody, came among King Noah's people and prophesied, "Behold, thus saith the Lord, and thus hath he commanded me, saying, Go forth, and say unto this people, thus saith the Lord—Wo be unto this people, for I have seen their abominations, and their wickedness, and their whoredoms; and except they repent I will visit them in mine anger" (Mosiah 11:20). Abinadi uses the same language that Lehi does, except he adds another term of opprobrium. Noah, of course, does not like this one bit; the scriptures say that he was "wroth," and he complained, "Who is Abinadi, that I and my people *should be judged of him?*" (Mosiah 11:27). The problem, according to Noah, is not that he is doing wrong but that Abinadi has judged him. If Abinadi had just been nonjudgmental, then things would have been just perfect. Noah had authority and power and Abinadi did not and therefore should not have been judging those who had the right to judge.

The third example is when Noah's priests, whom King Mosiah later described as Noah's "friends in iniquity" (Mosiah 29:22), got in the act and told the king, "O king, what great evil hast thou done, or what great sins have thy people committed, that we should be condemned of God or *judged of this man?* And now, O king, behold, we are guiltless, and thou, O king, hast not sinned; therefore, this man has lied concerning you" (Mosiah 12:13–14). They could not see that Noah had done anything bad. The fault was Abinadi's for having judged them. Judging them was such a bad thing that they declared that Abinadi was "worthy of death" (Mosiah 17:7).

The fact is that the only people in the Book of Mormon who complain about moral judgments are the wicked, who object to their wickedness being pointed out. On the other hand, Mormon tells his hearers, "behold, my brethren, *it is given unto you to judge,* that ye may know good from evil" (Moroni 7:15). We are both *allowed* to make judgments and *required* to make them so that we can distinguish good from evil. Mormon continues, "The way to judge is as plain. . . . For behold, the Spirit of Christ is given to every man, that he may know good from evil; wherefore, I show unto you the way to judge; for every thing which inviteth to do good, and to persuade to believe in Christ, is sent forth by the power and gift of Christ; wherefore ye may know with a perfect knowledge it is of God. But whatsoever thing persuadeth men to do evil, and believe not in Christ, and deny him, and serve not God, then ye may know with a perfect knowledge it is of the devil" (Moroni 7:15–17). This passage comes at the beginning of Mormon's sermon on faith, hope, and charity because, according to Mormon's argument, one cannot have faith, hope, or charity without first judging. Charity, far from being nonjudgmental, requires the individual who has charity to make judgments. Charity, after all, "thinketh no evil, and rejoiceth not in iniquity but rejoiceth in the truth"

> Charity, far from being nonjudgmental, requires the individual who has charity to make judgments.

(Moroni 7:45), which means that charity is both capable of judging and has judged things to be evil, or iniquitous, or true. Judging is a requirement for charity.

Mormon himself is an example of this charity. Looking back on his life as a leader of the people, he said, "Notwithstanding their wickedness I had led them many times to battle, and had loved them, according to the love of God which was in me, with all my heart; and my soul had been poured out in prayer unto my God all the day long for them" (Mormon 3:12). But for all this, he tells his son, Moroni, "I cannot recommend them unto God lest he should smite me" (Moroni 9:21). He claims that "my heart has been filled with sorrow because of their wickedness, all my days" (Mormon 2:19), because "a continual scene of wickedness and abominations has been before mine eyes ever since I have been sufficient to behold the ways of man" (Mormon 2:18). Mormon uses the same judgmental vocabulary, wickedness and abominations, that Lehi and Abinadi use, but he still loved his people.

Having charity, the pure love of Christ, thus is not the same thing as being nonjudgmental. One can have charity and be judgmental, point out others' wickedness, and call them to repentance. Indeed, one wonders how much of the pure love of Christ one can have and not invite people to repentance.

Judgment is also an essential part of the gospel. Jesus defined his gospel as follows:

> **This is the gospel** which I have given unto you—that I came into the world to do the will of my Father, because my Father sent me. And my Father sent me that I might be lifted up upon the cross;

and after that I had been lifted up upon the cross, that I might draw all men unto me, that *as I have been lifted up by men even so should men be lifted up by the Father, to stand before me, to be judged of their works, whether they be good or whether they be evil*—And for this cause have I been lifted up; therefore, according to the power of the Father I will draw all men unto me, *that they may be judged according to their works.* And it shall come to pass, that whoso repenteth and is baptized in my name shall be filled; and if he endureth to the end, behold, him will I hold guiltless before my Father *at that day when I shall stand to judge the world.* And he that endureth not unto the end, the same is he that is also hewn down and cast into the fire, from whence they can no more return, *because of the justice of the Father.* And this is the word which he hath given unto the children of men. And for this cause he fulfilleth the words which he hath given, and he lieth not, but fulfilleth all his words. And *no unclean thing can enter into his kingdom;* therefore nothing entereth into his rest save it be those who have washed their garments in my blood, because of their faith, and the repentance of all their sins, and their faithfulness unto the end. Now this is the commandment: Repent, all ye ends of the earth, and come unto me and be baptized in my name, that ye may be sanctified by the reception of the Holy Ghost, that ye may stand spotless before me at the last day. Verily, verily, I say unto you, **this is my gospel**. (3 Nephi 27:13–21)

The declarations "this is my gospel" (3 Nephi 27:13, 21) serve as bookends, enclosing the definition that Jesus gave of his gospel. In that definition judgment plays a crucial role. Jesus will judge the world and every individual in it. The standards and criteria of judgment are specifically laid out. Thus, according to the gospel, there are clear standards of morality and those standards are not left up to the individual. To deny judgment or to allow individuals to define their own morality is to deny the gospel as Jesus defines it.

Judgment is not just an integral part of the gospel—it is an inescapable part of life. Neurological studies have shown that we humans judge everything, instantaneously, continually. It takes us only a fraction of a second. "Neuroimaging evidence suggests there is an automatic valuation system that encodes values for preferences under all circumstances." It is automatic. *"We constantly judge."*[38] Whether we want to or not, we judge. Moral individualism may tell us that we should not judge, but we do so anyway. Even moral individualists judge.

Tolerance

Yet not being judgmental is seen as part of being tolerant, and tolerance is seen by many to be a secular virtue that every reasonable person should accept.[39] The meaning of the secular term itself, however, has changed over time. Originally it meant "to endure" something. In recent times it has taken on two distinctive meanings. This has been laid out with some clarity by D. A. Carson. Carson notes that there are two general views held in Western society and that both are given the label *tolerance*. One of these views precedes the other historically:

> Under the older view of tolerance, a person might be judged tolerant if, while holding strong views, he or she insisted that others had the right to dissent from those views and argue their own cases. This view of tolerance is in line with the famous utterance often (if erroneously) assigned to Voltaire: "I disapprove of what you say, but I will defend to the death your right to say it." This older view of tolerance makes three assumptions: (1) there is an objective truth out there, and it is our duty to pursue that truth; (2) the various parties in a dispute think that they know what the truth of the matter is, even though they disagree sharply, each party thinking the other is wrong; (3) nevertheless they hold that the best chance of uncovering the truth of the matter, or the best chance of persuading most people with reason and not with coercion, is by the unhindered exchange of ideas, no matter how wrongheaded some of those ideas seem. This third assumption demands that all sides insist that their opponents must not be silenced or crushed.[40]

Carson explores some of the implications of this view:

> The older view of tolerance held *either* that truth is objective and can be known, and that the best way to uncover it is bold tolerance of those who disagree, since sooner or later the truth will win out; *or* that while truth can be known in some domains, it probably

cannot be known in other domains, and that the wisest and least malignant course in such cases is benign tolerance grounded in the superior knowledge that recognizes our limitations.[41]

Over the second half of the twentieth century this view has subsequently changed both subtly and significantly:

The new tolerance argues that there is no one view that is exclusively true. Strong opinions are nothing more than strong preferences for a particular version of reality, each version equally true.... We must be tolerant, not because we cannot distinguish the right path from the wrong path, but because all paths are equally right.[42]

And here the trouble begins:

If you begin with this new view of tolerance, and then elevate this view to the supreme position in the hierarchy of moral virtues, the supreme sin is intolerance. The trouble is that such intolerance, like the new tolerance, also takes on a new definition. Intolerance is no longer a refusal to allow contrary opinions to say their piece in public, but must be understood to be questioning or contradicting the view that all opinions are equal in value, that all worldviews have equal worth, that all stances are equally valid. To question such postmodern axioms is by definition intolerant. For such questioning there is no tolerance whatsoever, for it is classed as intolerance and must therefore be condemned. It has become the supreme vice.[43]

Under the new understanding of tolerance, judging someone or something is wrong because all values are equally right, and so forming a judgment about something or someone is intolerant.[44] According to this way of thinking Lehi and Abinadi were intolerant and deserved to be killed. Those who advocate the new understanding of tolerance point to studies showing prejudice among the very religious:

Research linking religion to prejudice suggests that highly religious individuals, especially those taking a fundamentalist approach to religion, may be particularly susceptible to demonstrating prejudice toward dissimilar others. It is perhaps unsurprising that a belief system that claims "inerrant truth about existential and ethereal existence" leads to prejudice as adherents attempt to vigorously defend the validity and vitality of their religious beliefs; however, extant research on fundamentalism and prejudice paints a one-sided picture that fails to capture the variety of ways in which nonreligious and nonfundamentalist individuals may similarly be motivated to express negative attitudes toward attitudinally dissimilar others (e.g., religious fundamentalists).[45]

In a bizarre twist on this theme, 40% of millennials think that disagreeing with someone is the same as judging them.[46] Thus disagreeing with someone is viewed as being intolerant. In this way tolerance becomes accepting someone's point of view and agreeing with it. In this line of thinking tolerance becomes a way to force one's own opinions on others without having to come up with an argument or evidence to persuade them.

Carson sees the need "to think carefully about tolerance and intolerance" because

> every culture and every age necessarily displays *some* tolerance and *some* intolerance. No culture can be tolerant of everything or intolerant of everything: it is simply not possible. A culture that tolerates, say, genocide (e.g., the Nazis) will not tolerate, say, the Jews it wants to kill or homosexual practice. A culture that tolerates just about every sexual liaison may nevertheless balk at, say, rape, or pedophilia, or in many cases bigamy and polygamy.[47]

Thus much of what parades as tolerance comes across as intolerance, particularly to Christians.[48] Because it is simply not possible to be tolerant of everything, different individuals show tolerance of different things. Boundless tolerance is thus not some sort of ideal state that those who strive for can attain. Ironically, "groups typically defined by their tolerance will still be prejudiced toward dissimilar others."[49] The question is not whether one is tolerant, but what one is tolerant of. Recent studies have proposed that "people on both the left and the right of the ideological spectrum will be prejudiced toward and express a willingness to discriminate against those with different actual or perceived ideological beliefs."[50]

One study found that, counter to a prevailing narrative about how intolerance is associated with religion,[51] "those low in religious belief

Antonio Ciseri, *Ecce Homo*. Elder Neal A. Maxwell warned, "Irreligion as the state religion would be the worst of all combinations. . . . Its majorities—when faced with clear alternatives—would make the Barabbas choice, as did a mob centuries ago when Pilate confronted them with the need to decide." Courtesy of Wikimedia Commons.

(and, thus, low in religious fundamentalism) may also demonstrate greater absolute intergroup bias."[52] Another study found that while atheists and agnostics are less likely to *claim* to be dogmatic or certain of their beliefs, in actual practice they could be more dogmatic, close-minded and intolerant of other opinions than believers.[53] In other words, the irreligious may actually be more intolerant than those who are religious. Elder Neal A. Maxwell warned about this state of affairs decades ago: "Irreligion as the state religion would be the worst of all combinations. Its orthodoxy would be insistent and its inquisitors inevitable. Its paid ministry would be numerous beyond belief. Its Caesars would be insufferably condescending. Its majorities—when faced with clear alternatives—would make the Barabbas choice, as did a mob centuries ago when Pilate confronted them with the need to decide."[54] Elder Maxwell went on to warn,

Your discipleship may see the time come when religious convictions are heavily discounted. . . . This new irreligious imperialism seeks to disallow certain of people's opinions simply because those opinions grow out of religious convictions. Resistance to abortion will soon be seen as primitive. Concern over the institution of the family will be viewed as untrendy and unenlightened. In its mildest form, irreligion will merely be condescending toward those who hold to traditional Judeo-Christian values. In its more harsh forms, as is always the case with those whose dogmatism is blinding, the secular church will do what it can to reduce the influence of those who still worry over standards such as those in the Ten Commandments. It is always such an easy step from dogmatism to unfair play—especially so when the dogmatists believe themselves to be dealing with primitive people who do not know what is best for them. It is the secular bureaucrat's burden, you see.[55]

> Advocates of tolerance sometimes manifest something of a double standard. They ask for tolerance of their actions, but toward others' different opinions they demand complete capitulation and abandonment, anything but tolerance.

Others have emphasized the importance of thinking carefully about tolerance because the prevalent "moral relativism and complete tolerance for every other point of view actually do not respect or honor those points of views; quite the opposite." When people say they are being tolerant, "what they are really, if unintentionally, saying is, 'I don't care enough about what you think or believe to pay it any attention. Your view doesn't make any difference, it doesn't deserve to be taken seriously.'"[56] For many in the population at large, tolerance is simply a respectable name for apathy. For others "'religious tolerance' really amounts to 'embarrassed silence.'"[57] This is not a new situation. Long ago the Dutch reformed minister, later prime minister of the Netherlands, Abraham Kuyper (originally Kuijper) (1837–1920), wrote,

For the sake of tolerance the [liberal elite] seeks to remove every conviction that raises itself above the superficial. . . . A specific, settled conviction is in its eyes a "prejudice," an "outdated," an "immoderate notion." . . . Tolerance, yes, but tolerance out of indifference, out of superficiality, out of lack of principles. . . . It is the undermining of any solid conviction, under the slogan of the struggle against witch-hunts and sectarian conflict and religious hatred.[58]

Advocates of tolerance sometimes manifest something of a double standard. They ask for tolerance of their actions (by which they mean in this case unconditional acceptance and positive affirmation), but toward others' different opinions they demand complete capitulation and abandonment, anything but tolerance.

The scriptures never use the term *tolerance* or the verb *tolerate*. The only form of the root the scriptures use is the adjective *tolerable*, as in "it shall be more tolerable for Tyre and Sidon at the day of judgment, than for you" (Matthew 11:22). This is in the oldest English sense of tolerance as endurance.

Tolerance is not a Christian virtue. What the scriptures ask us to have is not tolerance but charity. Charity is not tolerance under any of the definitions of the English term. On the one hand, charity "beareth all things, believeth all things, hopeth all things, endureth all things" (Moroni 7:45). In this way, charity encompasses the original definition of tolerance as endurance but surpasses it since it is more than just endurance. One can tolerate—that is, endure—something without hope. On the other hand, charity "rejoiceth not in iniquity but rejoiceth in the truth" (Moroni 7:45), which implies that there is truth and there is iniquity and that the person possessing charity can discern between them. This runs counter to what Carson describes as the new view of tolerance: "A commonplace among those who support the new tolerance is that the enemies of tolerance are guilty of adopting strongly asserted positions. They [the enemies of tolerance] claim to know the Truth (with a capital "T"), and that is precisely what makes them most likely to be intolerant."[59]

This seems to suggest that the problem of intolerance might simply be in holding religious views strongly and that a less dogmatic approach might promote more tolerance. But research on intolerance does not support this: "the content of belief played a much stronger role than the style of belief [that is, whether beliefs were taken literally or metaphorically]." Specifically, "belief dissimilarity is the primary driver of prejudice, but that belief style can exacerbate the effects." In other words, what one believes makes one the subject of intolerance rather than one's meekness or lack thereof. This is not to say that meekness plays no role: "When people treat their religious belief and disbelief in a literal style it appears much more likely to lead to bias and prejudice than when people take a more symbolic and less strident approach to both religious belief and disbelief." Style can change the intensity. But the researchers hypothesize that "cognitive and motivational styles lead people to adopt particular religious beliefs."[60] Thus the style of the believer (or nonbeliever) changes the content of one's beliefs; and this change works in both directions. Adopting a moderating style will thus change the content of the beliefs, and this, historically, has proven a bad thing for religious faith.

The history of Dartmouth College provides an interesting case study. William Jewett Tucker, the president of Dartmouth from 1892 to 1906, helmed the transition of Dartmouth from a religious to a secular university. According to Tucker, "we have changed the emphasis from the content of faith to the tone of faith." Tucker outlines his rationale: "The question in the popular mind in regard to any man in whom it is interested religiously is not, so much as formerly, what he believes, but much more than formerly, how he believes. Formerly the distinction was, Is a man orthodox or heterodox?" But Tucker, and Dartmouth, had moved past all that. "Our religious beliefs and denials are experienced in shades and colors rather than in sharp and rigid outlines. And this means that we believe, or doubt, or deny, much more according to our experience of the world than according to logic."[61] Tucker summoned his students to "reach moral maturity" beyond the law, the prophets, or even Jesus. He wished for "a Bible set free from the last bondage to literalism, no longer the bulwark of divine ecclesiastical dogmas."[62] Although Dartmouth had begun as a Congregationalist school, the year Tucker left it balked at being included in a list of Congregationalist institutions of higher learning, saying, "Dartmouth College has no relation whatsoever with any religious denomination. The choice of trustees, officers, or professors depends in no way upon denominational considerations. In faculty and in students practically

What one believes often makes one the subject of intolerance rather than one's meekness or lack of meekness. Courtesy of Free-Photos/Pixabay.

all denominations are represented."[63] The emphasis on the tone rather than the content of faith was a rhetorical strategy for abandoning the content and abandoning the faith. Dartmouth's next president, "Hopkins, Tucker's protégé, cut this to half strength with neutral spirit and put forward 'friendliness and good will' as 'the essence of the religion Jesus taught' (1921)." The emphasis on religion as mere friendship, as simply getting along, has proven an abandonment of faith. "Somehow the turbulence required by religious fidelity and self-definition became so distasteful, so mortifying, that these colleges found it preferable to lay serious religious studies aside."[64] The change in the style of their religion changed its content.

Researchers on tolerance hypothesize that "prejudice helps people defend the sense of meaning, validity, and vitality of their religious beliefs and disbeliefs."[65] Thus, in order to maintain belief, some intolerance is necessary. This, in turn, is scriptural. Without "an opposition in all things, . . . all things must needs be a compound in one; wherefore, if it should be one body it must needs remain as dead" (2 Nephi 2:11). In order to have a viable belief, there must be boundaries and distinctions and some degree of intolerance. Boundless tolerance is not scriptural.

While the term *tolerance* does not appear in the scriptures, at least in the King James Version, it does appear in some other versions. In Revelation 2:2, Jesus commends the Saints at Ephesus because "I know that you cannot tolerate evil people" (Revelation 2:2 International Standard Version). Yet Jesus also tells the Saints at Thyatira, "I have this against you: You tolerate that woman Jezebel, who calls herself a prophet and who teaches and leads my servants to practice immorality and to eat food sacrificed to idols" (Revelation 2:20 International Standard Version). Jesus was clear that tolerance of iniquity or evil was not good. This mirrors the stance in the Book of Mormon.

MORAL RELATIVISM

Moral individualism is dependent upon relativism, the notion that there are no absolute truths but that all truth is dependent on the position of the observer. The NSYR noted that "not all morally individualistic emerging adults subscribe to strong moral relativism. But many do. Moral individualism does seem to have strong intellectual affinities with moral relativism. And those who avoid moral individualism seem to have more to work with intellectually in order to resist relativism, if they in fact want to resist it." The NSYR provides a helpful quantification of the prevalence of moral relativism, but because youth are not necessarily able to articulate their positions, many fall into more than one category, which is why the percentages are well over one hundred percent. About three out of ten (30%) of the emerging adults believe in strong moral relativism.[66]

> Two-thirds of emerging adults, however, were not strong moral relativists; they stopped short of that radical position. This remaining two-thirds of emerging adults wished to resist the radical implications of strong moral relativism. We might think of many of them as reluctant moral agnostics or skeptics. They were not, to be sure, firm moral realists or absolutists. Few of them, in fact, took clear moral stands that they could defend. The majority of emerging adults could not accept total moral relativism, but many of them also could not clearly explain or defend the moral claims that they wished to make or say why moral relativism is actually wrong.

Some—more than one-quarter (27 percent) of the emerging adults we interviewed simply waffled on these questions.[67]

This still leaves a large group unaccounted for—

those who took a "situationalist" approach to morality. All of the same things could be right or wrong, these emerging adults said, depending on the particular context or circumstances. About four in ten emerging adults we interviewed (41 percent) mentioned situations as complicating moral evaluations.[68]

Another sizable group took a different approach:

Yet another way that some emerging adults—about one in three (27 percent) of those we interviewed—resolve their reservations about strong moral relativism is to say that, while most moral beliefs are relative, a small number of moral truths are not relative. . . . [So some of them] distinguished between universal moral truths and more relative beliefs that require more interpretation.[69]

The NSYR cautions that "it would be wrong to interpret these more or less morally relativistic voices as mere self-indulgent rationalizations for emerging adults to live as (im)morally as they please."[70] But it has been shown that "even priming people with moral relativism increases their tendency to behave immorally,"[71] which was defined as engaging in behavior that was "either illegal or morally unacceptable to the larger community," including lying and cheating.[72] Moral relativism seems to "shape people to become more trusting yet less trustworthy (i.e., more unethical)."[73] Immoral behavior can be a consequence but apparently is not the dominating cause of moral relativism.

In fact, there are powerful institutional reasons why emerging adults think like this. And the moral reasoning of emerging adults has deep roots in American history and society. . . . These messages are well intentioned and, at least in certain ways, we think, important, valuable, and effective. . . . Unfortunately, at least some of this tolerance-promoting, multiculturalist educational project also seems to have been based upon some shoddy moral reasoning, which it reinforces in turn. Thus emerging adults in our interviews are simply parroting to us what they have been taught by the adults who have educated them. That does not make sloppy and indefensible moral reasoning acceptable, but it does help make it understandable.[74]

Researchers "propose that one way to counteract the potential toll of moral relativism on ethical behavior is committing to

> Researchers propose that one way to counteract the potential toll of moral relativism on ethical behavior is committing to values and codes of conduct.

values and codes of conduct."[75] In other words, if one is interested in increasing moral behavior then one must emphasize absolute moral values that must be consistent across cultures and countries, not moral relativism.

Latter-day Saint youth are less likely to be moral relativists than the general population. The NSYR found that 18% of Latter-day Saint teenagers believed that morals were relative.[76] They are not likely to have learned moral relativism from general Church leaders. Elder Boyd K. Packer told this experience about one form of moral relativism:

A few weeks ago I was returning from the East with President Hinckley. We conversed with a passenger who said something to the effect that all churches lead to heaven. How often have you heard that—the parallel path to heaven philosophy?

They claim one church is not really better than another, just different. Eventually the paths will converge. One is, therefore, quite as safe in any church as in any other.

While this seems to be very generous, it just cannot be true.

I find it so interesting that those who condemn us reject the parallel path philosophy themselves when it comes to non-Christian religions.

For if they do not, they have no reason to accept the Lord as our Redeemer or regard the Atonement as essential. And what could they do with his statement that "he that believeth and is baptized shall be saved; but he that believeth not shall be damned"? (Mark 16:16.)

While the converging path idea is very appealing, it really is not reasonable.

Suppose schools were operated on that philosophy, with each discipline a separate path leading to the same diploma. No matter whether you study or not, pass the tests or not, all would be given the same diploma—the one of their choice.

Without qualifying, one could choose the diploma of an attorney, an engineer, a medical doctor.

Surely you would not submit yourself to surgery under the hands of a graduate of that kind of school!

But it does not work that way. It cannot work that way—not in education, not in spiritual matters. There are essential ordinances just as there are required courses. There are prescribed standards of worthiness. If we resist them, avoid them, or fail them, we will not enter in with those who complete the course.

Do you realize that the notion that all churches are equal presupposes that the true church of Jesus Christ actually does not exist anywhere?

Now, others may insist that this is not the true church. That is their privilege. But to claim that it does not exist anywhere, that it does not even need to exist, is to deny the scriptures.[77]

General relativism

Relativism initially tried to take its authority from science. Albert Einstein published the special theory of relativity in 1905—it specified that even if time and length were relative to the position and motion of the observer, the speed of light was constant. By 1930 one psychologist could already talk about "a new movement in psychology with the principle of relativity made current and popular by the great physicist Einstein." This was explained as follows: Because "for Einstein, these [space and time] values depend directly on the position of the observer," so in Gestalt psychology "every perception, whether of a person's face or of anything else, exists in its own right, is itself." "Just as Einstein gave an impetus to physics by expounding the relative nature of space and time, so the champions of the configuration psychology have been assiduously engaged in the attempt to demonstrate the relative character of our mental life." Whereas "the traditional psychology taught that a color possesses a more or less absolute, unchanging character . . . [the newer psychology] would seem to show conclusively that color quality is a matter relative to the meaning borne by the quality." The relativism imported into psychology was explicitly antireligious: "Primitive man saw in human purpose the expression of the will of good and evil spirits. In nature, the lightning and the whirlwind voiced the wrath of a god. The coming of modern science has enabled us to understand the events of physical nature in terms of natural causes, but the struggle to interpret human action without reference to supernatural agencies has been long drawn out and severe."[78] Relativism was brought into psychology explicitly to support naturalism and reject the idea of God. This is yet another example of how "from its very inception modern science was used to underpin political ideologies."[79]

> Relativism thus denies that there are absolute truths. Under relativism there is truth only from a certain point of view, and a change in that point of view changes truth.

Relativism thus denies that there are absolute truths. Under relativism there is truth only from a certain point of view, and a change in that point of view changes truth. One of the results of this philosophy, taken to its logical conclusion, is that science is not a way of discovering truth. "Through a lens of cultural relativism, [science] becomes another way of producing knowledge. . . . While this should not seem terribly threatening, it nevertheless proved to be surprisingly threatening to one segment of the scientific community—the segment that had grown accustomed to having its authority on virtually all matters stand without scrutiny. Presumably this was because such relativistic approaches to knowledge contain an implicit repudiation of science as a source of unquestioned truth about the world. They certainly highlight the role of science as a cultural authority."[80] Relativism also undermines history: "If all knowledge is relative, this suggests that history cannot make any truth claims. In conclusion, history becomes fiction. . . . History is merely a series of interpretations."[81] Not only does relativism undermine science and history, it undermines itself. If there are no privileged points of view, there is no particular reason to privilege relativism. Relativism cannot be used to say that a religious point of view is wrong. If all points of view are valid, certainly any particular religious point of view must be valid as well.

Gospel arguments against relativism

The Book of Mormon provides arguments against relativism. It asserts that the Spirit "speaketh of things as they really are, and of things as they really will be; wherefore, these things are manifested unto us plainly, for the salvation of our souls. But behold, we are not witnesses alone in these things; for God also spake them unto prophets of old" (Jacob 4:13). In spite of various competing claims, the Book of Mormon asserts that some things are real (compare Alma 32:35) and that we can learn of them through the Spirit and through various witnesses provided by God, including prophets of old. Through these means we can come to know the truth ourselves.[82] These assertions of the existence of an absolute truth contradict the assertions of relativism that no such truth exists.

We can see the dangers of relativism by looking at what relativism does to the gospel as the Book of Mormon describes it. For the Book of Mormon, the gospel, or doctrine of Christ, is specific and consists of faith in Jesus Christ, repentance, the covenant of baptism, the receipt of the Holy Ghost, and enduring to the end.[83]

Faith in God constitutes more than merely an intellectual assent that God exists—it encompasses a trust in him and the promises that he has made and a loyalty to him based on that trust. Relativism argues against faith in God since it argues that all points of view are equally valid. To relativists, a point of view that rejects the existence of God is equally valid and equally true to the one that accepts the existence of God. Thus relativism can be opposed to having faith in God.

Repentance is the means by which we set our lives right with God. In this way it can be seen as dependent on faith (compare Alma 34:15-17). Repentance involves both a change of mind (or heart) and a change in behavior. From a relativistic perspective, there is no reason to change our point of view since it is equally as good and valid as any other. The result of a relative point of view is that we avoid the cognitive dissonance of not having our behavior match our beliefs by simply changing our beliefs to match our behavior and relativistically arguing that our new beliefs are as valid as any others. Relativism, in its own way, undermines repentance.

Baptism is a covenant with God, an agreement with him that we will do certain things and act in certain ways, and in return God will grant certain promises. According to relativism, any point of view is equally valid, and so it is equally valid if we choose not to keep our covenant or not to make it in the first place—and God should honor our point of view since it is equally true. In this way, relativism interferes with the making and keeping of covenants.

> According to the gospel, it is not enough to trust in Christ and change our ways once or for a short time, but we must endure or continue in this way of life to the end.

The gift of the Holy Ghost promises that God, through the Holy Ghost, will provide us with the inspiration that we need in our daily lives. It promises that communication from God to us is possible and available. Relativism denies that seeking and receiving inspiration from the Holy Ghost is any more true or valid than following our own predilections. Relativism keeps us from following the Holy Ghost.

According to the gospel, it is not enough to trust in Christ, change our ways, make and keep sacred covenants, and follow the Holy Ghost once or for a short time, but we must endure or continue in this way of life to the end. Relativism is a stumbling block to our enduring to the end because it asserts that someone else's path is no more valid or efficacious than the one we choose. There is no one way or truth (compare John 14:6).

In these and other ways relativism runs counter to the gospel of Jesus Christ, and an adoption of a relativistic point of view interferes with our ability to accept and keep the gospel of Christ.

Moral Sources

Where do young adults think that morality comes from? The NSYR examined "how emerging adults think about moral sources—that is, the grounds or basis for moral truths."[84] The NSYR made two important observations about those sources:

> First, most of the accounts of morality's sources offered by emerging adults . . . are not reasonably defensible. They might make some sense to some at first glance. But when analyzed, much of what follows simply does not work; it cannot hold up to basic critical scrutiny. Second, despite claiming to be strong moral individualists . . . most emerging adults' accounts of the sources of morality turn out to be not all that individualistic. Almost all of the accounts examined . . . , in fact, turn out to be highly oriented to the interests, needs, or desires of social relations. We are not simply representing different voices here. Rather, this is another instance of emerging adult thinking being not particularly internally consistent.[85]

We begin with one of the more sobering statistics:

> Fully one in three (34 percent) of the emerging adults we interviewed said that they simply did not know what makes anything morally right or wrong. They had no idea about the basis of morality. Tellingly, some of these stumped interviewees could not even understand our questions on this point. No matter how many different ways we posed them or tried to explain or clarify them, our very questions about morality's sources did not or could not make sense to them.[86]

The confusion about the source of morality provides one more example of individuals who "took no thought."

On the other hand, "about four out of ten (40 percent) of the emerging adults we interviewed referred to how other people would think of them as (at least partly) defining what for them would be morally right and wrong." These young adults "professed to believe in moral right and wrong. Yet their morality does not itself have an objective reference or basis but was defined instead primarily by what other people would think about someone. If others would think the worse of a person for doing something, then that would be morally wrong for them to do. Positive and negative social perceptions, in other words, are morality's ultimate ground."[87] In Book of Mormon terms, they consider morality to be whatever the great and spacious building embraces.

There are other perceived sources of morality. Six out of ten emerging adults interviewed (60%) "described the basis or grounds of morality as whether or not anything functionally improved people's situations. If a thought, attitude, or action created a better functional situation, then it was moral, they essentially said. If it made a situation worse, then it was morally bad."[88] This type of thinking creates problems for these adults:

> Because situational consequences can often turn out differently than expected, at least some of these emerging adults are not able to govern their lives with moral systems, maps, philosophies, or worldviews that can reliably tell them in advance what is right and wrong. Instead, right and wrong are only figured out after the fact, when one sees the actual consequences of living.[89]

As a result, the moral systems of over half of young adults are failing them:

> The crucial distinction that these emerging adults are missing is the difference between the basis or reason for some moral truth and the effects of living according to that moral truth. Right moral living should normally have certain positive, patterned effects, at least over the long run. But that does not make those effects per se the reason why those things are morally right in the first place. If they are indeed morally right, they should remain so even if they sometimes fail to have those effects. Furthermore, sometimes right moral action does not improve people's situations. At times, in fact, it creates major problems. Sometimes right moral action involves real costs and sacrifices—which is exactly why it can be so hard to live morally. . . . So defining morality as that which functionally improves people's situations really does not work.[90]

Just over half (53%) of those interviewed define morality as "whether it hurts other people." For them, "a moral violation per se is essentially defined as anything that hurts other people physically, emotionally, financially, or otherwise." Those who understood morality this way "did not agree, however, on whether hurting oneself would also be morally bad or whether that was one's prerogative that had no moral implications."[91]

> For some emerging adults, not only is each individual entitled to define their own personal moral code, but it is also only the hurting of individual persons that could make anything morally wrong. For them it was only wrong to hurt individuals, and not particularly wrong to cheat or steal from an organization, such as a business.[92]

The NSYR saw this approach as problematic:

> Again, without going into much depth, we must observe that whether or not something harms people simply cannot serve as a defensible explanation for morality's source. One reason is that acting morally sometimes involves hurting other people in some ways—think of certain situations that require telling a hard truth, for instance, or of enforcing certain kinds of justice concerning the fair distribution of goods in situations when some people will get less so that others can have more. Another, more basic reason is that even being able to know or define in the first place what hurts or helps other people often itself requires reference to certain moral standards and understandings of what is good and bad. . . . In many such cases, it is only knowledge of the moral good that determines what is truly hurtful and helpful to other people. So morality itself cannot be dependent on perceptions of help and hurt as the basis of its very definition.[93]

About 12% of those interviewed held a view "that can best be described as a 'social-contract theory' of morality."

> In essence, according to this view, moral truth does not really enjoy any objective existence—nothing that critiques a belief or practice, such as slavery, that is embraced by the majority in a society. Rather, morality is simply the name of a collective social invention agreed to by people in a group or society to advance the hedonic and functional goods of those submitting to the social compact. Their mutually policing moral norms may come to be seen erroneously as

objective, natural or universal. But in reality they are merely agreements by contact—pure social constructions.[94]

The study's authors point to major problems with social-contract theory, including its failure to explain human rights and that "if everyone in a society must agree to establish a social contract, then no morality will ever be defined, since never in human history has everyone in a society agreed to anything."[95]

Almost one in four "of the contemporary emerging adults we interviewed (23 percent) referenced obedience to the laws of the land as one, if not the, key way to define morality. The essential idea expressed was that if something is in the law or regulations, then it is moral, and if it is not law, then it is outside the realm of morality." The authors also note the problems with such a view: "What such a view lacks, of course, is the capacity to successfully advance a moral critique of any existing laws, rules, or regulations."[96]

The concept of karma was also put forward:

A surprising (to us) number of emerging adults we interviewed— nearly one in six (17 percent)—spontaneously referred to "karma" as a way to explain how morality works, why it's best to act morally, and why the universe is ultimately a morally just place. In invoking karma, they meant that good attitudes and behavior will be rewarded in this life and bad people will get what they deserve too.[97]

Lastly, about 40% of those interviewed "claimed that their own moral views were somehow based in God's commands, the Bible, or other religious knowledge or sensibilities."[98]

For those keeping track, these opinions account for 279% of emerging adults and reflect overlapping approaches to morality, not mutually exclusive categories. We can rank them in terms of popularity:

- 60% define their morals depending on the situation.
- 53% base morals on whether actions hurt other people.
- 40% base morals on what other people would think.
- 40% base morals on religious knowledge.
- 34% could not say whether anything was right or wrong.

- 23% base morals on laws or rules.
- 17% base morals on karma.
- 12% base morals on social contracts.

This indicates that most young adults do not think about these matters.

MORAL INSTINCTS AND HAPPINESS

When the NSYR asked what young adults would do in a situation where they were unsure of what was right, they got the following answers:

- 9% said they would do what would help them get ahead.
- 18% said they would do what God or the scriptures said was right.
- 34% said they would follow the advice of a parent or teacher.
- 39% said they would do what they thought would make them happy.

This makes it sound as though it were some deliberative process, but 72% of young adults say they would act on instinct. They "speak about moral knowledge as being instinctive, automatic, prerational, embodied, common sense, and perhaps genetically rooted."[99] There is a difference between some sort of instinctive knowledge of good and evil and the influence of the Holy Ghost. Mormon in the Book of Mormon says that "the Spirit of Christ is given to every man, that he may know good from evil," but immediately follows with "wherefore, I show unto you the way to judge" (Moroni 7:16), indicating that moral instincts need training to be most useful.

> While happiness may be the object and design of our existence, doing what we think will make us happy may not be the most reliable guide.

While happiness may be the object and design of our existence because "men are, that they might have joy" (2 Nephi 2:25), doing what we think will make us happy may not be the most reliable guide.

Arnold Friberg, *Samuel the Lamanite Prophesies*. These Nephites, like over a third of American youth, did what they thought would make them happy but deceived themselves in the process. Courtesy of churchofjesuschrist.org. © 1951 IRI.

Samuel the Lamanite pointed out that the Nephites of his day "have sought all the days of [their] lives for that which [they] could not obtain; and [they] have sought for happiness in doing iniquity, which thing is contrary to the nature of that righteousness which is in our great and Eternal Head" (Helaman 13:38). These Nephites, like over a third of American youth, did what they thought would make them happy but deceived themselves in the process.

It is not as though youth today are a generation of Korihors who think that "every man fared in this life according to the management of the creature; therefore every man prospered according to his genius, and that every man conquered according to his strength; and whatsoever a man did was no crime" (Alma 30:17). Only about one in eleven indicated that they would act according to what would get them ahead. On the other hand, only about one in six even thought of turning to the scriptures, while about twice as many would turn to their parents, the two best sources for training their moral instincts.

Relying on untrained instincts can lead to moral relativism. Evangelicals, who have greater numbers than Latter-day Saints and a stronger cultural tendency toward relying on instincts, have noticed this tendency and its results. "The strong individualistic subjectivism in the emerging adult religious outlook—that 'truth' should be decided by 'what seems right' to individuals, based on their personal experience and feelings—also has deep cultural-structural roots in American evangelicalism."[100] But some evangelicals are noticing that this propensity has a downside. An evangelical pastor reported that he would conclude an extensive catechetical class for teenagers by asking them about the divinity and resurrection of Jesus Christ. For six years he received the same response from every pupil—that "the deity and resurrection of Christ are . . . mere matters of personal opinion."[101]

Moral Dilemmas

The NSYR asked young adults to come up with some moral dilemmas that they had faced. "One-third of the emerging adults who we interviewed (33%) simply could not think of any moral dilemmas or difficult situations that they had personally confronted in recent years. . . . Nearly one in three (29 percent) of the emerging adults we interviewed offered what they thought were examples of moral dilemmas that they had faced. But these in fact turned out to be not moral dilemmas having to do with right and wrong, but rather some other kind of practical decision they had had to make. These situations or problems they described to us actually had little or nothing to do with moral conflicts."[102] Only about a third could accurately bring up specific examples of moral dilemmas.

This could be an indicator of a number of things. It might indicate that young adults have led sheltered lives and have never really faced serious temptations or moral dilemmas. It might indicate that having successfully overcome their moral dilemmas, they have not looked back or rehashed their previous temptations. It might also be an indication that they simply have never given any serious thought to moral reasoning and thus are unable to recognize moral dilemmas. Such would leave them vulnerable to stumbling into moral compromises.

Moral Compromises

While most young adults believe that people ought to obey the law and do what they think is morally right, a number did not. One in three of those interviewed "said that they might do certain things they considered morally wrong if they knew they could get away with it."[103] Does this group overlap with the one in three who cannot tell what is right or wrong? If it does not at all, then it means that one in three do not know what is right or wrong and one in three will do the wrong thing if they think no one will notice.

Among Latter-day Saints only 2% said that they would do wrong if they knew they could get away with it. We appear to be doing a good job at teaching children to choose the right. But the question was hypothetical anyway. Many people think that they will resist temptation if they encounter it only to cave when the actual temptation appears. This is one of the reasons we are here on earth, to determine whether we will actually obey God when doing so is not easy or when we think we can get away with it.

Conclusions

The NSYR had a number of conclusions on the moral reasoning of young adults. Some bear highlighting:

> [First,] it is not that emerging adults are a morally corrupt lot (although some of them are). The problem is more that many of them are simply lost. They do not adequately know the moral landscape of the real world that they inhabit. And they do not adequately understand where they themselves stand in that real moral world. They need some better moral maps and better-equipped guides to show them the way around.[104]

> [Second,] the families, schools, religious communities, sports teams, and other voluntary organizations of civil society are failing to provide many young people with the kind of moral education and training needed for them even to realize, for example, that moral individualism and relativism make no sense, that they cannot be reasonably defended or sustained, that some alternative views must be necessary if we are to be at all reasonable when it comes to moral concerns. Colleges and universities appear to be playing a part in this as well.[105]

The NSYR has some particularly interesting conclusions about what can and should be done about the problems that emerging adults face. They note the following basic causes:

Poor moral reasoning comes significantly from poor teaching of thinking skills in schools, families, religious communities, sports teams, and other youth-socializing settings. Damaging sexual experiences have connections to things like the way colleges and universities are run and the lifestyle scripts disseminated by advertising and the mass media. Mass consumer materialism is of course deeply rooted in the structure of the American capitalist economy and the advertising industry. Intoxicating habits have much to do with the financial motives of the alcohol industry ("Drink Responsibly" ads notwithstanding) and the structures of college life, among other things. And disconnection from civic, communal, and political life surely has something to do with the many real dysfunctions of American politics and the lure of private, mass consumerist, media-stimulated lifestyles.[106]

> The NSYR has consistently noted that the family has the biggest impact of any institution on shaping the lives and especially the religious lives of teenagers and emerging adults.

College life, particularly, can create certain problems:

Structurally, most emerging adults live this crucial decade of life surrounded mostly by their peers—people of the same age and in the same boat—who have no more experience, insight, wisdom, perspective, or balance than they do. It is sociologically a very odd way to help young people come of age, to learn how to be responsible, capable, mature adults.[107]

After discussing (mostly infeasible) nationwide initiatives to address these problems, they come down to practices on the smaller scale that can help—indeed, one of the themes running through the books is that small actions in families matter most:

Families, for example, can be intentional about their values, commitments, and lifestyles in ways that can have significant effects on their members. Not every American household, for instance, must watch television a great deal of the time. It is actually possible to find recreational activities besides going to the shopping mall. Often families can choose, for example, to eat more meals together than they typically do. Heads of families can in fact decide to practice and model for children generosity in the form of greater charitable and religious financial giving, volunteering, giving blood, and so on. Such choices are within the hands of families.[108]

The NSYR has consistently noted that the family has the biggest impact of any institution on shaping the lives and especially the religious lives of teenagers and emerging adults.[109]

As we examine possible intellectual reasons why youth might be sliding into secularism, doubts about particular historical or doctrinal issues do not appear in the sociological data. Perhaps Latter-day Saints are an anomaly in that regard. Instead, assumptions and intellectual or philosophical positions seem to provide a basis for encouraging doubt. The NSYR provides a map of the terrain and points to some problems that the NSYR thought were serious enough to need to be addressed. It is important to put these intellectual concerns in larger context. Based on the amount of coverage they give these topics, the NSYR seems to indicate that the sex lives of emerging adults and their use of alcohol and drugs play a larger role than intellectual issues. Materialism also plays a role. We can see all of these issues (to a greater or lesser degree) among Latter-day Saints.

It is also important to realize that the NSYR gave percentages for categories of the young adults at large, not Latter-day Saint young adults. The statistics about Latter-day Saints sometimes mirror the national trends and sometimes are very skewed. Since Latter-day Saint young adults were among those interviewed, they fit somewhere in the statistics. Probably the biggest problem is that many of the young adults (as is true for many adults in general) have given such matters little if any thought. They have not worked through the issues themselves and cannot necessarily deal with them in an intelligent or coherent fashion. This is not just a problem among emerging adults— some adult members of the Church have also not taken the time to think these matters through. Although mortality gives us only a limited amount of time, some matters are of sufficient importance that they need to be thought through.

One reason to give these matters some thought is to enable us to take moral stands on issues, both individually and as a church, and to articulate the reasoning behind those moral stands. Though the different assumptions of different audiences may necessitate different lines of reasoning to those in the Church and those outside the Church, we will not be able to articulate any argument if we have not thought things through.

Muddy thinking on moral issues may be a bigger problem than any particular source of doubt. Behavioral actions may constitute an even larger problem than intellectual issues.

NOTES

1. Christian Smith and Melinda Lundquist Denton, *Soul Searching: The Religious and Spiritual Lives of American Teenagers* (Oxford: Oxford University Press, 2005), 32, 311–12n1.

2. Smith and Denton, *Soul Searching*, 162–63.

3. Smith and Denton, *Soul Searching*, 163.

4. Nicolette D. Manglos, "Faith Pinnacle Moments: Stress, Miraculous Experiences, and Life Satisfaction in Young Adulthood," *Sociology of Religion* 74, no. 2 (2013): 178.

5. Lisa D. Pearce, Jessica Halliday Hardie, and E. Michael Foster, "A Person-Centered Examination of Adolescent Religiosity Using Latent Class Analysis," *Journal for the Scientific Study of Religion* 52, no. 1 (2013): 60; David Voas, "The Rise and Fall of Fuzzy Fidelity in Europe," *European Sociological Review* 25, no. 2 (2009): 155–68; Ingrid Storm, "Halfway to Heaven: Four Types of Fuzzy Fidelity in Europe," *Journal for the Scientific Study of Religion* 48, no. 4 (2009): 702–18.

6. Pearce, Hardie, and Foster, "Person-Centered Examination," 59; Storm, "Halfway to Heaven," 702.

7. Nancy T. Ammerman, "Spiritual but Not Religious: Beyond Binary Choices in the Study of Religion," *Journal for the Scientific Study of Religion* 52, no. 2 (2013): 272; Pearce, Hardie, and Foster, "Person-Centered Examination," 59.

8. Ammerman, "Spiritual but Not Religious," 272.

9. Smith and Denton, *Soul Searching*, 163

10. Smith and Denton, *Soul Searching*, 163–64.

11. Smith and Denton, *Soul Searching*, 164. Compare Donna Freitas, *Sex and the Soul: Juggling Sexuality, Spirituality, Romance, and Religion on America's College Campuses* (Oxford: Oxford University Press, 2008), 29: "God doesn't have much to say about Amy's sexual and romantic life, either. When Amy talks so explicitly to me about her sexual past and present, her spiritual leanings aren't even a whisper, and this 'man with a plan' disappears from our conversation. For Amy, and for many of her peers, keeping prayer private and spirituality personal amounts to the separation of religion from their social lives. When it comes to her stories about sex, Amy's intense spiritual identity and devotion to God simply go missing. . . . To Amy, the girl with the strong relationship with God who prays all the time and sees God everywhere, sex is a personal choice that each individual must face without reference to religion, a decision she imagines she must face without the help of the man with the plan."

12. Smith and Denton, *Soul Searching*, 165.

13. Mark Larrimore, "Religion and the Promise of Happiness," *Social Research* 77, no. 2 (2010): 574.

14. Smith and Denton, *Soul Searching*, 166.

15. D. Todd Christofferson, "Abide in My Love," *Ensign*, November 2016, 48: "One of the terms we hear often today is that God's love is 'unconditional.' While in one sense that is true, the descriptor *unconditional* appears nowhere in scripture. Rather, His love is described as 'great and wonderful love,' 'perfect love,' 'redeeming love,' and 'everlasting love.' These are better terms because the word *unconditional* can convey mistaken impressions about divine love, such as, God tolerates and excuses anything we do because His love is unconditional, or *all* are saved in the kingdom of God because His love is unconditional. God's love is infinite and it will endure forever, but what it means for each of us depends on how we respond to His love. . . . God will always love us, but He cannot save us in our sins."

16. Smith and Denton, *Soul Searching*, 168, 167.

17. Christian Smith and Patricia Snell, *Souls in Transition: The Religious and Spiritual Lives of Emerging Adults* (Oxford: Oxford University Press, 2009), 154–55.

18. Smith and Denton, *Soul Searching*, 162–63.

19. Smith and Denton, *Soul Searching*, 162–63.

20. *Oxford English Dictionary*, s.v. "nice."

21. Arthur C. Brooks, *Love Your Enemies: How Decent People Can Save America from the Culture of Contempt* (New York: HarperCollins, 2019), 49.

22. Lazar Stankov and Jihyun Lee, "Nastiness, Morality and Religiosity in 33 Nations," *Personality and Individual Differences* 99 (2016): 56–66.

23. Smith and Denton, *Soul Searching*, 162–63. If that were really the case, then advocates of Moralistic Therapeutic Deism should be pushing both religiosity and political conservatism since "both right-wing political orientation and religiosity are associated with increased happiness, both in the United States and across numerous nations around the world"; Michael T. Bixter, "Happiness, Political Orientation, and Religiosity," *Personality and Individual Differences* 72 (2015): 10.

24. "History, 1838–1856, volume D-1 [1 August 1842–1 July 1843] [addenda]," p. 3 [addenda], The Joseph Smith Papers, https://www.josephsmith papers.org/paper-summary/history-1838-1856-volume-d-1-1-august -1842-1-july-1843/284. The letter this statement is taken from is only attested in a copy by John C. Bennett and may be a forgery.

25. *Teachings of Presidents of the Church: Brigham Young* (Salt Lake City: The Church of Jesus Christ of Latter-day Saints, 1997), 183; citing Brigham Young, *Discourses of Brigham Young*, 235.

26. Smith and Denton, *Soul Searching*, 162–63.

27. C. S. Lewis, *Mere Christianity* (New York: Macmillan, 1960), 174.

28. Deuteronomy 8:5; 2 Samuel 7:14; Job 5:17; Psalms 94:12; 118:18; Proverbs 3:11; 1 Corinthians 11:32; Hebrews 12:5–6, 10–11; Revelation 3:19; 1 Nephi 16:25, 39; Mosiah 23:21; Helaman 15:3; Ether 2:14; Doctrine and Covenants 1:27; 75:7; 87:6; 90:36; 93:50; 95:1–2, 10; 97:6; 98:21; 100:13; 101:4–5, 41; 103:4; 105:6.

29. Smith and Denton, *Soul Searching*, 162–63.

30. Christian Smith, Kari Christofferson, Hillary Davidson, and Patricia Snell Herzog, *Lost in Transition: The Darker Side of Emerging Adulthood* (Oxford: Oxford University Press, 2011).

31. Smith et al., *Lost in Transition*, 11.

32. Smith et al., *Lost in Transition*, 20.

33. Janie Harden Fritz, Naomi Bell O'Neil, Ann Marie Popp, Cory Williams, and Ronald C. Arnett, "The Influence of Supervisory Behavioral Integrity on Intent to Comply with Organizational Ethical Standards

and Organizational Commitment," *Journal of Business Ethics* 114, no. 2 (2013): 252.

34. Smith et al., *Lost in Transition*, 21.

35. Smith et al., *Lost in Transition*, 23–24.

36. Smith et al., *Lost in Transition*, 26–27.

37. Smith et al., *Lost in Transition*, 27. For such admonitions in literature directed toward Latter-day Saints, see Benjamin R. Hertzberg, "Just War and Mormon Ethics," *Mormon Studies Review* 1 (2014): 150; and Patrick Q. Mason, *Planted: Belief and Belonging in an Age of Doubt* (Provo, UT: Neal A. Maxwell Institute for Religious Scholarship; Salt Lake City: Deseret Book, 2015), 17.

38. Carmen Simon, *Impossible to Ignore* (New York: McGraw Hill, 2016), 214–25; emphasis in original.

39. Jean-Marc Ferry, "Conviction religieuse et responsabilité politique: La question d'une implication des religions dans nos espaces publics," *Archives de sciences sociales des religions* 60, no. 169 (2015): 108.

40. D. A. Carson, *The Intolerance of Tolerance* (Grand Rapids: Eerdmans, 2012), 6–7.

41. Carson, *Intolerance of Tolerance*, 11.

42. Carson, *Intolerance of Tolerance*, 11.

43. Carson, *Intolerance of Tolerance*, 11–12.

44. For example, Nancy T. Ammerman, *Sacred Stories, Spiritual Tribes: Finding Religion in Everyday Life* (Oxford: Oxford University Press, 2014), 217.

45. Mark J. Brandt and Daryl R. Van Tongeren, "People Both High and Low on Religious Fundamentalism Are Prejudiced toward Dissimilar Groups," *Journal of Personality and Social Psychology* 112, no. 1 (2017): 76.

46. https://www.barna.com/research/millennials-oppose-evangelism/.

47. Carson, *Intolerance of Tolerance*, 47.

48. *American Views on Intolerance and Religious Liberty in America* (Nashville: LifeWay Research, 2015), 4–5.

49. Brandt and Tongeren, "People Both High and Low," 77.

50. Brandt and Tongeren, "People Both High and Low," 77.

51. Joanna Blogowska, Vassilis Saroglou, and Catherine Lambert, "Religious Prosociality and Aggression: It's Real," *Journal for the Scientific Study of Religion* 52, no. 3 (2013): 532–34; Ain Simpson, Jared Piazza, and Kimberly Rios, "Belief in Divine Moral Authority: Validation of

a Shortened Scale with Implications for Social Attitudes and Moral Cognition," *Personality and Individual Differences* 94 (2016): 264; Patty Van Cappellen, Barbara L. Fredrickson, Vassilis Saroglou, and Olivier Corneille, "Religiosity and the Motivation for Social Affiliation," *Personality and Individual Differences* 113 (2017): 24–31; George Yancey, "Who Has Religious Prejudice? Differing Sources of Anti-Religious Animosity in the United States," *Review of Religious Research* 52, no. 2 (2010): 159–60; Stefanie Doebler, "Relationships between Religion and Intolerance towards Muslims and Immigrants in Europe: A Multilevel Analysis," *Review of Religious Research* 56, no. 1 (2014): 61–86.

52. Brandt and Tongeren, "People Both High and Low," 84.

53. Filip Usarevic, Vassilis Saroglou, and Magali Clobert, "Are Atheists Undogmatic?," *Personality and Individual Differences* 116 (2017): 164–70; cf. Yancey, "Who Has Religious Prejudice?," 166–68.

54. Neal A. Maxwell, "Meeting the Challenges of Today," in *The Inexhaustible Gospel* (Provo, UT: BYU Studies, 2004), 69.

55. Maxwell, "Meeting the Challenges of Today," 69–70.

56. Smith et al., *Lost in Transition*, 67–68.

57. Freitas, *Sex and the Soul*, 184.

58. Quoted in James T. Burtchaell, *The Dying of the Light: The Disengagement of Colleges and Universities from Their Christian Churches* (Grand Rapids, MI: Eerdmans, 1998), 783–84.

59. Carson, *Intolerance of Tolerance*, 81.

60. Brandt and Tongeren, "People Both High and Low," 85, 93, 85, 94.

61. William J. Tucker, "The Religion of the Educator," quoted in Burtchaell, *Dying of the Light*, 36–37.

62. J. Tucker, *The Function of the Church in Modern Society*, quoted in Burtchaell, *Dying of the Light*, 37–38.

63. Burtchaell, *Dying of the Light*, 39.

64. Burtchaell, *Dying of the Light*, 825–26.

65. Brandt and Tongeren, "People Both High and Low," 94.

66. Smith et al., *Lost in Transition*, 27.

67. Smith et al., *Lost in Transition*, 29.

68. Smith et al., *Lost in Transition*, 30.

69. Smith et al., *Lost in Transition*, 31–32.

70. Smith et al., *Lost in Translation*, 34–35.

71. Jackson G. Lu, Jordi Quoidbach, Francesca Gino, Alek Chakroff, William W. Maddux, and Adam D. Galinsky, "The Dark Side of Going Abroad: How Broad Foreign Experiences Increase Immoral Behavior," *Journal of Personality and Social Psychology* 112, no. 1 (2017): 2.

72. Lu et al., "Dark Side of Going Abroad," 3. The authors note that it is the breadth of exposure to foreign cultures rather than the depth that is the predictive factor: Lu et al., "Dark Side of Going Abroad," 2–14. Missionaries are typically given an experience in depth in a foreign country.

73. Lu et al., "Dark Side of Going Abroad," 13.

74. Smith et al., *Lost in Translation*, 34–35.

75. Lu et al., "Dark Side of Going Abroad," 14.

76. NSYR wave 1 data. Some writings by Latter-day Saints espouse moral relativism; see, for example, Rosalynde Welch, "The New Mormon Theology of Matter," *Mormon Studies Review* 4 (2017): 72: "Truth is conditioned by time and place."

77. Boyd K. Packer, "The Only True Church," *Ensign*, November 1985, 82.

78. P. C. Squires, "A New Psychology after the Manner of Einstein," *The Scientific Monthly* 30 (January–June 1930): 156–57, 160–62.

79. Jonathan Marks, *Why I Am Not a Scientist* (Berkeley: University of California Press, 2009), 47.

80. Marks, *Why I Am Not a Scientist*, 63.

81. Carl Olson, *The Allure of Decadent Thinking: Religious Studies and the Challenge of Postmodernism* (Oxford: Oxford University Press, 2013), 130–31.

82. Alma 5:45–46, 48; 34:8; 36:4–6; Helaman 7:29; 15:7–8; Moroni 10:5.

83. 3 Nephi 11:27; Noel B. Reynolds, "The Gospel of Jesus Christ as Taught by the Nephite Prophets," *BYU Studies* 31, no. 1 (1991): 31–50.

84. Smith et al., *Lost in Transition*, 35.

85. Smith et al., *Lost in Transition*, 35.

86. Smith et al., *Lost in Transition*, 36.

87. Smith et al., *Lost in Transition*, 37–38.

88. Smith et al., *Lost in Transition*, 38.

89. Smith et al., *Lost in Transition*, 39.

90. Smith et al., *Lost in Transition*, 39.

91. Smith et al., *Lost in Transition*, 39–40.

92. Smith et al., *Lost in Transition*, 41.

93. Smith et al., *Lost in Transition*, 42.
94. Smith et al., *Lost in Transition*, 42.
95. Smith et al., *Lost in Transition*, 44.
96. Smith et al., *Lost in Transition*, 44–45.
97. Smith et al., *Lost in Transition*, 45–46.
98. Smith et al., *Lost in Transition*, 46–47.
99. Smith et al., *Lost in Transition*, 51–52, 55.
100. Smith and Snell, *Souls in Transition*, 290.
101. Ron Sider, *The Scandal of the Evangelical Conscience* (Grand Rapids, MI: Baker Books, 2005), 91.
102. Smith et al., *Lost in Transition*, 56–57.
103. Smith et al., *Lost in Transition*, 47.
104. Smith et al., *Lost in Transition*, 69.
105. Smith et al., *Lost in Transition*, 61.
106. Smith et al., *Lost in Transition*, 233.
107. Smith et al., *Lost in Transition*, 234.
108. Smith et al., *Lost in Transition*, 241.
109. Smith and Denton, *Soul Searching*, 111–12; Jasper van de Pol and Frank van Tubergen, "Inheritance of Religiosity among Muslim Immigrants in a Secular Society," *Review of Religious Research* 56, no. 1 (2014): 87–88.

A strong correlation exists between religiosity and sexual activity. Sexual misconduct may not be at the root of every loss of faith, but it nevertheless plays a role in many individual accounts. Courtesy of Elle Stallings/Pixabay.

7 | THE RUTHLESS WAR OF PROMISCUITY

The focus on intellectual issues and other social factors in diminishing faith sometimes overshadows the role that sexual morality plays in influencing the faith of youth. Many who lose faith after sexual misconduct wish to minimize the role that their actions have played and put the burden on intellectual issues. Others, knowing that not every loss of faith is caused by immoral behavior, claim that the role of sexual morality has been overemphasized. As a result, they deemphasize immorality. One researcher, however, noted multiple instances of individuals who went from devout to "spiritual but not religious" who "got there by experimenting with sex."[1] Sexual misconduct may not be at the root of every loss of faith, but it nevertheless plays a role in many individual accounts.

A strong correlation exists between sexual activity and religiosity,[2] so much so that the NSYR devoted a whole book to religiosity and sexuality.[3] This and other studies help us to understand the role of sexuality on the religion of youth. This is one area where the data about Latter-day Saints stands in stark contrast to the data from those of other denominations. Latter-day Saints do things very differently from others, and it shows in the data, almost always in ways that are sociologically better. It is important to understand what the typical patterns of behavior are and how behaviors differ for Latter-day Saint youth, as well as things Latter-day Saints do that contribute to those results.

THE NATURAL MAN

In considering this subject, it is worth setting practices of Latter-day Saints in the context of what the Book of Mormon terms "the natural man" (Mosiah 3:19), using the older English generic sense of *man* to include both male and female. (It should be remembered that the Book of Mormon is translated into an Early Modern English idiom older than the King James idiom.[4] "In all the Teut[onic] lang[uages] the word had a twofold sense of 'human being' and 'adult male human being,'" and thus it is "used explicitly as a designation equally applicable to either sex."[5]) The natural man displays the typical patterns of sexuality in the world around us.

The biological consequences of gender

In humans, sexual reproduction has historically and biologically required two individuals of different gender to be successful. "Biological sex (the binary categories of male and female) is a fixed aspect of human nature, even though some individuals affected by disorders of sex development may exhibit ambiguous sex characteristics. By contrast, gender identity is a social and psychological concept that is not well defined, and there is little scientific evidence that it is an innate, fixed biological property."[6] Though these scientists are using different language than the proclamation on the family, they are making the same argument. What the proclamation describes as "gender" they call "biological sex."[7]

Human beings are anomalous in the animal kingdom for being one of the few mammals whose sexual behavior is not controlled by the estrous cycle. In most mammals, the estrous cycle means that the female of the species engages in sexual activity only during the estrus

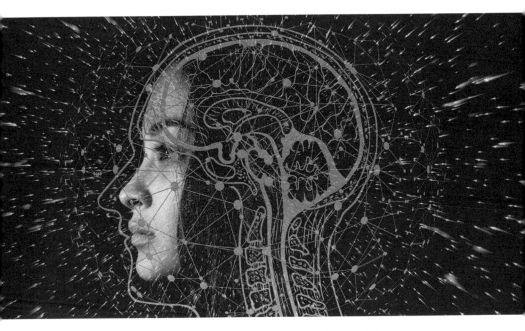

Development of the cerebral cortex that controls executive function in the brain lags behind a few years, so youth often have the ability to reproduce without necessarily having the mental equipment to do so in a wise manner. Courtesy of Gerd Altmann/ Pixabay.

phase of the cycle, also called being in heat.[8] Humans, on the other hand, normally choose whether and when to engage in sexual activity. Both the choice and the concomitant accountability are part of human sexual relations. "It takes comparatively little thought or discipline to have sexual intercourse. Eroticism is probably the lowest common denominator in human relations because it requires only appetite, the opportunity to gratify it, and normal physiological functioning."[9]

Puberty is marked, if not defined, by specific physiological changes in the human organism that prepare the body for reproduction. Unfortunately, neurological development, particularly development of the cerebral cortex that controls executive function in the brain, lags behind a few years.[10] So youth often have the ability and proclivity to reproduce without necessarily having the mental equipment to do so in a wise manner. But just because the prefrontal cortex is not fully developed does not mean that it is completely inoperable, nor does it mean that humans are not accountable for their choices in relation to sexual activity.

The brains of men and women generally work similarly in sexual activity,[11] but there are some significant neurological differences between men and women in this regard. Men are generally more aroused by appearances than women are.[12] This is one reason that men tend to be more susceptible to pornography than women.[13] In males the part of the brain responsible for thinking logically and planning ahead shuts down during arousal.[14] In aroused females the part of the brain responsible for inhibitions, fear, and guilt turns off.[15] In both, the part of the brain responsible for self-consciousness and worrying also shuts down.[16] The lack of clear thinking and concern for consequences are both good rea-

> **The lack of clear thinking and concern for consequences are both good reasons for safeguards on sexual behavior.**

sons for safeguards on sexual behavior. The shutting down of parts of the brain manifests itself in a number of ways. For those in search of sexual gratification, "concerns for the welfare of others and the world, as well as existential questions regarding the meaning of the world and one's individual life, may appear irrelevant in that specific moment or at least be temporarily considered of secondary importance."[17] Thus the heat of passion clearly does not create the best circumstances for making wise decisions.

Virginity

The initiation of sexual experience—called variously in the literature: loss of virginity, coitarche, or first sex—marks a particular turning point in the life of most humans. At the beginning of the twentieth century young women viewed their virginity as something of value, but young men esteemed their own much less. Starting about 1920, young people were increasingly likely to lose their virginity before marriage, though usually to their future spouse. Beginning in the 1960s young people were increasingly likely to engage in sex with people they had no intention of marrying.[18] Since that time, the age of first sexual experience has decreased.[19] Thus, in the twenty-first century, 9.8% of thirteen-year-olds have had sex, 32.6% of fifteen-year-olds,

61.3% of seventeen-year-olds, and 71.5% of eighteen-year-olds.[20] Still, for most, though not all, an individual's loss of virginity is a moment of particular significance.[21]

Just because it is significant does not mean that it is necessarily positive. As one young woman put it, "Well, when I had sex the first time, I felt horrible about myself after. I just felt dirty, and I think definitely if people are not doing it with the right person, and they are not ready for it, . . . they'll definitely regret their decision."[22] Although social scientists have noted that "the emotional pain that lingers after poor sexual decision making, at any age, is evidence of the complex morality inherent to human sexuality,"[23] one does not need to be a social scientist to notice that, but merely a thoughtful observer of humans. "Very many Americans reflect negatively on the circumstances in which—or the timing of when—they lost their virginity. Most emerging adults—70 percent in [one] study—think they were too young to have lost their virginity when they did."[24] One researcher records, "Women are ambivalent about this, seeing sexual experience as something of a loss. But guys are different. . . . They don't value virginity as much as women do, and it's really difficult to find a guy on campus who's still a virgin—or at least one who will admit it. For guys, virginity is 'something you want to get over with.' Women want something else. They don't want to 'waste' their first time having sex."[25]

The negative reflection among sexually active emerging adults about loss of virginity is part of a larger trend. Although "they clearly do not want to see themselves as having regrets," teenagers and young adults appear to "harbor regrets about the past even when they deny that they do."[26] As one put it, "For the most part, I don't regret it because I know it happened for a reason, but in a way I *do* regret it. But I don't *let* myself regret it. I just try to look on the positive side."[27] Their reflection presents "emotional dueling when enthusiasm battles disgust." At least 78% of women and 73% of men express regrets over at least one sexual relationship, and "over 80 percent reported having experienced ambivalence about a recent sexual relationship." The regrets afflict women more than men: "75 percent of those who reported no regrets were men, while two-thirds of those who did were women."[28] "Sex simply does not come without emotional strings for the majority of American adolescents, especially girls."[29] Some studies show that women are much more likely to feel regret for casual sex than men and that this effect is not culturally dependent.[30] And so "many adolescents do a good deal of mental labor and normative affirmation in order to convince each other that coupled sexual activity during adolescence—a period of relational instability and immaturity—is, in fact, a good idea. Arousal may come naturally during adolescent development, but sexual happiness does not."[31] Thus after a bad sexual experience, individuals "tend to blame themselves for getting into such a situation. So they hide their feelings, which does nothing to alter popular ideas and scripts" that led them to the bad experience in the first place. The popular notions do not change in part because "researchers have published . . . very little on the emotional-health consequences of sexual decision making."[32] Breakups among the sexually active are devastating:

> These splits are not your run-of-the-mill middle school and high school breakups that sweep the local rumor mill, create lots of drama, and leave somebody crying for a few days. The breakups that many emerging adults recounted instead sounded much more serious. They often happened in the context of couples living together or semicohabiting and, in any case, being sexually involved. They often resulted in serious emotional and physical distress—dumped partners told tales of days spent sleeping and crying or lying in bed debilitated with depression, of anguish suffered at being cheated on or otherwise betrayed, of profound struggles with self-doubt, self-criticism, and hopelessness lasting for months, of uncertainty about being able to trust another man or woman whom they might love in the future. . . . Their accounts suggested the experience of getting a hard divorce without ever even having gotten married.[33]

The emotional consequences of sex for sexually active young adults "vary wildly but can include guilt, regret, temporary self-loathing, rumination, diminished self-esteem, a sense of having used someone else or been used, a sense of having let yourself down, discomfort about having to lie or conceal sex from family, anxiety over the depth and course of the relationship, and concern over the place or role of sex in the relationship. Others experience more intense versions of these, which can include obvious depressive symptoms, crying more than normal, difficulty shaking 'the blues,' and extreme anxiety over the future of

Breakups among the sexually active are devastating; "their accounts suggested the experience of getting a hard divorce without ever even having gotten married." Courtesy of Victoria Borodinova/Pixabay.

the relationship."[34] Another study reported that "those who've ever reported concurrent sexual partners were also more apt to report taking medication for depression or anxiety than those who haven't (18 percent vs. 12 percent), and reported significantly less overall happiness. It isn't clear if concurrent sexual relationships cause psychological harm, detrimentally affecting happiness, or if depression or dissatisfaction with life causes people to 'self-medicate' by seeking out multiple sexual partners (or both)."[35] One researcher, looking at the effects of sex among college students wrote, "Positive student stories—stories of pleasurable sex, self-approval, and happiness with past experiences— were rare. . . . Most of what students talked about was negative."[36] This is also reflected in the vernacular idioms where expressions for sex almost always have a negative connotation of being damaged or used. For most people, media portrayals of the positive and satisfying sexual life of singles are disconnected with reality as they know it. The context of the sex matters a great deal since "when it's within a stable, romantic context, sex is seldom associated with depressive symptoms."[37]

Promiscuity

For the natural man, "solitary instances of sexual intercourse are unusual. Instead, virginity loss tends to commence a pattern of paired sexual activity, most commonly with more than one partner."[38] This is more desirable for the natural male than the natural female: "Researchers have reported that men want an average of fourteen sexual partners in their lifetime, while the women said that they wanted an average of one or two."[39] If that is the case, then 56.2% of never-married 18- to 26-year-old women have already exceeded their desired average. Two-thirds (67.0%) of men in that category have had more than one sexual partner, and almost an equal number (68.1%) of women report the same.[40] Norms have bent toward the desires of the natural male. "The number of sex partners people have over a lifetime—or how long those relationships last—is increasingly considered less important to emerging adults than is their monogamous conduct while in those relationships."[41] But even if the natural young man wants more partners, obtaining them is another matter. The median number of lifetime sexual partners for both natural males and females is between four and six. Only about 26% of heterosexual men have more than ten partners in their life and only 3% have more than fifty.[42] "Men are game for more sexual partnerships than women are, on average. . . . But a man's partner count generally cannot rise *as rapidly* as a woman's can—since, all other things being equal, her sexual marketability is consistently greater than his."[43] Rapid or not, an increase in sexual partners correlates with worse emotional health in women, though not men.[44]

If the goal is an elevated number of sexual partners, then the natural man should start having sexual partners before age 16, be popular, take risks, get drunk, not go to college, be politically liberal, use pornography, and have an abortion (or have one's partner get an abortion), since all of these factors are associated with a greater likelihood of increasing the numbers of sexual partners.[45] (Being politically conservative and in college or being a college graduate has the opposite effect.)[46] While this might seem desirable to the average natural male, it does not seem all that desirable to the average natural female. Even for men, it may not be as ideal as imagined: "Men often appear to lose track—or not care enough to recall correctly—after 6 or 7 partners."[47] It is not as though these individuals consider themselves promiscuous; they only consider someone to be promiscuous if they have had more sexual partners than they themselves have had.[48]

The morals in America have shifted: "You're only allowed one sexual partner at a time, and to overlap is to cheat, and cheating remains a serious norm violation that gives the victimized party not just the uncontested right but often a perceived moral obligation to end the relationship."[49] The natural man might acknowledge moral parameters, but they are for others. The natural man is *selectively permissive*: the moral rule remains right and good and in effect, yet it does not apply to them at present, for reasons too nuanced and difficult for them to adequately describe."[50] Accordingly, "a sizeable group of Americans (34 percent of men and 28 percent of women) . . . report having had concurrent sexual relationships at least once in their lifetimes."[51]

> Sex and commitment go together, and to try to get one without the other typically leaves the natural man without either.

With increased age and additional sexual partners, sexual activity is initiated more quickly within successive relationships. "Fully 36 percent of all young men's relationships become sexual in less than two weeks, and 70 percent in less than six months. Women's claims are slightly more conservative: 22 percent of their relationships become sexual early, within two weeks, while 61 percent of them do so before the six-month mark." The relationships of young adults not in college tend to become sexual faster than those in college.[52] Ironically, the earlier that sex commences in a relationship, the less likely the relationship is to last.[53] This, however, creates a "problem that may uniquely plague emerging-adult relationships": "many couples lack a clear, shared, and suitable role for the sex they experience within a romantic relationship, especially when sex is introduced relatively early." Many of them find it difficult to talk about. "Apart from relationship security, familiarity, and a shared domicile, sex has a difficult time playing a supportive role in fostering intimacy and building love. Instead it wants to be the lead character. But when left to sustain a relationship, sex typically falters."[54] Marriage changes the situation.[55] Sex and commitment go together, and to try to get one without the other typically leaves the natural man without either.

For the natural man, relationships tend to follow a particular script: "plenty of sex, starting early (before expressions of love but not necessarily before feelings of and hopes about it), underdeveloped interest in sacrificing on behalf of the other (especially but not exclusively discernable in men), accounts of 'overlapping' partners, much drama, and in the end nothing but mixed memories and expired time."[56] Consequently, "people commence relationships, enjoy them for a time, then await the sure signs of their fatal condition." The relationships tend to be brief. Two-thirds (67%) of nonromantic sexual relationships among 18- to 23-year-olds last less than a month.[57] But the majority of relationships are not of this sort. Of the same demographic group, under a third (29%) of men's relationships and just under a fifth (18%) of women's relationships can be classified that way. Some of the gap in perception can be explained by noting that there must have been more cases where the women have viewed the relationship as romantic while the men did not.[58] Yet even the romantic relationships do not last very long: Over half (54.7%) do not last six months, and over three-quarters (76.4%) do not last a year. Ironically, "sexual activity declines in frequency as the duration of the relationship increases" and so does the satisfaction with the sexual activity.[59] There are other adverse side effects as well. "High numbers of sexual partners, as well as concurrent sexual partners, are not only a public health concern because of the risk of spreading sexually transmitted infections, but have also been linked to higher rates of depression, anxiety, and substance abuse."[60]

> "The bottom line is this: *women are the sexual gatekeepers in their relationships*," even if many of them do not recognize that role.

Selfishness

The natural man has "come to think of sex as an individual action that happens to involve another person."[61] It is thus, unsurprisingly, an overwhelmingly selfish act. For the natural man, sex is about *me*, not about *us*.[62] The unmarried who dwell on sexual experience manifest an inherent self-centeredness. "Sexual pleasure and satisfaction may involve a self-centered dimension that prevents people from being fully open to the world and caring for the needs and well-being of many others. The opposition between hedonistic motives and prosocial concerns thus may not be a residual of old-style traditional morality but may point to the very nature of sexuality as a self-enhancing experience." The researchers also note that sex within marriage seems to work differently.[63] Though many believe that "it's nobody else's business as long as everyone directly involved consents,"[64] "sex is not an entirely private matter between two people." It never was. "Instead, it becomes part of an economic and social system in which couples participate."[65]

Economics

Even in the natural man, there are generally differences between the sexes. "On average—and that is always a critically important caveat to keep in mind—men and women desire sex for different reasons, show differing levels of interest in sex, and experience sex differently." Because women are generally less interested in casual sex than men are, "women can have sex when they wish to; men can only hope for it."[66] Thus "the bottom line is this: *women are the sexual gatekeepers in their relationships*,"[67] even if many of them do not recognize that role.

Other factors also play into sexual activity. To understand those factors, it is worthwhile to consider sex as an economic activity—certainly not the only way or perhaps not the best way to view the subject, but useful nonetheless. Consensual sexual access is granted on conditions agreed upon by the various parties. Because men are usually more interested in casual sex, the demand comes from the men while the supply is fulfilled by the women. The price is negotiated between them in the context of the local market. But the local market is overestimated: individuals estimate that 50–77% more sexual activity is going on than actually is, and the desire for abstinence is usually estimated at half the actual level.[68] People tend to think that they are more inhibited and ambivalent about sex than their peers are.[69] This leads individuals to act in the way they think is the norm rather than according to their own preferences, a form of self-fulfilling prophecy.[70] In this way "there's really no such thing as entirely discreet sex, even if a couple never mentions it to another soul, because every sexual act is a data point for both men and women in establishing the cost of sex in subsequent relationships." Thus the actual price can vary widely. "Although the 'cost' of sex is negotiated between partners *and* reflects the narratives about sex within the community at large, in the end a woman must agree to the transaction (in a consensual relationship)." Her consensual agreement on the price makes her the gatekeeper. "The highest price a man can pay is a lifetime promise to share all his wealth, income, and affection with a woman exclusively."[71] Over the last half century, the cost and communal value of sex have generally dropped.

Viewed as an economic enterprise, the percentage of women to men plays an important role. In markets where men outnumber women, men have to compete harder for the available women, and women can afford to be more selective and thus are able to dictate more in the way of commitment in return for sexual access.[72] In markets where women outnumber men, such as on most college campuses, women have to compete harder for the available men. When women outnumber men, "women have less power to demand relational commitment—upon which they are more reliant because of their more limited structural power—in return for sexual access";[73] men, on the other hand, "are thought to be more enabled to pursue sex while avoiding long-term relationship commitments."[74] Women also have a harder time finding an appropriate potential partner at all since there are not enough men to go around.[75] This might explain why 66.4% of never-married women in the 18- to 23-year-old age bracket are dating and having sex, whereas only 52.5% of men in the same bracket are.[76] As more women compete for fewer desirable men, they lower the price to the men in terms of monogamous commitment and not only allow men to have sexual access before marriage but also may end up having to endure cheating. Thus on college campuses where women outnumber men, women are more likely to remain virgins—because they could not find a partner—but when they have found a partner, they are more likely to be sexually active. With the increase in the percentage of women on campus the chances of sexual activity increase,[77] and "men are less likely to commit to women on campuses where there are more alternatives available to them outside of a relationship."[78] Thus "women who attend college on campuses where they are more numerous tend to view men as less interested in commitment and less trustworthy. They are less likely to expect much from men, find it more difficult to locate the right kind of men, and are more likely to report that their relationships do not work out and that a woman cannot have a boyfriend if she will not have sex."[79] Thus the increase of women in higher education has an unintended negative consequence for women.

> **"In the ruthless war of promiscuity women are at a double disadvantage. They play for higher stakes and are also more likely to lose."**

C. S. Lewis ended his last published work with the following observation, which still seems relevant:

A society in which conjugal infidelity is tolerated must always be in the long run a society adverse to women. Women, whatever a few male songs and satires may say to the contrary, are more naturally monogamous than men; it is a biological necessity. Where promiscuity prevails they will therefore always be more often the victims than the culprits. Also, domestic happiness is more necessary to them than to us. And the quality by which they most easily hold a man, their beauty, decreases every year after they have come to maturity, but this does not happen to those qualities of personality— women don't really care twopence about our looks—by which we hold women. Thus in the ruthless war of promiscuity women are at a double disadvantage. They play for higher stakes and are also more likely to lose.[80]

The quest of the natural man is not exactly romantic love: "in romantic love there may be stops and starts, but the quest is for settled-ness, the destination is a family, and the assumption is distinctiveness (and magnetism) between men and women."[81] Instead the quest is for ephemeral encounters. One cultural consequence of the prevalence of this point of view is the demise of the romantic comedy as a genre for films since such films typically ended with the marriage and stabilization of the relationship. Movies are typically aimed at a youth audience whose lives no longer resemble that genre but reflect more the endless episodic nature of a soap opera in a rerun rut.

COHABITATION

For adolescents and emerging adults, the initiation of sexual experiences usually leads to promiscuity that sometimes settles into longer-term liaisons, such as living together, or cohabitation. Emerging adults view cohabitation as a possible prelude to marriage. It is estimated that between 50 and 70% of couples cohabit before marriage.[82] Many emerging adults "maintained with complete assurance that one would be stupid to get married without first having lived together for six months to a year. . . . By cohabiting for the good part of a year, one is able to 'test drive' the relationship and confirm before it is too late that the marriage really will work."[83] Almost half (44%) of Americans agree with this philosophy.[84] This is, however, a fantasy; the reality is quite different. Only one in five cohabiting relationships actually ends in marriage, and that number is decreasing. Cohabiting to test out the relationship is less likely to result in marriage than cohabiting for other reasons.[85] Both men and women in a cohabiting relationship are more than twice as likely to report wanting to leave the relationship than those that are married.[86] The most successful cohabiting couples are those who view cohabitation as a step toward marriage[87] and who get married before children come into the picture,[88] but "the longer a cohabiting relationship continues, the less likely it is that the outcome is ever going to be marriage."[89]

Not only is cohabitation less likely to end in marriage, but those couples who marry are more likely to divorce than those who married without cohabiting. While 76% of young adults think that cohabitation is fine,[90] "none of the emerging adults who are enthusiastic about cohabiting as a means to prevent unsuccessful marriages seem aware

Not only is cohabitation less likely to end in marriage, but those cohabiting couples who marry are more likely to divorce than those who married without cohabiting. Courtesy of Steve Buissinne/Pixabay.

that nearly all studies consistently show that couples who live together before they marry are more, not less, likely to later divorce than couples who did not live together before their weddings."[91] Cohabitation significantly increases the risk of divorce. "The divorce rates of women who cohabit are nearly 80 percent higher than the rates of those who do not."[92] The divorce rates for those women who cohabit more than once are twice as high as those who cohabit only once.[93] "In fact, either something about living together before marriage itself or the very notion of approaching marriage with the mentality of hedging one's bets by shaking out the relationship with a provisional uncommitted marriage-like test, or both, significantly increases the probability of subsequently divorcing. But emergent adults are oblivious to these facts."[94] For example,

One college professor described a survey that he had conducted over a period of years in his marriage classes. He asked guys who were living with a girl, point blank, "Are you going to marry the girl that you're living with?" The overwhelming response, he reports, was "NO!" When he asked the girls if they were going to marry the guy they were living with, their response was, "Oh, Yes!" The professor asked "Why?" The girls usually replied, "Because we love each other and we are learning how to be together." The guys, however, explained that they would not marry the girl they were living with because, "She was easy for me. How can I trust her to be faithful in marriage?"[95]

> In terms of the economic view of mating, cohabiting men are already getting sexual access at a cheaper price in terms of commitment, and thus there is less incentive to pay a higher price.

The NSYR data backs up the professor's anecdotal claims; 61% of cohabiting women thought that their cohabitation was very likely to end in marriage, but only 43% of the men did.[96] National surveys show that cohabiting women are more interested in marriage than cohabiting men.[97] In terms of the economic view of mating, cohabiting men are already getting sexual access at a cheaper price in terms of commitment, and thus there is less incentive to pay a higher price.

The men in the professor's anecdote cited lack of trust as a reason for not proceeding to marriage, and they have a reason to think this way. "Not surprisingly, partners in a cohabiting relationship are more likely to be unfaithful to each other than married couples: . . . men in cohabiting relationships were 4 times more likely to be unfaithful than husbands and . . . women in cohabiting relationships were 8 times more likely to cheat than wives."[98]

The ones who really suffer in cohabitation, however, are the children. Children born to cohabiting couples are twice as likely to experience some form of parental union transition (either the creation or dissolution of a pairing) than those born to married couples.[99] "Older children (6 to 11 years of age) exhibited the highest number of behavioral problems living in cohabiting-partner households (16.4 percent) [where one of the biological parents is cohabiting with someone else]; cohabiting-parent households [where both biological parents are cohabiting] were next highest at 14 percent with single parent households at 9.0 percent as compared with only 3.5 percent among those living with married parents. For teens, the situation is similar." Behavior is not the only problem; poverty is also a factor: "In the mid-1990s, the poverty rate for children in cohabiting households was 31 percent, whereas that for children living in married couple families was about 6 percent." More tragic still are the rates of abuse. "Women are 62 times more likely to be assaulted by their live-in boyfriends than they are if living with their husband."[100] A more recent survey showed that the rate of *recurrent* abuse is about three times as likely in cohabiting couples as in married couples.[101] "Rates for serious abuse of children are lowest in the intact family, six times higher in stepfamilies, 14 times higher in the always-single-mother family, 20 times higher in cohabiting biological parent families, and an astonishing 33 times higher when the mother is cohabiting with a boyfriend."[102]

Even moving in together is no longer necessarily required for cohabitation. "Cohabiting does not always take the 'standard' form of two people deciding to move into a new apartment together—rather, some simply spend every weekend living together when one is away at college but otherwise live separate lives; and others basically move into the house where the boyfriend or girlfriend is still living with a parent or parents, simply sleeping in the friend's bedroom, hanging out, and coming and going as they please."[103]

Yet still the practice of cohabitation has become more prevalent in general society. "Nearly three in five American women cohabit by the age of 24."[104] Cohabitation is much more likely than marriage to produce adverse results for individuals, families, and society in terms of poverty, abuse, and behavioral problems in children. If nearly half of cohabiting men think that it is highly likely that their cohabitation will end in marriage, then, from a sexual economics point of view, they are willing to pay more in terms of commitment for sexual access. Given that the price of sex is generally considered lower than it actually is, women could expect more in terms of commitment than they currently do.

How many Latter-day Saint emerging adults are involved in cohabitation? "Mormon youths are unlikely to have sex before age 18 in the first place, but if they do have sex, they're more likely to try it once and then refrain from further sexual activity." Less than 6% qualify as promiscuous,[105] so one would expect the number to be less than 6%. These statistics, however, refer to adolescents, who are less likely to cohabit than emerging adults. Among Latter-day Saint emerging adults 8% cohabit (with 12% having ever cohabited).[106] If one includes results across all age spectra, then 3% of Latter-day Saint adults cohabit,[107] and only 1% of active Latter-day Saints. On the other hand, 13% of former members of the Church cohabit.[108] Flipping the statistical question on its head, since members of the Church outnumber former members of the Church, it would appear that cohabiting tends to turn Latter-day Saints into former members of the Church. This would go along with other research showing that both cohabitation and frequent extramarital sex cause a decrease in church attendance and increase the likelihood of disaffiliation with a religion.[109]

Homosexuality

Homosexuality is a sensitive topic to many people and also a bit confusing. "Sexual orientation and gender identity resist explanation by simple theories."[110] It does not help that "there is often poignant and bitter struggle over words and terms around sex, and the politics of using them or avoiding them."[111] When someone claims to be homosexual, are they referring to their sexual behavior with members of the same sex, their sexual identity or self-conception, their sexual attraction to those of the same sex, or their physiological sexual arousal to members of the same sex?[112] The subject can be especially confusing to those experiencing it.[113] Because sexually transmitted diseases are at elevated levels among those who engage in homosexual behavior, the United States Centers for Disease Control have had an interest in being clear on the topic but have found no objective criteria to determine who was homosexual. Perhaps one could just accept an individual's own identification as homosexual, but some men who identify themselves as homosexuals paradoxically claim that they are attracted only to women.[114] Self-reported identifications "can sometimes be inaccurate or incomplete, especially when people want to conceal their sexual orientations or when they are confused or conflicted about their sexual feelings."[115] Because "sexual attraction and identity correlates closely but not completely with reports of sexual behavior,"[116] when an individual identifies as homosexual, others may incorrectly assume that behavior is indicated; homosexual feelings usually precede homosexual behavior by about three years. The plethora of slang terminology only further complicates the picture, even though the common scientific terms "are historically and culturally specific, and they do not necessarily translate to other times and places." All proposed methods for determining whether an individual is homosexual are problematic: either ineffective, onerous, or subject to manipulation.[117]

The prevalence of homosexuality has been politicized. Those in favor of it cite a higher incidence, while those opposed cite lower numbers.[118] The prevalence depends on the study. According to one study, nationally "only 2.3 percent of all men and 1.3 percent of all women . . . self-identify as homosexual."[119] Another study also claimed that those who classify themselves as gay, lesbian, or bisexual account for only 2.3% of the population in the United States.[120] "A recent survey of 34,557 U.S. adults yielded rates of 96.6% heterosexual, 1.6% gay or lesbian, and 0.7% bisexual."[121] Another survey found that about 4% of the U.S. population was homosexual but that Americans thought the number was one in four (25%), showing a huge gap between perception and reality.[122] There is little reason to assume that the percentages among Latter-day Saints significantly exceed the national figures.[123] The prevalence or popularity of homosexuality misses an important point. "If homosexuality is wrong, then it is wrong even if it is common; if it is not wrong, then nonheterosexual people deserve their rights regardless of how rare they are."[124] The Church has taken the position that the practice of homosexuality is wrong and a sin—those who engage in homosexual behavior cannot remain members of the Church in good standing, but nonheterosexual people nevertheless still deserve basic rights.[125]

Causes

Researchers have found that "there are perceptible linear associations between all same-sex measures (except bisexual identity) and the two religiosity measures (church attendance and importance of religion)." Thus "there is simply very little evidence of same-sex anything among the most religious boys," while "the categories 'no religion' and 'other religion' tend to exhibit the highest percentages in most of the same-sex outcomes."[126] Perhaps the data should be taken as an indication

> A persistent problem with scientific studies of homosexuality is the pervasive assumption that there must be a single cause.

of self-selection: "Youth who experience same-sex attraction or wish to identify themselves as something besides heterosexual likely self-select away from extensive religious participation."[127] The data, however, can also be read as indicating that the more religious the upbringing, the more likely it is for a youth to be heterosexual. Such an explanation, however, is usually discounted.[128] As Professor Camille Paglia, herself a lesbian, observes,

> After the American Psychiatric Association, responding to activist pressure, removed homosexuality from its list of mental disorders in 1973, psychological inquiries into homosexuality slowly became *verboten*. To even ask about the origins of homosexuality was automatically dubbed homophobic by gay studies proponents in the '80s and '90s. Weirdly, despite the rigid social constructionist bias that permeated the entire left, gay activists in and out of academe now leapt on the slightest evidence that could suggest a biological cause of homosexuality. . . . Yet the intricate family dynamic of every single gay person I've ever known seems to have played some kind of role in his or her developing sexual orientation.
>
> The widespread desire to find a biological basis for homosexuality seems to me very misconceived. It will inevitably lead to claims that gays are developmentally defective at the prenatal level. I myself believe . . . that exclusive homosexuality is an adaptation to spe-

cific social conditions. When a gay adult claims to have been gay since early childhood, what he or she is actually remembering is the sense of being different for some reason, which in boys often registers as shyness or super-sensitivity, leading to a failure to bond with bumptious peers. This disjunction, with all its painfully stifled longings, becomes overt homosexuality much later on. But retrospective psychohistory is out these days, and the only game in town is pin the tail on the oppressor.[129]

It is not clear how helpful it is to stereotype how any individual may have come under the homosexual classification. No single cause for homosexuality has been discovered,[130] and a persistent problem with scientific studies of homosexuality is the pervasive assumption that there must be a single cause. This has resulted in serious scientific proposals that appear rather bizarre at first glance, such as the now discredited proposal that whether one was homosexual or not was dependent on the ratios between the lengths of various fingers.[131]

A number of potentially different routes may lead to a homosexual classification. For example, females with congenital adrenal hyperplasia have been exposed to increased testosterone in the womb and report elevated rates of homosexual orientation as adults; nevertheless, most females affected are still exclusively heterosexual, "thus, the high levels of prenatal androgens do not ensure homosexuality in these women."[132] Researchers have hypothesized that 15–28% of homosexual males may be a result of the number of older brothers that they have, "each additional older brother causing an increase in the chances of a man's being homosexual . . . by an estimated 33% to 34%."[133] Another study, however, found no correlation in the same data.[134]

A number of years ago one scientist argued that part of the brains of homosexual males—the third interstitial nucleus of the anterior hypothalamus (INAH-3)—was half the size of heterosexual males. Presumably both sides of the debate could be happy: homosexual advocates could argue that there was nothing that homosexuals could do about their sexual orientation, while opponents could argue that there is something wrong with homosexuals' brains. Unfortunately, another study failed to reproduce the results. Furthermore, both studies suffered from small sample sizes. They are unlikely to be replicated: "The

INAH-3 is so small—about the size of a grain of sand—that it cannot be accurately measured without dissecting brain tissue." The two studies found too many exceptions for the size of the INAH-3 for it to be the sole determining factor in determining homosexuality.[135] The studies specifically did not show that homosexuality was genetic (that is, that homosexuals were born that way), nor did it locate a "gay center in the brain."[136]

Genetics may play a role, but not as much a role as is generally thought. After a thorough review of the literature, one group of researchers reported,

> Our best estimate of the magnitude of genetic effects is moderate—certainly not overwhelming. In contrast, the evidence for environmental influence is unequivocal. . . . Based on the evidence from twin studies, we believe that we can already provide a qualified answer to the question "Is sexual orientation genetic?" That answer is: "Probably somewhat genetic, but not mostly so." . . . There can be little doubt that sexual orientation is environmentally influenced.[137]

Exactly which environments influence sexual orientation is a question the researchers left open. Another set of researchers concurred with this assessment: "While the genetic component of homosexual behavior is far from negligible, non-shared environmental factors play a critical, perhaps preponderant, role."[138] A massive genetic study of the sexual orientation of nearly 24,000 individuals "yielded no significant effects."[139] No genetic predictors were discovered. Even if genetics may predispose individuals to a certain sexual orientation, "there is no reliable scientific evidence that sexual orientation is determined by a person's genes."[140] Another study may have put the genetic theory permanently to rest. A genome-wide association study of nearly half a million (477,522) individuals concluded that "there is certainly no single genetic determinant (sometimes referred to as the "gay gene" in the media)."[141] Even combinations of various groups of single-nucleotide polymorphisms (SNP) in the genome could account for no more than 25% of those engaged in same-sex behaviors.[142] The notion that homosexuals were born that way does not appear to be scientifically supported.

One study posited at least one environmental factor. It showed "a sizable difference in rates of male homosexual behavior among individuals who spent their adolescence in rural as compared to large metropolitan cities in America, suggesting the influence of social and cultural environments." Whereas only 1.2% of those who had spent their adolescent years in rural environments had had a homosexual partner in the year of the survey, 4.4% of those who had lived in metropolitan areas had—over three times the rate.[143]

Some have proposed that pathological parent-child relationships, such as emotionally distant fathers or overbearing mothers, cause homosexuality. The "correlations between retrospective ratings of parent-child relationship characteristics and the child's eventual sexual orientation in adulthood" are at best small and mostly nonsignificant.[144] If such factors play a role, the role is mostly undetectable. This is not to say that family dynamics might not play a role: "41% of non-heterosexual males and 42% of non-heterosexual females reported childhood family dysfunction, compared to 24% and 30% of heterosexual males and females, respectively."[145] Family dysfunction is related to parent-child relationships, but they are not the same thing.

In a few notable cases individuals have claimed to have chosen to be homosexual; as one famously put it, "For me it's a choice, and you don't get to define my gayness for me."[146] The individual continued, "Why can't it be a choice? Why is that any less legitimate?"[147] Given the taboos of the prevailing narrative, it is unlikely that any research study would dare tackle the question of how common such a situation is. Since there are individuals who are willing to claim that their homosexuality is a deliberate choice, it seems best to take them at their word and allow for that possibility in at least some cases.

The possibility that homosexuality might be freely chosen also raises the possibility that some homosexuals might be recruited. Reports of such exist in the scholarly literature.[148] Unfortunately, many of the studies that supposedly demonstrate recruitment often examine phenomena that can have other explanations as well. It is thus not clear what percentage, if any, of the people who exhibit the phenomena studied exhibit them because of recruiting and what percentage exhibit them because of another explanation.[149] One researcher reported that "pornography is indirectly shaping (and increasing) the sexualization of situations, what people are willing to try, and what they come to desire sexually" and thus "is blurring the lines between sexual orientations, contributing to the growth of what is sexually attractive." It may not be coincidence that those who use pornography more frequently are more likely to support homosexuality.[150] Support, however, does not necessarily translate into participation. Another study showed that confusion over gender could be transmitted through social contagion via peer groups that resulted in sudden confusion of identity and radical rewriting of childhood memories that supported the new identity.[151] Such a line of investigation invites further research. One study found that a fifth of men who have sex with men were initiated into this practice when they were young by an older man.[152]

To sum up, so far studies have shown neither one specific cause of homosexuality nor a specific factor that precipitates homosexuality in most cases when it is present. It seems likely that there are a number of different ways that an individual can come to consider themselves homosexual.

Are there early predictors of homosexuality? "Retrospective studies suggest that some degree of childhood gender nonconformity is a common precursor of adult homosexuality in both sexes." For boys, gender nonconformity means "cross-dressing, desiring to have long hair, playing with dolls, disliking competitive sports and rough play, preferring girls as playmates, exhibiting elevated separation anxiety, and desiring to be—or believing that one is—a girl. In girls, gender nonconformity comprises dressing like and playing with boys, showing interest in competitive sports and rough play, lacking interest in conventionally female toys such as dolls and makeup, and desiring to be a boy." These traits usually emerge by preschool age, perhaps as young as two. "It is important to add that children are usually considered to be gender-nonconforming only if they persistently engage in a variety of these behaviors, as opposed to engaging in a single behavior once or twice."[153] The studies are fraught with problems; it takes about the same amount of space to list the problems as it does to describe the studies and list the findings. Gender nonconformity does not necessarily predict that an individual will grow up to become homosexual any more than gender conformity will predict that an individual will become heterosexual.

Abuse

Homosexuality is related to childhood sexual abuse. A study of 33,902 individuals found that "nonheterosexual adults of both sexes were much more likely than heterosexual adults to have experienced childhood sexual abuse, defined as 'sexual experiences with an adult or any other person younger than 18 years when the individual did not want the sexual experience or was too young to know what was happening.' . . . The risk was much higher for nonheterosexual respondents: 38.1% for lesbians, 43.5% for bisexual women, and 14.2% for heterosexual women; 18.6% for gay men, 19% for bisexual men, and 4.6% for heterosexual men,"[154] though some studies found significantly higher numbers.[155] Because a number of different causes and effects are combined in this study, specific causation is not demonstrable and so the results need to be interpreted cautiously. Nonheterosexuals are about twice as likely as heterosexuals to have suffered emotional, physical, or sexual abuse as children.[156] While "the vast majority of individuals who suffer childhood trauma do not become gay or bisexual," it is still a viable hypothesis "that adverse childhood experiences may be a significant—but not a determinative—factor in developing homosexual preferences."[157] Victims of sexual abuse deserve compassion and assistance. They also deserve special care because they are more likely to become sexual abusers of children.[158]

> The rates that homosexuals have been victims of sexual assault are horrific.

The rates that homosexuals have been victims of sexual assault are horrific. Because different studies vary widely in the rates reported, I will give only the median numbers of the various studies.[159] Among homosexual men, more than one in five (22.7%) have been the victim of sexual abuse as a child, one in seven (14.7%) as an adult, almost one in three (30.4%) sometime during their lifetime, and almost one in eight (12.1%) from a sexual partner. Among homosexual women, more than one in three (34.5%) were the victim of sexual abuse as a child, almost one in four (23.2%) as an adult, more than three out of seven (43.4%) at some point in their life, and more than one in eight (13.3%) from a sexual partner. Homosexuals thus suffer nearly twice the rate of posttraumatic stress disorder as heterosexuals[160] and have from 2.7 to 2.8 times the likelihood of suffering from depression as heterosexuals do.[161]

The sad fact is that nonheterosexual individuals are much more likely to suffer from a number of adverse effects. British researchers found that

> lesbian, gay, and bisexual individuals had a 2.47 times higher lifetime risk than heterosexuals for suicide attempts, that they were about twice as likely to experience depression over a twelve-month period, and approximately 1.5 times as likely to experience anxiety disorders. Both non-heterosexual men and women were found to be at an elevated risk for substance abuse problems (1.51 times as likely), with the risk for non-heterosexual women especially high—3.42 times higher than for heterosexual women. Non-heterosexual men, on the other hand, were at a particularly high risk for suicide attempts: while non-heterosexual men and women together were at a 2.47 times greater risk of suicide attempts over their lifetimes, non-heterosexual men were found to be at a 4.28 times greater risk.[162]

Studies in other countries have replicated these findings, "confirming a consistent and alarming pattern." Among women, the prevalence of lifetime mood disorders was "was 44.4% in lesbians, 58.7% in bisexuals, and 36.5% in women unsure of their sexual identity, as compared to 30.5% in heterosexuals." Homosexual men had more than twice the prevalence of lifetime mood disorders (42.3%) as heterosexual men (19.8%). Homosexuals, especially women, "appear to be likelier than heterosexuals to smoke, use or abuse alcohol, and abuse other drugs."[163] One study concluded that homosexual men have a pooled lifetime prevalence of suffering violence from an intimate partner of 48%, with a prevalence within the last five years of 32%. Other studies came to similar conclusions.[164] Homosexual men have, on average, many more partners; over 30% have more than fifty sexual partners over their lifetime and the median homosexual male reports between sixteen and twenty.[165] The rates of being battered are higher even than among women who are cohabiting.[166] Regrettably, "sexual orientation is one of the strongest predictors of suicide."[167]

Astute readers will have noticed that both heterosexual females and homosexual males suffer from the same set of problems as a result of their sexual activity with men outside of heterosexual marriage. Both have an increased likelihood of suffering from depression and physical abuse. The difference is a matter of degree, not of kind. Homosexuals suffer from these outcomes at higher rates. Additionally, they are more likely to commit suicide.

Stereotypes

In 2011 the Center for Disease Control published a study that provided statistics shedding light on some common stereotypes about homosexuals. About 82% of women who have engaged in some form of homosexual activity have also engaged in sexual activity with at least three different men; and about 61% of men who have engaged in some form of homosexual activity have also engaged in sexual activity with at least three different women.[168] All told, 96% of women who have had sex with women have also had sex with men, and 84% of men who have had sex with men have also had sex with women. These statistics apply to those who have engaged in homosexual behavior at some point. What about those who identify themselves as homosexual? More than two-thirds (70%) of men who identify themselves as homosexual have nevertheless had some type of sex with women. Most women (92%) who identify as homosexual have had some form of sex with men.[169] Women are more likely to identify as heterosexual the more education they have, while men have a greater chance of identifying as homosexual (up to 3%) the more education they have.[170] A different study found the opposite among women: "women who attended college were nine times more likely to identify as lesbians than women who did not."[171] More than two-thirds (69%) of men who identify as being homosexual have been to college.[172]

A different survey found that "a notable share of lesbian women (70 percent) and gay men (30 percent) who report attraction exclusively to members of their own sex also report having had at least one opposite sex sexual partner in their lifetimes."[173] Because the Center for Disease Control's study revealed statistics that contradicted certain stereotypes and narratives, the information on the heterosexual sexual behavior of homosexuals was omitted from the 2016 version of the report.[174] A study from Argentina reported that of men who had sex with men "over two thirds reported also having sex with women in the past year."[175] One factor that might be at play here is that bisexuality, an attraction to both sexes, is both understudied[176] and underreported because of "negative stereotypes about bisexuality, perpetuated within the gay community as well as in the culture at large."[177] While the standard narrative that homosexual men are completely unattracted to women might apply in some and even many cases, the Center for Disease Control's statistics show that the majority who identify as homosexual have sufficient appetite, opportunity to gratify it, and normal physiological functioning for heterosexual sexual activity. As unexpected as it may be, given the data, it is difficult to escape the conclusion that either (1) bisexuality is far more prevalent than homosexuality, or (2) for at least 70% of those who self-identify as homosexual, homosexuality is a choice, or (3) both.

Here we should be clear about which aspects of homosexuality are associated with choice and which are not,[178] and comparing them with heterosexuality can be instructive. Researchers have pointed out that homosexuality, or nonheterosexuality, is an umbrella term that covers four interrelated aspects,[179] though these aspects are not as closely interrelated as commonly assumed.[180] The first is one's degree of sexual attraction to a particular sex. One may not have much control or choice about whether one finds members of a particular sex sexually attractive.[181] The second (perhaps a variant of the first) is "one's relative physiological sexual arousal to men versus women." Again, though this aspect is more prominent in men than women, one may not have much control or choice about one's physiological reactions. "Sexual arousal comprises both subjective and genital response to a sexual stimulus."[182] One may expect to have more control

> Researchers have pointed out that homosexuality, or nonheterosexuality, is an umbrella term that covers four interrelated aspects.

and choice over the subjective response. The third aspect is one's sexual identity—that is, "one's self-conception (sometimes disclosed to others and sometimes not) as a homosexual, bisexual, or heterosexual person."[183] One has more control and choice in this matter. Fourth, one's personal sexual behavior—the sexual behavior that an individual initiates or voluntarily participates in, as opposed to something like rape where sexual situations are forced upon a victim—is a matter in which the individual has a choice and can be held accountable for that choice. We can illustrate the choices with a heterosexual male: A man may not have any choice about whether he is sexually attracted to women, or whether he is physiologically aroused when exposed to pornography. He has some choice in how he identifies himself. But whether he is a loving and faithful husband, an adulterer, an ascetic monk, or something else is entirely his choice.[184] The sin comes with the behavior.[185]

Reorientation

Can sexual orientation change? The whole notion of sexual orientation is to some extent a vague and poorly defined cultural construct useless for scientific research.[186] "While labels such as 'heterosexual' and 'homosexual' are often taken to designate stable psychological or even biological traits, perhaps they do not. It may be that individuals' affective, sexual, and behavioral experiences do not conform well to such categorical labels because these labels do not, in fact, refer to natural (psychological or biological) kinds."[187] The evidence on changing sexual orientation is mixed. Some literature claims that for males "there is no evidence to suggest that individuals can consciously alter their genital arousal to fit a certain sexual identity label."[188] Other literature disputes this: "There is now considerable scientific evidence that sexual desires, attractions, behaviors, and even identities can, and sometimes do, change over time."[189] The National Longitudinal Study of Adolescent to Adult Health reported that "80% of the adolescent males who had reported same-sex attractions at Wave I later identified themselves as exclusively heterosexual as young adults at Wave IV," a dozen years later. "The data for the females surveyed were similar but less striking: for adolescent females who had both-sex attractions at Wave I, more than half reported exclusive attraction to males at Wave III."[190] The results so upset one pair of researchers that they accused the study participants of giving false answers.[191] If so, in which wave of the study were they lying? The idea that significant numbers of individuals independently falsified their answers on a large-scale random study seems at least improbable.

Another longitudinal study of 10,515 youth had similar results, "suggesting fluidity and plasticity of same-sex attractions among many adolescents."[192] A different longitudinal study of 80 nonheterosexual women showed that over an eight-year period, two-thirds "changed their sexual identities" though not necessarily to heterosexual.[193] The sexual orientation of men is also reported to be somewhat fluid.[194] Other studies of the general population have shown that sexual orientation can change with age with the general tendency being to become less homosexual with age.[195] Whatever their effectiveness in individual cases, various proposed therapies purporting to change sexual orientation have not been shown to be widely effective in studies and are opposed by most professional organizations.[196] The studies that these professional organizations rely on state only that "there is little in the way of credible evidence that could clarify whether SOCE [sexual orientation change efforts] does or does not work in changing same-sex sexual attractions," and "the data presented in this study do not provide information on the incidence and prevalence of failure, success, harm, help, or ethical violations in conversion therapy."[197] While it may be possible to change one's sexual orientation, no one really knows why and how this happens. Change in sexual orientation is not necessarily reproducible and certainly not coercible.

AN ENEMY TO GOD

In the Book of Mormon, King Benjamin points out that "the natural man is an enemy to God" (Mosiah 3:19). It is thus not altogether surprising that the sexual scripts outlined in the previous sections have a deleterious effect on the faith of those who follow them. "Sexual behavior is a powerful force that ensures survival but is tightly regulated in all human societies. The biological mechanisms underlying sexual behavior are constrained and changed by these cultural forces. . . .

Gary L. Kapp, *King Benjamin Preaches to the Nephites*. In the Book of Mormon, King Benjamin taught that "the natural man is an enemy to God" (Mosiah 3:19). Courtesy of churchofjesuschrist.org.

In humans this versatility [of sexual behavior] interacts with higher human brain functions such as morality. Cultural variations in sexual mores invariably create tension across cultures."[198] Creating tension is simply a euphemism for the enmity described more plainly in the Book of Mormon.

Among emerging adults, sex is generally in tension with religion. Two researchers observed,

> Most of them want to party, to hook up, to have sex in relationships, and to cohabit; or if they do not do these things now, many at least want to keep them as options for the future. . . . Many want to have sex with a boyfriend or girlfriend, or to at least be free to do so if the occasion arises, and many want to be able to hook up with someone they meet to whom they may feel attracted. Many also want to cohabit with current or future serious partners or fiancés before getting married. And all of this, emerging adults are aware, contradicts the teachings of most religions. So they simply avoid religion and thereby resolve the conflict.[199]

More than half of high school students who had sexual intercourse said that their religion had no effect at all on their decision to have sex.[200] Wanting to have the option of engaging in sex might be misinterpreted as indiscriminate hedonism, but that is not the case with most young adults. College "students may indeed want to have sex and hook up, but they do not want to do so with anonymous strangers." They "sense that meeting someone with whom you have *no prior real-life connection* is reckless."[201]

> Framed as a social-psychological causal mechanism: most emerging adults reduce a certain cognitive dissonance they feel—arising from the conflict of religious teachings against partying and sex before marriage versus their wanting to engage in those behaviors—by mentally discounting the religious teachings and socially distancing themselves from the source of those teachings. In this simple way, the role of sex, drinking, and sometimes drugs is often important in forming emerging adults' frequent lack of interest in religious faith and practice.[202]

The conflict between an individual's aspirations and behavior emerges with the first sexual experience.

> Sexual status and behavior do matter for rapid and significant religious decline. Youth who reported already having had sex (i.e., being a non-virgin) are more likely to report a large decrease in both attendance and personal religious salience. The act of first sex (i.e., virginity loss between study waves) does not appear to alter attendance habits but did correspond significantly with a large decrease in the importance that adolescents accord to religion. Thus one's sexual status and behavior appear unrelated to whether or not adolescents increase their religiosity, but they correspond to their likelihood of considerable religious decline (especially that of personal religious salience). Sex is, however, the only behavioral association noted in this study. Alcohol and drug use display no such patterns of association.[203]

While a decline in church attendance is not associated with a decline in the importance of religion, frequency of extramarital sex is.[204] Initiating sexual activity outside of marriage generally does not reduce

While a decline in church attendance is not associated with a decline in the importance of religion, frequency of extramarital sex is. Courtesy of Matthias Böckel/Pixabay.

church attendance but does reduce the importance of religion in an individual's life; frequent sexual activity outside of marriage, however, does reduce church attendance.

How this alienation works is illustrated in part by a story told by one researcher: She reported an interview with a religious young woman who chose to have sex with her boyfriend during a summer: "Her decision to have sex almost destroyed her faith. [She] finds it difficult to live with the fact that she is no longer pure—that she has given away her physical virginity to someone who is not her husband." She reported,

> "I definitely felt like I was running from God, trying to hide what I was doing," she says, recalling the summer she first had sex. "It took me a long time to get back to a relationship with God."
>
> "How long?" I ask.
>
> "A year and a half," she answers. . . . "God does forgive you, and it is forgotten. I don't think you ever forget about it, but you are given a second chance." . . . During this period, she experienced lots of doubt, terrible regret, and deep alienation from God. At times, she believed that God would never forgive her for having sex and that she would never forgive herself. This period *began* with a vow not to have sex again outside of marriage, but it also entailed many hours in personal prayer and working closely with a mentor.[205]

The causal association, however, works both ways. "There is strong evidence that the relationship between religiosity and sexual debut is causal."[206] The more religious one is, the more likely one is to postpone sexual debut. Studies find that, like those who view pornography, those who leave religion "were more liberal in their attitudes regarding sex."[207]

Only about 16% of emerging adults between 18 and 23 years old are virgins. Virginity is more likely among those in college or college graduates, those who are more religious, those who do not get drunk, and those who do not consider themselves popular.[208] Men who regularly go to church and women who are politically conservative are more likely to remain virgins. They tend to be very religious, adverse to risk, oriented toward marriage, and generally less tolerant of deviant behavior. Being very religious is the most common reason (44%) that individuals who maintained their virginity into their twenties cited as the reason they were still virgins. This is not particularly surprising. "All ideas—no matter how new or old or popular or unpopular—require social support and control in order to stay relevant and persuasive. Churchgoing and religiosity often provide social support and social control for those who remain virgins into young adulthood."[209]

> Initiation of sexual activity commences a pattern of ongoing behavior that is at odds with most religious teachings.

As we have seen, initiation of sexual activity commences a pattern of ongoing behavior that is at odds with most religious teachings. Emerging adults who live a more or less hedonistic life do not want to think about religion. As one individual put it, "If I think about that stuff too much I'm gonna be miserable."[210] Thus "some students do not even try to reconcile their sexual lives with their faith lives because they do not believe it is possible to do so within traditional organized religion." For them, "faith is faith and sex is sex and never the twain shall meet; the idea of allowing religious beliefs to affect one's sex life is silly if not laughable."[211] "For many youth, therefore, initiating sexual activity is a significant turning point in pulling away from religion, in part because of the mental and emotional dissonance that willfully having sex on an ongoing basis causes in the religious contexts of their lives, even when nobody religious knows they are having sex."[212] Some researchers argue that "sexual experience, even when not currently being undergone but simply remembered, decreases religious/spiritual aspirations." The effect is not just among the religious or among Americans; European researchers found "the negative association in people's minds between sexuality and religion may be shared among believers and nonbelievers." To them this suggests that "the 'conflict' between sexuality and social order, in particular religious and moral order, . . . is probably, to some extent, an intrinsic conflict and not only historical, traditional, and confined to conservative contexts" because "this 'conflict' seems to be present even today in Western secularized societies and among young people of modest average religiosity."[213]

A surprising finding is that dwelling on sexual experiences by unmarried individuals tends to lessen both honesty and generosity. "Sexual thoughts . . . not only diminish active interest in the existential and spiritual/religious domain, which in a way could be more easily understood given some traditional conflict between religion/spirituality and sexuality, they also lessen concerns for others and for the common goal, i.e., care-based, prosocial, and integrity-based, honest, moral behaviors. These findings are particularly interesting given that in contemporary Western societies, sexuality, even if dissociated from marriage and parenting, is explicitly considered as not incompatible with (interpersonal) morality." Thus "the effects of sexuality on morality were independent from participants' religiosity."[214] Another study found that "religious guilt" did not explain the increased incidents of depression among those who were cheating on their partners.[215]

Various religions have made efforts to decrease the sexual activity before marriage among their adherents, though not necessarily with the desired outcomes. While "it is popularly held that evangelical Protestants are the most conservative American religious tradition with respect to sexual attitudes," it comes as a surprise[216] that "evangelical Protestant youth are not the religious group least likely to have sex."[217] Evangelical programs to encourage chastity in youth, like True Love Waits, the Silver Ring Thing, and Purity Balls, which solicit public commitments from youth not to have sex before marriage, are not working particularly well, since 88% of those who participated in such programs

Various religions have made efforts to decrease the sexual activity before marriage among their adherents, though not necessarily with the desired outcomes. Courtesy of Free-Photos/Pixabay.

engaged in sexual intercourse before marriage[218] and "in up to 7 of 10 cases, it is not with their future spouse."[219] These are well-intentioned programs that seem, on the face of it, ideal for generating the commitment necessary to resist temptation; it is something like making a covenant. "Given conservative Protestants' vocal promotion of restrictive sexual scripts, their failure to stand out from mainliners, Catholics, and those from other religions may surprise some. But other evidence from studies of adolescents suggests conservative Protestants do not differ from others in their premarital sexual activity, only in their attitudes toward premarital sex. Conservative Protestants are typically sent out from their religious communities armed only with the message of 'don't have sex until marriage,' which may not be particularly compelling when the opportunity for pre-marital sex presents itself."[220]

Part of the explanation for why such programs did not work is that adolescents who do not live "in a biologically intact, two-parent family" lack a "family advantage" and are almost twice as likely to engage in sexual activity,[221] and evangelicals are actually more likely than average to divorce.[222] Among evangelicals, "we see both high marriage rates and high divorce rates, together with elevated teenage pregnancy rates, etc."[223] This also helps to understand the high rate of promiscuity among Black Protestants, whose rate of illegitimacy is around 77%.[224] In general, "people who came from families where their parents were married, and stayed married until the present day (or who stayed married until the death of one of the parents) were far less likely to have ever reported being in overlapping sexual relationships (26 percent of those raised by parents who stayed married so report compared to 39 percent whose parents did not.)"[225] These statistics are not brought in to criticize others' misfortunes but to help understand the unusual position in which Latter-day Saints find themselves and to understand that some of the things that we think ought to work actually do not.

> The religion-and-premarital-sex story is largely about religiosity— or the strength of religious commitment—itself. Young adults who attended religious services weekly during adolescence—irrespective of their particular religious tradition—are far more likely to refrain from sexual intercourse until marriage, as are those who considered religion a very important part of their daily life. Even so, the findings here still indicate that the vast majority of young adults who were religious during their teenage years engage in sex before they are married. In fact, more than half engage in premarital sex with someone other than their future spouse. Certainly religion restricts premarital sex among the unmarried young adults, but not nearly to the extent that might please religious organizations (and parents). Even the most religious individuals will not be entirely isolated from secular messages about sex, and when religious sexual scripts are forced to compete against less restrictive ones (in addition to biological impulses), they seem to lose out most of the time.[226]

OUTLIERS

It is precisely in the area of sexual morality where Latter-day Saint youth and young adults stand out in contrast to the rest of the world. Our statistics when it comes to sexual morality among youth and young adults do not look like any other group. We are a peculiar people. A comparison of our statistics with those of other groups is in order to show how unusual Latter-day Saints are.

Latter-day Saint youth appear as statistical outliers. As teenagers, they are the most likely to be virgins (87.4%), compared to 71.9–85% for other denominations.[227] Most Latter-day Saint youth say they are "not in a hurry to have sex" (72.5%); somewhat fewer evangelicals follow suit (66.2%). Latter-day Saint youth are the second least likely to have sex even though they would like to (14.9%, after evangelical Protestants at 14.3%).[228]

Latter-day Saint youth who have had sex seem to be a mixture of those who follow the pattern of the world and those whose comparative behavior is unusual. Latter-day Saints have the highest mean age of sexual debut (19.2 years); Jews place second (17.5 years).[229] Where in most youth loss of virginity commences a pattern of multiple sexual partners, Latter-day Saint teenagers are the most likely to have had sex only once and not again (7.0%); the least likely to have continuing sex with one partner outside of marriage (0%); and the least likely to have multiple sex partners (5.6%). To see how strange this is, look at the numbers in each category as a percentage of nonvirgins belonging to a particular religion who engage in each behavior. Among Latter-day Saint youth who have had sex, 55.6% do so only once. The next closest to this are Catholics at 17.3%.[230] Latter-day Saint youth who have had sex that continue to have sex with one partner outside of marriage is 0% (which means only that it did not show up in the sample, not that it never occurs).[231] The next lowest occurrence is the catch-all category of other religions at 16.2%. While 44.4% of Latter-day Saint youth who have had sex have had multiple partners, no other religion was below 50%.[232] Latter-day Saint youth are the least likely to use pornography (6.2% use it monthly).[233] They are the least likely to engage in oral sex (9.0%), though Black Protestants are also outliers (11.9%).[234] Latter-day Saint youth who have sex are the most likely to use birth control the first time they have sex (91.8%), considerably more likely than the next closest religious group, which, ironically, is Catholics (67.7%). Perhaps "some parents are pushing sexual safety rather than abstinence, and their adolescent children are listening and obeying. Parental expectations are what shape their sexual values and scripts." Latter-day Saint youth are the least likely to think that others would believe them pro-

> As Latter-day Saints understand it, the law of chastity encompasses more than just refraining from sexual intercourse.

miscuous if they use birth control (8.6%), though Jews (9.2%) are also outliers.[235]

As Latter-day Saints understand it, the law of chastity encompasses more than just refraining from sexual intercourse. The Church's guidelines, as stated in *For the Strength of Youth*, put it this way: "Before marriage, do not participate in passionate kissing, lie on top of another person, or touch the private sacred parts of another person's body, with or without clothing."[236] While Latter-day Saint youth and young adults tend not to have sex, 61% of Latter-day Saint young adults have been involved in heavy petting (touching the private parts of another's body underneath or without clothes) before marriage, compared with 87% nationally.[237] Even as teenagers before graduating from high school, 41% of Latter-day Saint youth had been involved in heavy petting, as compared with the national statistic of 69%.[238] There is a gender difference in this statistic. In the teenage years Latter-day Saint young women are more likely than young men to have been involved in heavy petting (44% to 37%), but in the college years the men catch up and pass the women (63% to 59%).[239] As bad as this is, even in this case we are outliers. On a sobering note, of those Latter-day Saints involved, 38% seriously regret being sexually involved but an equal number have no regrets about their activities.[240]

Love and marriage

Among those who marry at an early age (before 25), 43% of Latter-day Saint young adults wait until marriage to have sex; this is almost three times as many as the next closest religious group. Almost 19% of Latter-day Saints had premarital sex but only with their future spouse, and 38% had premarital sex with someone else. (The next lowest religious group reported their rate of premarital sex with someone other than their future spouse at 61%). "Mormons, who report abstinence rates of about 43%, are more likely than anyone else to avoid sex before marriage, and less likely than members of any other group to report having had premarital sex with someone other than their future spouse."[241] This represents not all Latter-day Saint young adults but only those who marry at an early age. "As might be anticipated from earlier findings, . . . only Mormon young adults are more likely than mainline Protestants to have abstained from sex until marriage. The difference is quite substantial, however: Mormons are more than eight times as likely as mainline Protestants to abstain rather than have premarital sex with someone other than their spouse. No other religious group stands out from mainline Protestants, but those with no religious affiliation are significantly less likely than mainliners to abstain from premarital sex."[242]

Other surveys give similar results. Among all Latter-day Saints, only 21% of married Latter-day Saints had sex with their spouse before marriage, but that drops to 14% among those who were attending church at least three times per month. The next lowest religious group was Hindus at 29% and Muslims at 43%. "Those reporting their religion as 'Nothing' or 'Spiritual but not religious' report the highest levels of premarital sex [97%], while Mormons (LDS) report the lowest levels."[243]

By the time Latter-day Saint teenagers have become adults and enter college years, the picture changes a bit. By that time 39% have had sex, and half of those with more than one partner, but 22% of them are married.[244] This means that at least one in six has had sex outside of marriage. The majority (92%) of unmarried Latter-day Saint young adults are dating or in a romantic relationship, which on average lasted about a year (though the range varied from one week to five years).[245] Almost two-thirds (61%) of those think that their relationship is likely to end in marriage,[246] which, if not accurate, is at least optimistic.

Producing a peculiar people

The statistics where Latter-day Saints are outliers are generally seen as positive outcomes. What could account for them? "After controlling for frequency of religious service attendance and self-reported religious salience during adolescence, Mormons are still nearly five times as likely as mainliners to abstain." That is a significant difference, one so large that some researchers have called it the "Mormon effect." They note that the "Mormon effect" remains substantial even after con-

Latter-day Saint youth are the most likely to support waiting until marriage for sex. Photo courtesy of TréVoy Kelly/Pixabay.

trolling for all other variables. What accounts for the "Mormon effect"? In one study, when compared to Catholics, "Mormons are on the other end of the spectrum. These individuals are far more abstinent than every other group. Social control and differential exposure to sex seem to drive part—though not all—of this association. Mormon youth are enrolled in daily 'seminary' classes where sexual ethics are often taught, and participation in Mormon temple rituals is often contingent on sexual chastity. Furthermore, Mormon men may be removed from sexualized situations while they serve on a missionary journey (usually between the ages of 19 and 21), and their religion's emphasis on abstinence from alcohol may also limit their exposure to situations that are conducive to premarital sex."[247] This analysis may not be complete from the point of view of a Latter-day Saint—for example, it is not clear that missionaries are necessarily removed from sexualized situations— but the explanation does cover part of the differences.

Latter-day Saints are also outliers in some of their attitudes. Latter-day Saint youth are the most likely to support waiting until marriage for sex (77.3%) but are closely followed in that attitude by evangelical Protestants (73.7%), who have a much worse success rate. Latter-day Saints are the least likely to think that having sex would make them respected (2.2%) or attractive (6.1%); and the most likely to think they would feel guilty (77.1%), upset their mothers (96.4%), and make their parents "extremely mad" if they had sex (79.7%).[248] Only the last three items are statistically different enough from other religious groups to truly make Latter-day Saints outliers. Yet these effects are dependent on the family, not the Church; their parents will be upset, not their bishops. Latter-day Saints are the least likely by some margin to agree that "it is OK for two people to get together for sex and not expect anything further": "Mormons (80% of all Mormons and 89% of those who attend church three times a month or more) oppose casual sex the most, while Jewish respondents (54%) are the most tolerant of all religious groups. Approval rates for casual sex are highest among those who claim no religious affiliation, with 71% of those who say their religious affiliation is "Nothing/Atheist/Agnostic" approving of no-strings-attached sex."[249]

Latter-day Saints are also outliers in their views about cohabitation. "Religious affiliation plays a significant role in how cohabitation is perceived. Both Mormons (76%) and Muslims (56%) are far more likely to disagree than agree" that cohabitation is acceptable.[250] Latter-day Saints, along with Baptists, are the least likely to cohabit.[251] A related area in which Latter-day Saints are outliers is marriage. Latter-day Saint young adults are by far the most likely to be married, with 22% married by their early twenties. No other religion has over 10% married.[252] Of Latter-day Saint young adults, 65% think it is important to marry someone of the same religion.[253]

Parental communication

Although parents talking to youth about sex is generally thought to improve outcomes, Latter-day Saint parents do not generally stand out from the crowd in this regard[254] except in two areas: They are the second most likely to find it very difficult to talk with their children about

Parents talking to children about sex is generally thought to improve outcomes, although the current data do not necessarily support this. Courtesy of Anastasia Gepp/Pixabay.

the subject (29.1%, just under the 29.5% of mainline Protestants), and they are the most likely not to talk about birth control at all with their children (21.4%).[255] (This is ironic considering the statistic cited above that Latter-day Saint youth who have sex are most likely to use birth control.) Not discussing birth control may be of slight significance since children whose parents talk "a great deal" about birth control are more likely to become sexually active. But "talking about birth control is not as powerful an influence on subsequent virginity loss as the number of recent dating partners or the age of the child."[256]

Less-religious parents are clearer on the distinction between talking about mechanics and talking about values. "When devoutly religious parents say they are talking regularly with their adolescents about sex and birth control, it means they are talking with them about morality rather than sharing information."[257] For them, "talk about sex is talk about values," not mechanics.[258] Some suggest as an antidote that parents should talk more with their children: "We owe our children a more comprehensive sex education—moral advocacy and information—than most of them are getting. . . . Mothers and fathers have the power—and, I would argue, the responsibility—to break any legacies of secrecy about sex, to resist sexual double standards, to both instruct their adolescents about the beauty, pleasures, and complexities of sex and human anatomy as well as pass on to them their own moral assertions about sexual boundaries."[259] Although researchers are strongly in favor

> There are clear links between sexual behavior and religiosity.

of parents talking to their children about such matters, findings are not particularly encouraging about the effect of talking with adolescents about sex: "More frequent parent-child communication about sex slightly elevates the probability that an adolescent child will subsequently lose his/her virginity before adulthood."[260] Data also indicate that the religious group whose parents talk the most with their children about the subject[261] also have the most sexually active and promiscuous adolescents.[262] Parents talking to their children about mechanics seems not to be the major influence in promoting chastity. Indeed, sexual naïveté can be "understandable and may even be strategic." One young man, for example, described how he "uses his ignorance of how to have sex—that is, the script he'd be expected to follow if he were in a sexual situation—to delay the experience."[263] The surveys did not delve into the content, context, or manner of teaching, which might account for why more talk seems to lead to more behavior. Perhaps the strongest arguments for parents talking to their children about sexual matters is that (1) a majority of children would rather hear about such matters from their parents,[264] and (2) the Church encourages parents to talk to their children about the subject.[265] Latter-day Saint parents seem already to be doing generally well at teaching the morality of avoiding intercourse, but they could probably do a better job than they are at teaching their children to avoid heavy petting.

Cross-cultural comparisons

While some of these factors may contribute to the difference between Latter-day Saints and other religious groups, there seem to be other factors at work. In contrast to many other religions, Latter-day Saints emphasize sexual purity, define it clearly, and have methods of institutional accountability concerning it. Those semiannual interviews with the bishopric and temple recommend interviews are important. Latter-day Saints "outpace evangelicals in terms of the organization of sexual social control."[266] Latter-day Saint teenagers generally follow Church guidelines when it comes to dating; the median (and mode) age of starting to date is 16, though 38% begin to date before that time, starting as early as twelve.[267] Religiously devoted emerging adults tend to be involved in sexual activity later, less frequently out of wedlock, and less promiscuously. They are less involved in pornography and cohabitation.[268] The causality works both ways: on the one hand, "we have every reason to believe that the higher religious commitment of the most religious emerging adults causally reduces the amount of alcohol they consume and the sex in which they engage."[269] On the other hand, those who are less religious tend to have more "self-oriented reasons to have sex."[270]

Four things stand out in the sociological research on sexual behavior among various religions: (1) There are clear links between sexual behavior and religiosity. (2) Latter-day Saint youth and young adults are significantly different from those of other religious backgrounds, especially those from no religious background. (3) Social science has not really accounted for the differences; the right questions have not been asked. (4) Latter-day Saints have room for improvement.

There is a close association between keeping the law of chastity and keeping one's religion. While violations of the law of chastity may not account for every case of loss of faith, the role of sexual morality is far too prominent to be discounted. The behavior of Latter-day Saints usually stands in marked contrast to that of the world, marking us as outliers, a peculiar people. It is a distinction we would do well to maintain.

NOTES

1. Donna Freitas, *Sex and the Soul: Juggling Sexuality, Spirituality, Romance, and Religion on America's College Campuses* (Oxford: Oxford University Press, 2008), 157–58.

2. Lauren Olsho, Jessica Cohen, Deborah K. Walker, Andrew Johnson, and Gretchen Locke, *National Survey of Adolescents and Their Parents: Attitudes and Opinions about Sex and Abstinence* (Cambridge, MA: Abt Associates, 2010), 66–69.

3. Mark D. Regnerus, *Forbidden Fruit: Sex and Religion in the Lives of American Teenagers* (Oxford: Oxford University Press, 2007).

4. Stanford Carmack, "A Look at Some 'Nonstandard' Book of Mormon Grammar," *Interpreter: A Journal of Latter-day Saint Faith and Scholarship* [hereafter cited as *Interpreter*] 11 (2014): 209–62; Royal Skousen, "Tyndale Versus More in the Book of Mormon," *Interpreter* 13 (2015): 1–8; Carmack, "What Command Syntax Tells Us about Book of Mormon Authorship," *Interpreter* 13 (2015): 175–217; Carmack, "The Implications of Past-Tense Syntax in the Book of Mormon," *Interpreter* 14 (2015): 119–86; Carmack, "Why the Oxford English Dictionary (and Not Webster's 1828)," *Interpreter* 15 (2015): 65–77; Carmack, "The More Part of the Book of Mormon Is Early Modern English," *Interpreter* 18 (2016): 33–40; Carmack, "Joseph Smith Read the Words," *Interpreter* 18 (2016): 41–64; Carmack, "The Case of the {-th} Plural in the Earliest Text," *Interpreter* 18 (2016): 79–108; Carmack, "The Case of Plural Was in the Earliest Text," *Interpreter* 18 (2016): 109–37; Carmack, "How Joseph Smith's Grammar Differed from Book of Mormon Grammar: Evidence from the 1832 History," *Interpreter* 25 (2017): 239–59; and Carmack, "Barlow on Book of Mormon Language: An Examination of Some Strained Grammar," *Interpreter* 27 (2017): 185–96.

5. Oxford English Dictionary, s.v. "man."

6. Lawrence S. Mayer and Paul R. McHugh, "Sexuality and Gender: Findings from the Biological, Psychological, and Social Sciences," *New Atlantis* 50 (2016): 11.

7. See "The Family: A Proclamation to the World," *Ensign*, November 2010, 129.

8. William P. Brown, *The Seven Pillars of Creation: The Bible, Science, and the Ecology of Wonder* (Oxford: Oxford University Press, 2010), 104;

Mayer and McHugh, "Sexuality and Gender," 20; J. R. Giorgiadis and M. L. Kringelbach, "The Human Sexual Response Cycle: Brain Imaging Evidence Linking Sex to Other Pleasures," *Progress in Neurobiology* 98 (2012): 50.

9. Victor L. Brown Jr., *Human Intimacy: Illusion and Reality* (Salt Lake City: Parliament Publishers, 1981), 13; compare Giorgiadis and Kringelbach, "Human Sexual Response Cycle," 50.

10. Louann Brizendine, *The Male Brain: A Breakthrough Understanding of How Men and Boys Think* (New York: Broadway Books, 2010), 34, 48.

11. Timm B. Poeppl, Berthold Langguth, Rainer Rupprecht, Adam Safron, Danilo Bzdok, Angela R. Laird, and Simon B. Eickhoff, "The Neural Basis of Sex Differences in Sexual Behavior: A Quantitative Meta-analysis," *Frontiers in Neuroendocrinology* 43 (2016): 40.

12. David Sylva, Adam Safron, A. M. Rosenthal, Paul J. Reber, Todd B. Parrish, J. Michael Bailey, "Neural Correlates of Sexual Arousal in Heterosexual and Homosexual Women and Men," *Hormones and Behavior* 64 (2013): 682.

13. Mark D. Regnerus and Jeremy E. Uecker, *Premarital Sex in America: How Young Americans Meet, Mate, and Think about Marrying* (Oxford: Oxford University Press, 2011), 95. Frustratingly, while Sarah Ashton, Karalyn McDonald, and Maggie Kirkman, "Women's Experiences of Pornography: A Systematic Review of Research Using Qualitative Methods," *Journal of Sex Research* 55, no. 3 (2018): 342, report that some women are aroused by pornography, there is no indication of the prevalence of this phenomenon.

14. This is the prefrontal cortex. Giorgiadis and Kringelbach, "Human Sexual Response Cycle," 61, 63–65, 75.

15. This is the amygdala. Louann Brizendine, *The Female Brain* (New York: Morgan Road Books, 2006), 77–83. The amygdala in males functions differently; Sylva et al., "Neural Correlates of Sexual Arousal," 676; Giorgiadis and Kringelbach, "Human Sexual Response Cycle," 61.

16. This is the anterior cingulate cortex. Brizendine, *Male Brain*, 73, 75.

17. Caroline Rigo, Filip Uzarevic, and Vassilis Saroglou, "Make Love and Lose Your Religion and Virtue: Recalling Sexual Experiences Undermines Spiritual Intentions and Moral Behavior," *Journal for the Scientific Study of Religion* 55, no. 1 (2016): 25.

18. Regnerus, *Forbidden Fruit*, 119–20.

19. Regnerus, *Forbidden Fruit*, 120; Regnerus and Uecker, *Premarital Sex in America*, 18.

20. Regnerus, *Forbidden Fruit*, 121.

21. Regnerus and Uecker, *Premarital Sex in America*, 22.

22. Freitas, *Sex and the Soul*, 86.

23. Regnerus, *Forbidden Fruit*, 211.

24. Regnerus and Uecker, *Premarital Sex in America*, 22.

25. Freitas, *Sex and the Soul*, 85.

26. Christian Smith and Patricia Snell, *Souls in Transition: The Religious and Spiritual Lives of Emerging Adults* (Oxford: Oxford University Press, 2009), 41.

27. Freitas, *Sex and the Soul*, 142.

28. Regnerus and Uecker, *Premarital Sex in America*, 107, 105, 108, 136.

29. Regnerus, *Forbidden Fruit*, 41.

30. Mons Bendixen, Kelly Asao, Joy P. Wyckoff, David M. Buss, and Leif Edward Ottesen Kennair, "Sexual Regret in US and Norway: Effects of Culture and Individual Differences in Religiosity and Mating Strategy," *Personality and Individual Differences* 116 (2017): 246–51.

31. Regnerus, *Forbidden Fruit*, 41.

32. Regnerus and Uecker, *Premarital Sex in America*, 107, 114, 137.

33. Smith and Snell, *Souls in Transition*, 61–62.

34. Regnerus and Uecker, *Premarital Sex in America*, 137.

35. *Relationships in America Survey* (Austin, TX: The Austin Institute for the Study of Family and Culture, 2014), 26.

36. Freitas, *Sex and the Soul*, 24.

37. Regnerus and Uecker, *Premarital Sex in America*, 155.

38. Regnerus, *Forbidden Fruit*, 161; Freitas, *Sex and the Soul*, 150-51, provides examples.

39. Brizendine, *Male Brain*, 67.

40. Regnerus and Uecker, *Premarital Sex in America*, 25.

41. Regnerus and Uecker, *Premarital Sex in America*, 24.

42. *Relationships in America Survey*, 23.

43. Regnerus and Uecker, *Premarital Sex in America*, 25.

44. Regnerus and Uecker, *Premarital Sex in America*, 139–43.

45. Regnerus and Uecker, *Premarital Sex in America*, 26. For the influence of pornography, see Paul J. Wright, "U.S. Males and Pornography, 1973–

2010: Consumption, Predictors, Correlates," *Journal of Sex Research* 50, no. 1 (2013): 66.

46. Regnerus and Uecker, *Premarital Sex in America*, 212–13.

47. Regnerus and Uecker, *Premarital Sex in America*, 28.

48. Regnerus and Uecker, *Premarital Sex in America*, 28–30; compare Amy Adamczyk and Jacob Felson, "Friends' Religiosity and First Sex," *Social Science Research* 35 (2006): 928.

49. Regnerus and Uecker, *Premarital Sex in America*, 23.

50. Regnerus and Uecker, *Premarital Sex in America*, 35, 206–7; Regnerus, *Forbidden Fruit*, 200.

51. *Relationships in America Survey*, 25.

52. Regnerus and Uecker, *Premarital Sex in America*, 31, 60, 105.

53. Regnerus and Uecker, *Premarital Sex in America*, 82–83, 243.

54. Regnerus and Uecker, *Premarital Sex in America*, 74, 76.

55. Freitas, *Sex and the Soul*, 69–71.

56. Mark Regnerus, *Cheap Sex: The Transformation of Men, Marriage, and Monogamy* (Oxford: Oxford University Press, 2017), 5.

57. Regnerus and Uecker, *Premarital Sex in America*, 73.

58. Regnerus and Uecker, *Premarital Sex in America*, 67, 106.

59. Regnerus and Uecker, *Premarital Sex in America*, 73, 79–81.

60. *Relationships in America Survey*, 26.

61. Regnerus and Uecker, *Premarital Sex in America*, 51.

62. Regnerus and Uecker, *Premarital Sex in America*, 173; compare Spencer T. Zitzman and Mark H. Butler, "Wives' Experience of Husbands' Pornography Use and Concomitant Deception as an Attachment Threat in the Adult Pair-Bond Relationship," *Sexual Addiction & Compulsivity* 16 (2009): 231.

63. Rigo, Uzarevic, and Saroglou, "Make Love and Lose Your Religion," 35.

64. Freitas, *Sex and the Soul*, 147.

65. Regnerus and Uecker, *Premarital Sex in America*, 52, 245–46.

66. Regnerus and Uecker, *Premarital Sex in America*, 52, 56.

67. Regnerus and Uecker, *Premarital Sex in America*, 57; emphasis in original. This is also suggested by the data presented by Carlos J. Vélez-Blasini, "Evidence against Alcohol as a Proximal Cause of Sexual Risk Taking among College Students," *Journal of Sex Research* 45, no. 2 (2008): 123–24, though not his analysis. Another way of looking at the data is that the male arousal and perceptions of costs and benefits are

more or less constant, but sexual intercourse only happens when the woman is aroused, and perceives the benefits as high and the cost low. She is thus the gatekeeper.

68. Regnerus and Uecker, *Premarital Sex in America*, 118, 247; compare Susan M. Doornwaard, Tom F. M. ter Bogt, E. Reitz, and Regina van den Eijnden, "Sex-Related Online Behaviors, Perceived Peer Norms and Adolescents' Experience with Sexual Behavior: Testing an Integrative Model," *PloS ONE* 10, no. 6 (2015): 13.

69. David Dunning, Chip Heath, and Jerry M. Suls, "Flawed Self-Assessment: Implications for Health, Education, and the Workplace," *Psychological Science in the Public Interest* 5, no. 3 (2004): 75.

70. Regnerus and Uecker, *Premarital Sex in America*, 118–19.

71. Regnerus and Uecker, *Premarital Sex in America*, 63, 57, 59.

72. Jeremy E. Uecker and Mark D. Regnerus, "Bare Market: Campus Sex Ratios, Romantic Relationships, and Sexual Behavior," *Sociological Quarterly* 51, no. 3 (2010): 410.

73. Uecker and Regnerus, "Bare Market," 410.

74. Regnerus and Uecker, *Premarital Sex in America*, 121.

75. Uecker and Regnerus, "Bare Market," 428.

76. Regnerus and Uecker, *Premarital Sex in America*, 16.

77. Uecker and Regnerus, "Bare Market," 427–28; Regnerus and Uecker, *Premarital Sex in America*, 123–24.

78. Uecker and Regnerus, "Bare Market," 430.

79. Uecker and Regnerus, "Bare Market," 427; Regnerus and Uecker, *Premarital Sex in America*, 123.

80. C. S. Lewis, "We Have No 'Right to Happiness,'" *Saturday Evening Post*, December 21–28, 1963, 12.

81. Regnerus, *Cheap Sex*, 9.

82. Regnerus and Uecker, *Premarital Sex in America*, 199.

83. Smith and Snell, *Souls in Transition*, 62; Regnerus and Uecker, *Premarital Sex in America*, 200.

84. *Relationships in America Survey*, 44.

85. Regnerus and Uecker, *Premarital Sex in America*, 199, 200, 201–2.

86. *Relationships in America Survey*, 41.

87. Regnerus and Uecker, *Premarital Sex in America*, 202.

88. Laurie DeRose, Mark Lyons-Amos, W. Bradford Wilcox, and Gloria Huarcaya, "The Cohabitation-Go-Round: Cohabitation and Family Insta-

bility across the Globe," in *World Family Map 2017* (New York: Social Trends Institute, 2017), 6–7.

89.   Regnerus and Uecker, *Premarital Sex in America*, 202.

90.   Regnerus and Uecker, *Premarital Sex in America*, 202.

91.   Smith and Snell, *Souls in Transition*, 63.

92.   Janice Shaw Crouse, "Cohabitation: Consequences for Mothers, Children, and Society," in *The Family in the New Millennium*, ed. A. Scott Loveless and Thomas B. Holman, vol. 1 (Westport, CT: Praeger, 2007), 353.

93.   Regnerus and Uecker, *Premarital Sex in America*, 202.

94.   Smith and Snell, *Souls in Transition*, 63; Regnerus and Uecker, *Premarital Sex in America*, 203.

95.   Crouse, "Cohabitation," 353.

96.   NSYR wave 3 data.

97.   *Relationships in America Survey*, 39.

98.   Crouse, "Cohabitation," 353.

99.   DeRose et al., "Cohabitation-Go-Round," 9.

100.   Crouse, "Cohabitation," 351, 354, 357.

101.   *Relationships in America Survey*, 36.

102.   Crouse, "Cohabitation," 357.

103.   Smith and Snell, *Souls in Transition*, 59.

104.   Jeremy E. Uecker, Damon Mayrl, and Samuel Stroope, "Family Formation and Returning to Institutional Religion in Young Adulthood," *Journal for the Scientific Study of Religion* 55, no. 2 (2016): 389.

105.   Regnerus, *Forbidden Fruit*, 132–33.

106.   NSYR wave 3 data.

107.   According to the Pew Forum U.S. Religious Landscape Survey 2010, http://religions.pewforum.org/portraits#9.

108.   Stephen Cranney, "Who Is Leaving the Church? Demographic Predictors of Ex–Latter-day Saint Status in the Pew Religious Landscape Survey," *BYU Studies* 58, no. 1 (2019): 102.

109.   Jeremy E. Uecker, Mark D. Regnerus, and Margaret L. Vaaler, "Losing My Religion: The Social Sources of Religious Decline in Early Adulthood," *Social Forces* 85, no. 4 (2007): 1671–72, 1678–81.

110.   Mayer and McHugh, "Sexuality and Gender," 12.

111.   Regnerus, *Cheap Sex*, 8.

112. J. Michael Bailey, Paul L. Vasey, Lisa M. Diamond, S. Marc Breedlove, Eric Vilain, and Marc Epprecht, "Sexual Orientation, Controversy, and Science," *Psychological Science in the Public Interest* 17, no. 2 (2016): 48; Mayer and McHugh, "Sexuality and Gender," 21: "Should homosexuality, for example, be characterized by reference to desires to engage in particular acts with individuals of the same sex, or to a patterned history of having engaged in such acts, or to particular features of one's private wishes or fantasies, or to a consistent impulse to seek intimacy with members of the same sex, or to a social identity imposed by oneself or others, or to something else entirely?"

113. Freitas, *Sex and the Soul*, 155–57.

114. Anjani Chandra, William D. Mosher, Casey Copen, and Catlainn Sionean, "Sexual Behavior, Sexual Attraction, and Sexual Identity in the United States," *National Health Statistics Reports* 36 (March 2011): 31.

115. Bailey et al., "Sexual Orientation, Controversy, and Science," 49.

116. Chandra et al., "Sexual Behavior," 1.

117. Bailey et al., "Sexual Orientation, Controversy, and Science," 58, 64, 50–51.

118. Bailey et al., "Sexual Orientation, Controversy, and Science," 53.

119. Regnerus, *Forbidden Fruit*, 77.

120. Brian W. Ward, James M. Dahlhamer, Adena M. Galinsky, and Sarah S. Joestl, "Sexual Orientation and Health among U.S. Adults: National Health Interview Survey, 2013," *National Health Statistics Reports* 77 (July 2014): 3, 7.

121. Bailey et al., "Sexual Orientation, Controversy, and Science," 53.

122. *Relationships in America Survey*, 18.

123. The faulty method of gathering data skews the results reported in William S. Bradshaw, Tim B. Heaton, Ellen Decoo, John P. Dehlin, Renee V. Galliher, and Katherine A. Crowell, "Religious Experiences of GBTQ Mormon Males," *Journal for the Scientific Study of Religion* 54, no. 2 (2015): 315–16, 327: "Our findings are not necessarily generalizable."

124. Bailey et al., "Sexual Orientation, Controversy, and Science," 53.

125. *Handbook 2: Administering the Church* (Salt Lake City: The Church of Jesus Christ of Latter-day Saints, 2018), §21.4.6, available at churchofjesuschrist.org: "While opposing homosexual behavior, the Church reaches out with understanding and respect to individuals who are attracted to those of the same gender."

126. Regnerus, *Forbidden Fruit*, 77–78; emphasis in original.

127. Regnerus, *Forbidden Fruit*, 78.

128. See, for example, the debate: Paul Cameron, "Children of Homosexuals and Transsexuals More Apt to Be Homosexual," *Journal of Biosocial Science* 38, no. 3 (2005): 413–18; Todd G. Morrison, "Children of Homosexuals and Transsexuals More Apt to Be Homosexual: A Reply to Cameron," *Journal of Biosocial Science* 39, no. 1 (2006): 153–54; Paul Cameron, "Facts, Not Opinions, Drive Science: A Reply to Morrison," *Journal of Biosocial Science* 39, no. 1 (2007): 155–56; Walter R. Schumm, "Children of Homosexuals More Apt to Be Homosexuals? A Reply to Morrison and Cameron Based On an Examination of Multiple Sources of Data," *Journal of Biosocial Science* 42, no. 6 (2010): 721–42. I note that Cameron had previously been expelled from the American Psychological Association.

129. Camille Paglia, "Obama's Early Stumbles," January 14, 2009, http://www.salon.com/news/opinion/camille_paglia/2009/01/14/obama/index.html.

130. For a look at some of the logical problems, see Mayer and McHugh, "Sexuality and Gender," 41–42.

131. Bailey et al., "Sexual Orientation, Controversy, and Science," 70–71.

132. Bailey et al., "Sexual Orientation, Controversy, and Science," 70; Mayer and McHugh, "Sexuality and Gender," 35–36.

133. Bailey et al., "Sexual Orientation, Controversy, and Science," 79.

134. Mayer and McHugh, "Sexuality and Gender," 29–30.

135. Bailey et al., "Sexual Orientation, Controversy, and Science," 71–72.

136. Mayer and McHugh, "Sexuality and Gender," 14.

137. Bailey et al., "Sexual Orientation, Controversy, and Science," 76.

138. Mayer and McHugh, "Sexuality and Gender," 26–29.

139. Bailey et al., "Sexual Orientation, Controversy, and Science," 77; Mayer and McHugh, "Sexuality and Gender," 32–33.

140. Mayer and McHugh, "Sexuality and Gender," 31.

141. Andrea Ganna, Karin J. H. Verweij, Michel G. Nivard, Robert Maier, Robbee Wedow, Alexander S. Busch, Abdel Abdellaoui, Shengru Guo, J. Fah Sathirapongsasuti, 23andMe Research Team, Paul Lichtenstein, Sebastian Lundström, Niklas Långström, Adam Auton, Kathleen Mullan Harris, Gary W. Beecham, Eden R. Martin, Alan R. Sanders, John R. B. Perry, Benjamin M. Neale, and Brendan P. Zietsch, "Large-Scale

GWAS Reveals Insights into the Genetic Architecture of Same-Sex Sexual Behavior," *Science* 365, no. 6456 (2019): 6.

142. Ganna et al., "Large-Scale GWAS Reveals Insights," 3.

143. Mayer and McHugh, "Sexuality and Gender," 51.

144. Bailey et al., "Sexual Orientation, Controversy, and Science," 83.

145. Mayer and McHugh, "Sexuality and Gender," 47.

146. A prominent example is given in Mayer and McHugh, "Sexuality and Gender," 13.

147. Quoted in Mayer and McHugh, "Sexuality and Gender," 13.

148. Curtis Dolezal, Alex Carballo-Diéguez, Iván C. Balán, María A. Pando, Marina Mabragaña, Rubén Marone, Victoria Barredad, and María M. Avila, "Childhood Sexual Experiences with an Older Partner among Men Who Have Sex with Men in Buenos Aires, Argentina," *Child Abuse & Neglect* 38 (2014): 272.

149. Bailey et al., "Sexual Orientation, Controversy, and Science," 81–82; compare Mayer and McHugh, "Sexuality and Gender," 43.

150. Regnerus, *Cheap Sex*, 123, 124–26.

151. Lisa Littman, "Rapid-Onset Gender Dysphoria in Adolescents and Young Adults: A Study of Parental Reports," *PLoS ONE* 13, no. 8 (2018): e0202330.

152. Dolezal et al., "Childhood Sexual Experiences," 277.

153. Bailey et al., "Sexual Orientation, Controversy, and Science," 57.

154. Bailey et al., "Sexual Orientation, Controversy, and Science," 82–83; Mayer and McHugh, "Sexuality and Gender," 43. Compare Norman Doidge, *The Brain That Changes Itself* (New York: Viking, 2007), 98–100.

155. Dolezal et al., "Childhood Sexual Experiences," 272.

156. The exact rates vary depending on the type of nonheterosexuality and the type of abuse. For the exact figures, see Mayer and McHugh, "Sexuality and Gender," 45.

157. Mayer and McHugh, "Sexuality and Gender," 45–50.

158. Dieter Urban and Joachim Fiebig, "Pädosexueller Missbrauch: wenn Opfer zu Tätern werden: Eine empirische Studie," *Zeitschrift für Soziologie* 40, no. 1 (2011): 42–61.

159. Mayer and McHugh, "Sexuality and Gender," 45.

160. Mayer and McHugh, "Sexuality and Gender," 46.

161. Mayer and McHugh, "Sexuality and Gender," 46; compare Dolezal et al., "Childhood Sexual Experiences," 272.

162. Mayer and McHugh, "Sexuality and Gender," 61.

163. Mayer and McHugh, "Sexuality and Gender," 61, 62, 65.

164. Mayer and McHugh, "Sexuality and Gender," 71–73.

165. *Relationships in America Survey*, 23.

166. Mayer and McHugh, "Sexuality and Gender," 73.

167. Mayer and McHugh, "Sexuality and Gender," 68. Compare Freitas, *Sex and the Soul*, 157.

168. Chandra et al., "Sexual Behavior," 27. The figures given in the article are for numbers and percentages of those who have had a certain number of opposite-sex partners in their lifetime who have engaged in sexual activity with someone of the same sex. These numbers have been recalculated to determine the number of opposite-sex partners that those who have engaged in sexual activity with someone of the same sex have.

169. Chandra et al., "Sexual Behavior," 27, 31.

170. Chandra et al., "Sexual Behavior," 29, 30.

171. Mayer and McHugh, "Sexuality and Gender," 51.

172. Chandra et al., "Sexual Behavior," 30. This figure has been calculated from the statistics given in the table. Compare this to 63.7% of Latter-day Saint men who identify as homosexual being college graduates; Bradshaw et al., "Religious Experiences of GBTQ Mormon Males," 316.

173. *Relationships in America Survey*, 23.

174. See Casey E. Copen, Anjani Chandra, and Isaedmarie Febo-Vazquez, "Sexual Behavior, Sexual Attraction, and Sexual Orientation among Adults Aged 18–44 in the United States: Data from the 2011–2013 National Survey of Family Growth," *National Health Statistics Reports* 88 (January 2016): 1–13.

175. Dolezal et al., "Childhood Sexual Experiences," 277.

176. Bailey et al., "Sexual Orientation, Controversy, and Science," 59.

177. Bailey et al., "Sexual Orientation, Controversy, and Science," 60; an example is given in Mayer and McHugh, "Sexuality and Gender," 15.

178. Bailey et al., "Sexual Orientation, Controversy, and Science," 61–62.

179. Bailey et al., "Sexual Orientation, Controversy, and Science," 48. Note also the critique in Mayer and McHugh, "Sexuality and Gender," 16–19.

180. Mayer and McHugh, "Sexuality and Gender," 23–24.

181. Bailey et al., "Sexual Orientation, Controversy, and Science," 48; Mayer and McHugh, "Sexuality and Gender," 19: "The testimony of experience

suggests that one's experience of sexual desire and sexual attraction is not voluntary, at least not in any immediate way."

182. Bailey et al., "Sexual Orientation, Controversy, and Science," 48, 54.

183. Bailey et al., "Sexual Orientation, Controversy, and Science," 48.

184. Marriage, of course, is not entirely an individual choice; others with agency are involved. For the purposes of illustration, I have used married men as an example to show that what sort of married person one is, is something that an individual has a choice and consequent accountability about.

185. I am not discounting the importance of scriptures like Matthew 5:27–30 that describe lust as a sin. Lust leads to fornication and adultery and should be avoided. Our thoughts will condemn us at the last day (see Alma 12:14; Mosiah 4:30). The Church, however, does not discipline individuals unless and until the behavior occurs; *Handbook 2: Administering the Church*, §21.4.6: "Homosexual behavior violates the commandments of God, is contrary to the purposes of human sexuality, and deprives people of the blessings that can be found in family life and in the saving ordinances of the gospel. Those who persist in such behavior or who influence others to do so are subject to Church discipline. . . . If members feel same-gender attraction but do not engage in any homosexual behavior, leaders should support and encourage them in their resolve to live the law of chastity and to control unrighteous thoughts. These members may receive Church callings. If they are worthy and qualified in every other way, they may also hold temple recommends and receive temple ordinances."

186. Bailey et al., "Sexual Orientation, Controversy, and Science," 64–68; Mayer and McHugh, "Sexuality and Gender," 16.

187. Mayer and McHugh, "Sexuality and Gender," 25.

188. Bailey et al., "Sexual Orientation, Controversy, and Science," 54.

189. Mayer and McHugh, "Sexuality and Gender," 50; Doidge, *Brain That Changes Itself*, 95.

190. Mayer and McHugh, "Sexuality and Gender," 51.

191. Mayer and McHugh, "Sexuality and Gender," 53–54.

192. Mayer and McHugh, "Sexuality and Gender," 52.

193. Bailey et al., "Sexual Orientation, Controversy, and Science," 56; Mayer and McHugh, "Sexuality and Gender," 55–56. Compare Freitas, *Sex and the Soul*, 158–59.

194. Mayer and McHugh, "Sexuality and Gender," 56.

195. *Relationships in America Survey*, 18–19.

196. Bailey et al., "Sexual Orientation, Controversy, and Science," 86.

197. Christopher H. Rosik, Stanton L. Jones, and A. Dean Byrd, "Knowing What We Do Not Know about Sexual Orientation Change Efforts," *American Psychologist* 67, no. 6 (2012): 499.

198. Giorgiadis and Kringelbach, "Human Sexual Response Cycle," 52–53.

199. Smith and Snell, *Souls in Transition*, 83–84; compare Regnerus, *Forbidden Fruit*, 53–54; Carolyn McNamara Barry and Larry J. Nelson, "The Role of Religion in the Transition to Adulthood for Young Emerging Adults," *Journal of Youth and Adolescence* 34, no. 3 (2005): 247; Freitas, *Sex and the Soul*, 26.

200. Melanie A. Gold, Anya V. Sheftel, Laurel Chiappetta, Amanda J. Young, Allan Zuckoff, Carlo C. DiClemente, and Brian A. Primack, "Associations between Religiosity and Sexual and Contraceptive Behaviors," *Journal of Pediatric Adolescent Gynecology* 23 (2010): 295.

201. Freitas, *Happiness Effect*, 198.

202. Smith and Snell, *Souls in Transition*, 83–84; compare Regnerus, *Forbidden Fruit*, 53–54; Barry and Nelson, "Role of Religion in the Transition to Adulthood," 247; Freitas, *Sex and the Soul*, 26, 154.

203. Mark D. Regnerus and Jeremy E. Uecker, "Finding Faith, Losing Faith: The Prevalence and Context of Religious Transformations during Adolescence," *Review of Religious Research* 47, no. 3 (2006): 229; Regnerus, *Forbidden Fruit*, 125: "Adolescent virgins who exhibited rapid declines in attendance or religious salience were much more likely to report having had sex between study waves (the odds increase by 35–50 percent)."

204. Uecker, Regnerus, and Vaaler, "Losing My Religion," 1678–81.

205. Freitas, *Sex and the Soul*, 143.

206. Adamczyk and Felson, "Friends' Religiosity and First Sex," 925.

207. C. Harry Hui, Sing-Hang Cheung, Jasmine Lam, Esther Yuet Ying Lau, Shu-Fai Cheung, and Livia Yuliawati, "Psychological Changes during

Faith Exit: A Three-Year Prospective Study," *Psychology of Religion and Spirituality* 10, no 2. (2018): 115.

208. Regnerus and Uecker, *Premarital Sex in America*, 23, 19.

209. Regnerus and Uecker, *Premarital Sex in America*, 19–21.

210. Quoted in Regnerus, *Forbidden Fruit*, 36.

211. Freitas, *Sex and the Soul*, 145–46.

212. Smith and Snell, *Souls in Transition*, 240; Freitas, *Sex and the Soul*, 155.

213. Rigo, Uzarevic, and Saroglou, "Make Love and Lose Your Religion," 29–30, 34.

214. Rigo, Uzarevic, and Saroglou, "Make Love and Lose Your Religion," 29, 33, 34.

215. *Relationships in America Survey*, 26.

216. Regnerus, *Forbidden Fruit*, 153–61.

217. Regnerus, *Forbidden Fruit*, 153.

218. Ron Sider, *The Scandal of the Evangelical Conscience* (Grand Rapids, MI: Baker Books, 2005), 23; Freitas, *Sex and the Soul*, 70, 75–79.

219. Regnerus, *Forbidden Fruit*, 205.

220. Jeremy E. Uecker, "Religion, Pledging, and the Premarital Sexual Behavior of Married Young Adults," *Journal of Marriage and Family* 70 (2008): 741 (textual references omitted).

221. Regnerus, *Forbidden Fruit*, 155.

222. Sider, *Scandal of the Evangelical Conscience*, 18–20. This factor is downplayed in Regnerus, *Forbidden Fruit*, 157.

223. Regnerus, *Forbidden Fruit*, 157.

224. Paul E. Barton and Richard E. Coley, *The Black-White Achievement Gap: When Progress Stopped* (Princeton: Princeton Educational Testing Service, 2010), 35; compare 21–24.

225. *Relationships in America Survey*, 26.

226. Uecker, "Religion, Pledging, and Premarital Sexual Behavior," 741; Regnerus, *Forbidden Fruit*, 123–24.

227. Regnerus, *Forbidden Fruit*, 123. Also reported was a different, slightly older data set (Add Health) with slightly older teenagers, where 78.3% of Latter-day Saints were virgins, second to Jews, at 82.4%.

228. Regnerus, *Forbidden Fruit*, 133.

229. Regnerus, *Forbidden Fruit*, 127, gives the percentage as 18.0. This was based on earlier wave data. I have used the later NSYR wave 3 data here.

230. Regnerus, *Forbidden Fruit*, 133.

231. One suspects that this statistic is a feature of granularity and an arte-fact of the sample size. When Latter-day Saints are a fraction of the original sample and only a small percentage of them have had sex in the first place, the small percentage of those who continue to have sex with the same individual has appeared as zero. The granularity of the statistics makes it appear that the total number of Latter-day Saint youth in the sample who had engaged in sex at that point was nine.

232. Regnerus, *Forbidden Fruit*, 133. According to NSYR wave 3 data, no other religion was below 72%.

233. Regnerus, *Forbidden Fruit*, 176; but note page 175: "Evangelicals, Mor-mons, and youths who identify with another (non-Christian) religion display the lowest stated rates of pornography use here, though these numbers may be artificially low due to stronger than average social desirability bias."

234. Regnerus, *Forbidden Fruit*, 164, 169. Many American teenagers do not consider oral sex to be sex. Regnerus, *Forbidden Fruit*, 30. This is a cul-tural perception since ancient Romans considered oral sex to be mor-ally worse than vaginal intercourse.

235. Regnerus, *Forbidden Fruit*, 143, 181, 141.

236. *For the Strength of Youth* (Salt Lake City: The Church of Jesus Christ of Latter-day Saints, 2011), 36.

237. NSYR wave 3 data. Because the data was not published in the reports, the percentages, broken down by religion, are Muslim 100%, not reli-gious 90%, Catholic 88%, Jewish 87%, Protestant 86%, other religion 86%, Latter-day Saint 61%.

238. NSYR wave 3 data. Because this information was not available in the published reports, the percentages, broken down by religion, are Jew-ish 76%, not religious 72%, Catholic 68%, Protestant 66%, other religion 66%, Muslim 60%, Latter-day Saint 41%.

239. NSYR wave 3 data.

240. NSYR wave 3 data.

241. Uecker, "Religion, Pledging, and Premarital Sexual Behavior," 736–37.

242. Uecker, "Religion, Pledging, and Premarital Sexual Behavior," 737.

243. *Relationships in America Survey*, 32.

244. NSYR wave 3 data.

245. NSYR wave 3 data.

246. NSYR wave 3 data.

247. Uecker, "Religion, Pledging, and Premarital Sexual Behavior," 737, 739, 740–41.

248. Regnerus, *Forbidden Fruit*, 87, 104, 87.

249. *Relationships in America Survey*, 46, 55.

250. *Relationships in America Survey*, 47, 55.

251. Martha Gault-Sherman and Scott Draper, "What Will the Neighbors Think? The Effect of Moral Communities on Cohabitation," *Review of Religious Research* 54, no. 1 (2012): 48. According to NSYR wave 3 data, Jews (at 10%) are less likely to cohabit than Latter-day Saints.

252. NSYR wave 3 data.

253. NSYR wave 3 data.

254. Regnerus, *Forbidden Fruit*, 64–69.

255. Regnerus, *Forbidden Fruit*, 66, 65.

256. Regnerus, *Forbidden Fruit*, 71.

257. Regnerus, *Forbidden Fruit*, 67.

258. Regnerus, *Forbidden Fruit*, 67; emphasis in original.

259. Regnerus, *Forbidden Fruit*, 212–13; emphasis in original.

260. Regnerus, *Forbidden Fruit*, 71; emphasis in original.

261. These are Black Protestant parents (by at least 18 points); Regnerus, *Forbidden Fruit*, 65; compare Olsho et al., *National Survey of Adolescents and Their Parents*, x.

262. Regnerus, *Forbidden Fruit*, 123, 133, 135; Olsho et al., *National Survey of Adolescents and Their Parents*, ix, xi.

263. Regnerus and Uecker, *Premarital Sex in America*, 21.

264. Olsho et al., *National Survey of Adolescents and Their Parents*, 56–57.

265. *Handbook 2: Administering the Church*, §21.4.11: "Parents have primary responsibility for the sex education of their children. Teaching this subject honestly and plainly in the home will help young people avoid serious moral transgressions."

266. Regnerus, *Forbidden Fruit*, 23.

267. NSYR wave 3 data.

268. Smith and Snell, *Souls in Transition*, 271–75.

269. Smith and Snell, *Souls in Transition*, 277; compare Olsho et al., *National Survey of Adolescents and Their Parents*, x.

270. Rigo, Uzarevic, and Saroglou, "Make Love and Lose Your Religion," 24–25.

8 | **PROVIDING PROTECTION**

Parents, conscientious teenagers, and emerging adults might want to know how to protect themselves or their family members from the pitfalls that come in the college-age years. Some factors—such as personality, family, behavior, and context—influence decisions to forsake religion, but demography does not seem to be one of those causes. On the other hand, demographic factors do seem to play a role in *increases* in religiosity,[1] but because not much research has been done on increases in religiosity, the factors at play need to be explored further. Consequently, "religious decline is easier to predict than religious growth."[2] Although the literature on retaining or increasing faith is meager, it is still worth reviewing. It is also worth reviewing some approaches, like theology, that have been advocated as avenues for parents and others to reach youth and young adults.

While statistics predict the behavior of the masses but not the individual, there are a few behaviors that correlate with positive consequences for the individual's life and faith. The four indicators that seem to correlate most closely to the importance of faith in the lives of emerging adults are (1) weekly church attendance, (2) frequent prayer, (3) frequent scripture study, and (4) avoiding sexual activity outside of marriage. (The first three behaviors are necessary to place an individual in the NSYR's "devoted" category.)[3] Among Latter-day Saints, these variables are not independent (whether one prays is related to and partially dependent on whether one attends church meetings). If they were, we would expect only about 32% of Latter-day Saints to be in the devoted category[4] instead of the 56% who actually are.[5] The flip side is that 29–44% of Latter-day Saint emerging adults are not doing these things, and so their faith is in danger.[6] The factors influencing positive outcomes are behaviors, not beliefs. As one group of researchers mused, "Perhaps internal religious commitments and external religious behaviors are more intertwined than is typically thought."[7] "Fidelity receives expression through behavior, such as church attendance, that in turn is an observable indicator of one's ideological preferences and commitments."[8] While there is a connection between beliefs and practice, practices have a stronger influence on outcomes than mere beliefs. Actions matter.

While at an academic conference, I discussed the results of the NSYR with an evangelical who was also attending. Though he knew about the NSYR results, he rejected them as red herrings. He thought that there must be something else really responsible for the positive sociological outcomes of those in the devoted category rather than practices reported, which were something that he classified as good works. His theological position—that faith is more important than works—was incompatible with the results of the sociological research, and it was clear to him that theology should take precedence over sociology. In one sense, he is correct. The sociological research is only as good as the research study design and the questions the sociologists asked. It is perfectly possible that there are important facets that the sociologists neglected to study and that need to be considered. For example, the sociological literature is silent on the role of family home evenings and seminary and institute. On the other hand, the four factors mentioned above (church attendance, prayer, scripture study, and keeping the law of chastity) have been demonstrated to play a statistically significant

A family in Ghana holds family home evening and reads scriptures together. Courtesy of churchofjesuschrist.org.

role in preserving faith, and it would be foolish to ignore their importance simply because the list was incomplete.

Nothing in this list of behaviors is new to Latter-day Saints who have been paying attention. Back in 1986, for example, President Ezra Taft Benson addressed the young men of the Church and gave them the following counsel:

> In your own family, encourage family home evenings and be an active participant. Encourage family prayer and be on your knees with your family in that sacred circle. . . .
>
> Next, young men, may I admonish you to participate in a program of daily reading and pondering of the scriptures. . . . Of the four great standard works of the Church—the Bible, the Book of Mormon, the Doctrine and Covenants, and the Pearl of Great Price—I would particularly urge you to read again and again the Book of Mormon and ponder and apply its teachings. . . . Young men, the Book of Mormon will change your life. . . .

May I now direct your attention to the importance of attending all of your Church meetings. Faithful attendance at Church meetings brings blessings you can receive in no other way. . . .

We want you to live the clean life all of your life. We want the morally clean life to be your way of life. . . . It is not pleasing to the Lord prior to a mission, or at any time, to sow one's wild oats, to engage in sexual transgression of any nature, and then to expect that planned confession and quick repentance will satisfy the Lord.[9]

He gave similar advice to the young women of the Church.

Last April general conference I had a similar opportunity to speak to all the men of the Church on Saturday evening in general priesthood meeting. At that time, I spoke directly to the Aaronic Priesthood. Tonight, I would like to speak to you young women of corresponding age.

Some of what I say this evening will be exactly what I said to the young men six months ago, and which I want you to know likewise applies directly to you. . . .

In your own family, encourage family home evenings and be an active participant. Encourage family prayer. Be on your knees with your family in that sacred circle. . . .

Next, young women, may I admonish you to participate in a program of daily reading and pondering of the scriptures. . . . Of the four great standard works of the Church—the Bible, the Book of Mormon, the Doctrine and Covenants, and the Pearl of Great Price—I would particularly urge you to read again and again the Book of Mormon and ponder and apply its teachings. . . . Young women, the Book of Mormon will change your life. . . .

May I now direct your attention to the importance of attending all of your Church meetings. Faithful attendance at Church meetings brings blessings you can receive in no other way. . . .

> **Over thirty years ago the prophet specifically encouraged youth to do the four things that have been statistically demonstrated to help retain faith.**

I would now like to speak to you about personal purity.

Solomon said that the price of a virtuous woman "is far above rubies" (Proverbs 31:10). Young women, guard and protect your virtue as you would your very life. We want you to live the morally clean life all of your life. We want the morally clean life to be your way of life. . . . It is not pleasing to the Lord to sow one's wild oats, to engage in sexual transgression of any nature, and then expect that planned confession and quick repentance will satisfy the Lord.

In each case, over thirty years ago the prophet specifically encouraged youth to do the four things that have been statistically demonstrated to help retain faith. Such prophetic passages could be easily multiplied, but they demonstrate, in general conference addresses delivered by the President of the Church, that the advice given to the youth has not changed in the last generation and that prophets were giving this advice before the sociological studies that confirm them were even thought of.

Each of the four protective practices bears examination. How parents and teachers provide protection is also worth examining.

Weekly Church Attendance

Despite the demonstrated importance of weekly attendance at church in maintaining faith, relatively few studies investigate this particular action. To be sure, "church attendance is indicative of fidelity and identity commitment."[10] Besides being a public affirmation of our faith, getting ourselves out of bed and into the pews for two hours appears to be beneficial.

One study concludes that "compared with never attendance, at least weekly service attendance was subsequently associated with greater life satisfaction and positive affect, greater volunteering, greater sense of mission, more forgiveness, and lower probabilities of drug use and early sexual initiation," as well as having fewer sexual partners.[11] It also found weaker correlations with a number of other positive health outcomes. A different study found that those who attend church regularly tend to be happier and more satisfied with life than those who do not.[12]

Another study found "powerful and robust relationships between the belief in supernatural evil and four measures of religious commitment: church attendance, religious perception, giving, and faith sharing."[13] Believing in the existence of a devil is correlated with regular church attendance. While the two are correlated, preliminary evidence indicates that the belief might precede the action.[14]

Those who have researched switching religious affiliation in older adults have noticed that those who attend church regularly are less likely to switch religions. Researchers propose two explanations: "The link between low attendance and propensity to switch groups may be partly explained by the fact that less involved individuals have fewer social ties within the group, and hence face fewer social barriers to leaving. Low attendance may also be a sign of dissatisfaction with the group, which may be the real reason underlying propensity of leave [sic]."[15]

In spite of these results, it seems that researchers had little interest in understanding the relationship between attending church and keeping faith. The Book of Mormon, however, gives its own reasons for the practice. Moroni explains that those who "had been received unto baptism, and were wrought upon and cleansed by the power of the Holy Ghost, . . . were numbered among the people of the church of Christ; and their names were taken, [1] that they might be remembered and [2] nourished by the good word of God, [3] to keep them in the right way, [4] to keep them continually watchful unto prayer, relying alone upon the merits of Christ, who was the author and the finisher of their faith. And the church did meet together oft, [5] to fast and [6] to pray, and [7] to speak one with another concerning the welfare of their souls. And they did meet together oft [8] to partake of bread and wine, in remembrance of the Lord Jesus" (Moroni 6:4–6). These purposes are also echoed in the words of Jesus in 3 Nephi 18:22–25. The sacrament, the focal point of sacrament meeting, is a covenant ceremony centered on remembering Jesus Christ and what he has done for us.

Latter-day Saints emerge as the religious group most likely to attend church. According to the Relationships in America Survey, "Mormons report much higher attendance than any other group, at just over 80 percent weekly."[16] The Baylor Religion Survey puts the attendance lower at 64% attending weekly and 72% attending at least monthly.[17] The effect is so prominent that in addition to the Bible Belt, "the 'Mountain

Latter-day Saints emerge as the religious group most likely to attend church. Courtesy of churchofjesuschrist.org.

West' also exhibits high rates of church attendance. Of the top 10 states in church attendance, six are in the south, and three are in the Mountain West region. Utah, with its majority Mormon population, leads the nation in attendance—by far—at 65 percent in any given week. The second state, Arkansas, is 14 percentage points back, at 51 percent."[18] While in most religions there is a significant gap in church attendance between women and men, with more women attending than men, "Mormons are closer to numerical equality between men and women with 105 women at church for every 100 men."[19]

The NSYR found that 84% of Latter-day Saint teenagers attend church at least once a week.[20] This increased to 93% among Latter-day Saint young adults.[21] Two factors may be involved here. Either it shows an increase in faithfulness as time goes on, or some of those who stop attending may cease to affiliate. About three in four (74%) of Latter-day Saint young adults say that they have become more religious with time; only 4% say that they have become less religious.[22] Other statistics confirm this trend.

DAILY PRAYER

If church attendance is the public manifestation of worship, prayer is the private one. The two are related—prayer is positively correlated with church attendance.[23]

To a great extent, prayer is taught in the home. Children who grew up in a family where one of the parents was not religiously active have essentially the same odds of praying regularly as those who were raised in a single-parent family.[24] Researchers hypothesize that "aging . . . may bring about changes in spiritual maturity that help to shape these beliefs and behaviors over time." They point to studies that "found that four- and six-year-old children believed

The Church encourages the youth to develop a habit of prayer. Courtesy of churchofjesuschrist.org.

that prayer was used exclusively to express positive emotions, whereas eight-year-old children and adults believed that prayer was also used to cope with negative emotions." The importance of prayer tends to increase with age: "older adults engage in prayer more often than younger adults."[25] This is despite the fact that among educated Christians, the belief that prayers are answered tends to decline with age.[26]

One study found a number of positive benefits from praying: "Compared with never praying or meditating, at least daily practice was associated with greater positive affect, emotional processing, and emotional expression; greater volunteering, greater sense of mission, and more forgiveness; lower likelihoods of drug use, early sexual initiation, STIs, and abnormal Pap test results; and fewer lifetime sexual partners." Haphazard prayer, less than once a day, produced results that differed little from not praying at all.[27] Prayer for one's partner seems to improve relationship satisfaction over time.[28]

Again, the relationship between frequent prayer and keeping one's faith is insufficiently explored in the sociological literature, but it is well known in scripture. The injunction to "pray always" appears repeatedly.[29] These scriptures give a number of purposes for praying:

- that "I will pour out my Spirit upon you"
- that "I may unfold the [scriptures] to their understanding"
- "that ye may not faint"
- "that you may come off conqueror"
- so that "I will be with them even unto the end"
- so that "all things shall work together for your good"
- "lest they fall into temptation"
- "lest you enter into temptation and lose your reward"
- "lest that wicked one have power in you"
- "that you may escape the hands of the servants of Satan that do uphold his work"
- "or they shall be removed out of their place"[30]

This list is not exhaustive, but these scriptures give a number of desirable outcomes associated with praying always. Prayer also gives us the opportunity to communicate with God, with whom we have made covenants.

The Church encourages the youth to develop a habit of prayer. Young women participating in the Personal Progress program were required to "exercise your own faith by establishing a habit of prayer in your life. Begin by regularly saying your morning and evening prayers." As part of the Duty to God program, the Church invited each young man, whether deacon, teacher, or priest, to begin or strengthen a habit of daily prayer. Among Latter-day Saint youth, 79% pray more than once a week and 63% (almost two out of three) pray daily.[31] When they become young adults, 89% pray every day, and 96% pray at least weekly.[32] In general 68% of Latter-day Saints of all ages pray every day.[33]

DAILY SCRIPTURE STUDY

The sociological literature on prayer and church attendance, though meager, is relatively robust compared to the literature on scripture study. We do know that those who take the scriptures literally, or as historical—that is, to say as true—tend to have a stronger commitment to their religion.[34] Otherwise the practice of reading scriptures seems hardly to have drawn any sociological interest.

Knowledge of the connection between reading scriptures and faith is very old. In the book of Deuteronomy, the king is ordered to have a copy of the scriptures so that he may "read therein all the days of his life: that he may learn to fear the Lord his God, to keep all the words of this law and these statutes, to do them" (Deuteronomy 17:19). Moses also instructed that "when all Israel come to appear before the Lord thy God in the place which he shall choose, thou shalt read this law before all Israel in their hearing. Gather the people together, men, and women, and children, and thy stranger that is within thy gates, that they may hear, and that they may learn, and fear the Lord your God, and observe to do all the words of this law: and that their children, which have not known any thing, may hear, and learn to fear the Lord your God, as long as ye live in the land whither ye go over Jordan to possess it" (Deuteronomy 31:11-13). The purpose in both cases is that those who read the scriptures, or who hear them, may learn to fear God and keep his commandments.

There are other good reasons to study the scriptures. The scriptures "[contain] the covenants of the Lord" (1 Nephi 13:23) and are written "that [we] may know the covenants of the Lord" (Book of Mormon title page). The scriptures "have enlarged the memory of this people" (Alma 37:8). They help the reader to remember (Moroni 10:3), and they can be called up to remembrance (Jacob 5:1), serving as common ground between readers. A written, unchanging record prevents those who read it and believe it from dwindling in unbelief (Mosiah 1:5; 1 Nephi 4:13).

Some of the scriptures were written so that others "will present their supplication before the Lord, and will return every one from his evil way" (Jeremiah 36:6-7). It was, after all, reading a passage of scripture that prompted Joseph Smith to pray for the first time (Joseph Smith—History 1:11-14).

In a May 1829 revelation, Hyrum Smith was told:

Seek not to declare my word, but first seek to obtain my word, and then shall your tongue be loosed; then, if you desire, you shall have

Those who read the scriptures, or who hear them, may learn to fear God and keep his commandments. Courtesy of churchofjesuschrist.org.

my Spirit and my word, yea, the power of God unto the convincing of men. But now hold your peace; study my word which hath gone forth among the children of men [the Bible], and also study my word which shall come forth among the children of men, or that which is now translating [the Book of Mormon], yea, until you have obtained all which I shall grant unto the children of men in this generation, and then shall all things be added thereto. (Doctrine and Covenants 11:21–22)

Study of the Bible and Book of Mormon is necessary to have the words and Spirit to convince others. This process is reiterated in other words in a later revelation: "Treasure up in your minds continually the words of life, and it shall be given you in the very hour that portion that shall be meted unto every man" (Doctrine and Covenants 84:85).

The scriptures also contain some interesting statements about those who do not study the scriptures: "Your minds in times past have been darkened because of unbelief, and because you have treated lightly the things you have received—which vanity and unbelief have brought the whole church under condemnation. And this condemnation resteth upon the children of Zion, even all. And they shall remain under this condemnation until they repent and remember the new covenant, even the Book of Mormon and the former commandments which I have given them, not only to say, but to do according to that which I have written" (Doctrine and Covenants 84:54–57). Neglecting the scriptures, particularly the Book of Mormon, causes the mind to be darkened.

The Church encourages the youth to develop a habit of scripture study. As part of the Duty to God program, the Church invited each young man, whether deacon, teacher, or priest, to begin or strengthen a habit of daily scripture study. Young women were also admonished to "follow a pattern of regular scripture study and prayer" as part of the Personal Progress program. While only about one in four youth (26%) read the scriptures every day, 61% of them read them at least once a week.[35] This increases for young adults as 44% read the scriptures every day, and 81% read them at least once a week.[36] In general 64% of Latter-day Saints of all ages read the scriptures at least once a week.[37]

LIVING THE LAW OF CHASTITY

The previous chapter dealt with living the law of chastity in detail. It is one of the commandments and covenants that we keep.

The Church emphasizes chastity in a number of ways. One of the Young Women values emphasized in the Personal Progress program was virtue, and it included a number of required value experiences helping young women to understand what virtue is and how to develop that quality. For the young men, the Duty to God program had a required section on living worthily. For the deacons, the emphasis was on learning repentance; for the teachers and priests, the emphasis was on living the law of chastity, with an emphasis on keeping thoughts clean.

THE LITTLE THINGS

Most of the practices that help preserve faith are little things, small habits of the heart that seem to make a big difference in outcomes. "Out of small things proceedeth that which is great" (Doctrine and Covenants 64:33). Intentionally repeating these small things over time demonstrates how important faith is to us. When big decisions come, those whose religion is important to them are more likely to find that their faith plays a role in making decisions like whether and whom to marry, where to live, and how many children to have, while those to whom religion is of little importance are more likely to find it plays no role in those decisions.[38] For the most part, these private religious

practices end up influencing the public ones: "In adolescent populations, service attendance may be a marker of parental service attendance patterns that may not persist into later life, whereas private religious practices may more closely correspond to their own service attendance patterns later in life."[39]

HEARING THE MUSIC

Doing the little things is important, but one could simply go through the motions without actually having what Alma calls a "mighty change of heart" (Alma 5:14), much as one could go through the steps of a dance without really feeling or hearing the music. Elder Wilford Andersen expanded on this analogy:

> Sometimes in our homes, we successfully teach the dance steps but are not as successful in helping our family members to hear the music.... It is hard to dance without music. Dancing without music is awkward and unfulfilling—even embarrassing. Have you ever tried it? ... We learn the dance steps with our minds, but we hear the music with our hearts. The dance steps of the gospel are the things we do; the music of the gospel is the joyful spiritual feeling that comes from the Holy Ghost. It brings a change of heart and is the source of all righteous desires. The dance steps require discipline, but the joy of the dance will be experienced only when we come to hear the music."[40]

243

Studies show that accepting the teachings of a religion is more important in how one acts than how religious one is or whether one attends church.[41] One should not underestimate the impact that acting in accordance with teachings can have on the acceptance of those teachings. As Jesus taught, "If any man will do his will, he shall know of the doctrine, whether it be of God, or whether I speak of myself" (John 7:17). According to Jesus, doing comes before knowing. As we do, we can come to know, which then gives us the motivation to continue doing. Acting in accordance with the teaching before we know is not necessarily hypocrisy; it can be an act of faith.

MAKING IT MEMORABLE

While social science research has identified key factors in youth retaining their faith, those who teach the youth, such as parents and youth leaders, might wonder how they can motivate and inspire youth. Elder Neal A. Maxwell's biographer noted that as a young man he "had come alive with his excitement for fresh gospel teachings, both as a missionary and from his discovery as a student that the gospel could illuminate so many other issues. With his engine running in such high gear, he sometimes found it frustrating, or perhaps a little boring, to sit through classes and meetings that fell short of what he thought the gospel really had to say." As a university student he and a friend met with Elder Harold B. Lee because they "just wanted Elder Lee to know how disappointed they were with the quality of instructional manuals the students were finding in their Sunday School and other classes."[42] Elder Maxwell would later encourage leaders to improve their teaching: "Activation requires conversion. Believing requires gospel beliefs to be understood. Quorum instruction and Gospel Essentials classes must be of a high quality. Attendees must feel the Spirit as they are taught. These individuals need the bread of life, not crumbs from the table. After all, the father of the prodigal son prepared a feast for the returnee—he did not merely warm up some leftovers!"[43] One can look back at Elder Maxwell's output and eloquence as a desire to make the gospel and its instruction memorable rather than boring.

Even if we lack Elder Maxwell's way with words, there is research about what can make our teaching more—or less—memorable.

Theology

The NSYR has data on what sort of teaching is most effective among youth. The NSYR wanted to measure the impact of Catholic high schools on the theological interests of Catholic young adults. They did this by surveying the interest in mandatory theology courses at Notre Dame. They found that "having attended Catholic high school appears to make a sizeable difference in what young Catholics know about the Bible and theology and how much they care about theology and the Church."[44] This was a survey of "mostly first-year and sophomore, Catholic (or formerly Catholic) undergraduate college students at an elite Catholic university." True, what they found was that those who had attended four years of Catholic high school found theology more interesting, important, and relevant than those who did not, but even then, more than half said that they did not think theology was interesting, important, or relevant to their own lives.[45] Thus, even elite Catholic youth with some training in the subject seemed to find their theology boring, irrelevant, and unimportant. Even though this information concerns Catholics, there might be some useful insights for Latter-day Saints here.

Other Christians use the term *theology* differently than Latter-day Saints do. The first use of the term *theology* seems to have been in Plato's *Republic* to describe lies that men told about God to manipulate others for political purposes.[46] The term has changed meanings over the years, but interestingly it is never used in the scriptures. "The traditional task of theology (from the Greek *theos*, god, and *logos*, study of) is to seek understanding of God's reality, to describe divine things rationally, and to elaborate the present meaning of past manifestations of God, whether theoretically, practically, descriptively, or critically."[47] Since theology produces creeds, it is worth noting that Jesus labeled all the results of doing theology "an abomination in his sight" (Joseph Smith—History 1:19). Because Latter-day Saints have revelations from God, they "have little interest in theology in the sense of trying to discover divine things with the unaided resources of the human mind." Instead Latter-day Saints "sometimes informally borrow a Christian tendency to designate the whole of their beliefs and dogma by the label 'theology.'"[48] There is little reason to think that Latter-day Saint youth would respond any better than Catholic youth do to attempts to present divine things as a systematic application of human reason.

Religious studies

What if we used an approach that eschewed theology? Religious studies started out as a way to study religion that explicitly rejected theology. It represented the "liberation of the study of religion from theology,"[49] because it saw "religion as a universal phenomenon to be examined anthropologically."[50] Religious studies is "a direct outgrowth" of the pillars of Enlightenment philosophy with a "contempt for tradition and authority" originally represented by the Catholic Church.[51] One of the axiomatic premises of religious studies is that "there is no one religion that embodies absolute truth."[52] When "in the 'religious studies' mode, . . . students are invited to study the 'phenomenon' of religion as outsiders, rather than as believers."[53] Those involved in religious studies are asked to "minimize their ontological commitments"[54]—that is, any commitment to "supernatural causation."[55] Evolution and natural selection are the starting point for inquiry into religion.[56] That believers would see such an approach to religion as being counter to their religion would seem obvious; nevertheless, one individual with a PhD in religious studies was surprised to discover that "instead of provoking a thoughtful discussion, my idea of comparative religious studies seemed only to strike students as blasphemous."[57] Religious studies has since its establishment grown to "an artificially constructed discipline for the study of religious narratives, thoughts, actions, and phenomena by scholars."[58] Not only is the discipline artificially constructed but sometimes the subject matter is as well: "Religious Studies has also been plagued by an enthusiasm for imagining religious subcultures that 'must have' been there: orgiastic Gnostic cults in antiquity, diabolical witch-cults for the late medieval period, and even—among turn-of-the-century Russian scholars—Jews sacrificing Christian children" or Satanic ritual abuse.[59]

"Without a generally agreed upon method for the overall study of its subject, religious studies is characterized at present by the use of many methods, such as comparative, historical, theological, philosophical, phenomenological, psychological, sociological, anthropological, economical, feminist, hermeneutical, cognitive science, and post-modern." It thus tends to follow the latest fad and to be blown about by every wind of doctrine. Some of these intellectual trends tend "to disrupt or more subtly to subvert the type of thinking common in a discipline like religious studies."[60] Because "many scholars in Religious Studies have had a certain aversion to the positivistic use of evidence, borne of post-modern critiques of scientific verifiability and a general relativism toward truth-claims,"[61] they find it "easy to jump on the theoretical bandwagon of the latest trend and ride it until it fizzles out." This might explain why so many of them are "left alone to wander errantly and to return to repetitively deconstruct texts in a parasitic fashion."[62]

What many of the methods employed by religious studies scholars share is their reductionism. "A profound analysis of the religious data has to take into account political, historical, literary and other factors. . . . The downside was the [religion] was not only well described, but also explained, i.e. explained away into political, historical or literary factors,"[63] or, in another view, into genetically determined traits, environmentally determined traits, additive traits, and nonadditive traits.[64]

Some religious studies scholars are in the thrall of certain French philosophers such as Georges Bataille, whose "theory of religion is ahistorical and devoid of any relationship to evidence from any religious culture or based on any such data."[65] According to insiders, the "aversion" to evidence, the "uncritical perpetuation" of dubious theories, and the extent to which "imagination informs" the approach to the subject are unfortunately frequent in the religious studies field.[66] Since the theory is devoid of actual data it can be concluded that Bataille and his followers are "writing a book of fiction or book on religion as pornography."[67] In this way, "religious studies . . . treated [Christianity] as a phenomenon, a curiosity similar to Islam and shamanism."[68] One scholar from the discipline notes that religious studies tends to produce "rather superficial treatments of the covered religions"[69] that often get basic facts wrong[70] and thinks that it "has endured well past its usefulness."[71] This leads him to ask: "Does this mean that religious studies is dead? Or is it simply on life support with its death a future possibility?"[72] Whether the field is dead or not, it has been shown historically to kill off faith on an institutional level; religiously affiliated institutions that adopt the religious studies discipline for the instruction of religion lose their connection to the religion that sponsored them.[73] This is a good reason not to use it in teaching faith in the Church.

> **What theology and religious studies have in common is the rejection of inspiration and revelation.**

What theology and religious studies have in common is the rejection of inspiration and revelation. They do so for different reasons. Classical Christian theology assumes that revelation is in the past and so all that is left is human reasoning to apply to the word of God. Religious studies axiomatically eliminates revelation as a possibility—as a result only political, historical, or literary factors can be considered, and religion must be reduced to those. Neither approach is appropriate for studying or teaching the restored and revealed gospel of Jesus Christ.

Stories

The most important means of making teachings memorable is precisely the element that is missing from and denied by theology and religious studies: the inspiration and revelation from the Holy Ghost. When someone "receiveth the word by the Spirit of truth," they "receiveth it as it is preached by the Spirit of truth," then "he that preacheth and he that receiveth, understand one another, and both are edified and rejoice together" (Doctrine and Covenants 50:21–22). Unfortunately, social science has a hard time measuring the presence and influence of the Holy Ghost, but it does shed light on another practice in the Church that also helps make things memorable.

In the Church we have always had two different tendencies at work with each other—sometimes in tension and sometimes in tandem. One tendency is toward extracting general "principles" (which is superficially similar to theology), and the other is toward telling stories (which is superficially similar to history). They work together when we analyze stories to find the general patterns and then apply those to our particular situation. They work against each other when the principles are divorced from the application.

James Tissot, *Jesus Teaching on the Sea Shore*. Principles and stories work together when we analyze stories to find the general patterns and then apply those to our particular situation. Courtesy of Wikimedia Commons.

Theology, as practiced by other denominations, drains teaching of meaning, interest, importance, and relevance for most people. After all, "theology does not rely on narrative."[74] On the other hand, stories stick. "Stories are told and retold because they contain wisdom. Stories are effective teaching tools. They show how context can mislead people to make the wrong decisions. Stories illustrate causal relationships that people hadn't recognized before and highlight unexpected, resourceful ways in which people have solved problems."[75]

The scriptures of the Church of Jesus Christ are not theological treatises; they are stories. It cannot be coincidence that the Book of Mormon—which God gave for our instruction (Doctrine and Covenants 33:16), from which we are commanded to teach (Doctrine and Covenants 42:12), and the treating lightly of which brings the Church under the condemnation of God (Doctrine and Covenants 84:54–57)— is one big story compiled from a number of smaller stories. Some of the most memorable scriptural stories come from the Old Testament, but the lists and regulations and poetry tend to cause people's eyes to glaze over. The New Testament provides the story of Jesus; in fact, the English term *gospel* originally meant the "story (or spell) of God." After the book of Acts, the New Testament stops telling stories and tends to appeal to theologians and not so much to anyone else. The Doctrine and Covenants comes alive when placed in the context of the stories from Church history that relate to the individual revelations. Even Jesus himself told parables, which are stories designed to demonstrate a point by comparison (the word *parable* means "comparison"); he did not give theological discourses.

Jesus Christ's parables provide good examples of how stories can be powerful tools in teaching the gospel. "Stories have the amazing dual power to simulate and to inspire. And most of the time we don't even have to use much creativity to harness these powers—we just need to be ready to spot the good ones that life generates every day."[76] There are plenty of examples from everyday life because "ordinary experience manifests the complexity and richness of human existence, and does not represent an artificial construction of philosophical or scientific modes of thinking."[77] Jesus's parables are simple stories from everyday life designed to convey a specific point to his audience. "The hardest part of using stories is making sure they're Simple—that they reflect your core message. It's not enough to tell a great story; the story has to reflect your agenda."[78]

Why do stories work? "The story's power . . . is twofold: It provides simulation (knowledge about how to act) and inspiration (motivation to act). Note that both benefits, simulation and inspiration, are geared to generating *action*. . . . A *credible* idea makes people believe. An *emotional* idea makes people care. . . . The right stories make people act."[79] Additionally, "Human stories [foster] a deep understanding of others. Brain science tells us . . . we are wired for stories."[80]

Some might argue that it is more important to distill general principles that can be applied than it is to tell stories. The Book of Mormon provides an interesting argument to the contrary. Consider the famous statement in Moroni:

> Behold, I would exhort you that when ye shall read these things, . . . that ye would remember how merciful the Lord hath been unto the children of men, from the creation of Adam even down until the time that ye shall receive these things, and ponder it in your hearts. And when ye shall receive these things, I would exhort you that ye would ask God, the Eternal Father, in the name of Christ, if these things are not true; and if ye shall ask with a sincere heart, with real intent, having faith in Christ, he will manifest the truth of it unto you, by the power of the Holy Ghost. (Moroni 10:3–4)

What we call Moroni's promise comes in the last chapter of the Book of Mormon, but it comes after the Book of Mormon has provided many examples of stories of people following that very process, examples that start in the very first chapter:

> In the commencement of the first year of the reign of Zedekiah, king of Judah, . . . there came many prophets, prophesying unto the people that they must repent, or the great city Jerusalem must be destroyed. Wherefore it came to pass that my father, Lehi, as he went forth prayed unto the Lord, yea, even with all his heart, in behalf of his people. And it came to pass as he prayed unto the Lord, there came a pillar of fire and dwelt upon a rock before him; and he saw and heard much. (1 Nephi 1:4–6)

Some of the examples are far less dramatic:

> And it came to pass that I, Nephi, being exceedingly young, nevertheless being large in stature, and also having great desires to know of the mysteries of God, wherefore, I did cry unto the Lord; and behold he did visit me, and did soften my heart that I did believe all the words which had been spoken by my father. (1 Nephi 2:16)

These experiences provide one bookend in the Book of Mormon, and Moroni's distillation of a general procedure provides the other. Still other examples of the same process are found in its pages. Before Moroni states the general principle, it is illustrated by many stories showing a range of applications.

Stories not only demonstrate the application of principles, they help make them memorable. For years a Stanford university professor gave his classes an unusual assignment. First he gave the class a set of government statistics on crime patterns in the United States. Then he assigned half of the students to give the class a one-minute speech arguing that nonviolent crime is a problem and the other half were assigned to give a speech arguing that it is not. Immediately after the speech the listeners then rated each speaker. "What happens, invariably, is that the most polished speakers get the highest ratings. Students who are poised, smooth, and charismatic are rated at the top of the class." The exercise appears to be over, and the professor then plays a short video. Then abruptly, he asks the students to pull out a piece of paper and list every idea they remember from each speaker they had heard just ten minutes before. "The students are flabbergasted at how little they remember . . . [and] are lucky to recall one or two ideas from each speaker's presentation. Many draw a complete blank on some speeches—unable to remember a single concept." During presentations, students typically use 2.5 statistics in one minute; only one in ten students tells a story. But "when students are asked to recall the speeches, 63 percent remember the stories. Only 5 percent remember any individual statistic." And this is only about ten minutes later. No correlation appears between the speaker's talent as a public speaker and how memorable their message is: "A community college student for whom English is a second language could easily out-perform unwitting Stanford graduate students." Because "public speakers naturally want to appear composed, charismatic, and motivational," they have a "tendency to focus on the presentation rather than on the message."[81]

> **Stories not only demonstrate the application of principles, they help make them memorable.**

There is nothing wrong with wanting our presentations to be polished, but this should not come at the expense of the message. The content is more important than the presentation. As Elder Maxwell taught: "We should judge the warnings given to us by their accuracy and relevancy, not by the finesse or the diplomacy by which the warnings are given. The disciple's commitment to truth must be to truth, without an inordinate concern for the method of delivery. Of course, it takes real humility to listen under some circumstances. The Paul Reveres in our lives may have voices too shrill, use bad grammar, ride a poor horse, and may pick the oddest hours to warn us. But the test of warnings is their accuracy, not their diplomacy."[82] Stories, however, can put the plumber on par with the professor.

The stories we tell, however, should be true. Otherwise, we are doing theology in Plato's sense: telling lies about divine things to manipulate others. That is probably the worst possible way to do theology.

Reproof

Much has been said about the importance of listening. But demonstrating love requires more than just listening. We may listen, but we need to warn as well. Elder Neal A. Maxwell, who served for many years as dean of students at the University of Utah, reflected on his experiences dealing with troubled youth:

> A few dealings with student dissenters taught me (too late to help them, I'm sorry to say) that my silent disgust did not necessarily teach them. It often created distance. Unexplained indignation is not always communication. True, silence in some circumstances is a powerful reprover, but not in other situations. To withhold deserved reproof, and the reasons therefore, may be to withhold a warning that is urgently needed. Reproof is often a last railing before an erring individual goes over the edge of the cliff.[83]

Elder Maxwell points out that reasons need to be given for reproof along with the reproof itself. The Doctrine and Covenants points out that no power or influence can or ought to be maintained by virtue of one's position but that persuasion needs to be used (Doctrine and Covenants 121:41). That is, just because someone is a father or a mother or a bishop or a stake president or an administrator does not mean that one can insist on having one's own way just because one says so. One needs to "be ready always to give an answer to every man that asketh you a reason of the hope that is in you" (1 Peter 3:15). While that may not mean that the individual will accept that reproof, we have put forth the arguments for the reproof in a reasoned fashion. Elder Maxwell observed that "one of our needs in Church leadership is to legitimatize the necessity of giving specific reproof and commendation."[84]

In 1987 Elder Maxwell observed the following about "reproving betimes with sharpness" (Doctrine and Covenants 121:43):

> There are, for instance, a number of words in the scriptures that we assume we know the meaning of, but in our casualness we fail to search them. One such word occurs in the revelation given to the Prophet Joseph Smith in Liberty Jail. It declares that true leadership requires "reproving *betimes* with sharpness, when moved upon by the Holy Ghost; and then showing forth afterwards an increase of love toward him whom thou hast reproved, lest he esteem thee to be his enemy." Most of us casually assume the word betimes means "from time to time," or occasionally. Betimes actually means "early on."
>
> If we both identify a need early and are moved upon by the Holy Ghost to act before pride has hardened our attitudes, we have a greater likelihood of success. Our effectiveness in working with others depends not only upon our meekness but also upon theirs, and mutual meekness is more apt to be present "early on" rather than later.[85]

His observation about *betimes* meaning "early" is an observation he made on multiple occasions. The word *betimes* is not the only word that has changed meaning. In Joseph Smith's day *sharp* could mean "with keen perception; exactly; minutely." Reproving with sharpness thus meant reproving with exactness and keen perception, not necessarily severely. As Elder Maxwell also observed,

> If we seek to administer reproof properly, we must also be willing to listen and to respond after we have issued our reproof. The receiver will often need some time to test the accuracy of our reproof and the implications of that reproof. He needs to reassure himself that

we care for him, that he is still safely within our circle of concern. Thus even when we give deserved specific criticism in the spirit of love we must be willing to take added time, if necessary, to do some "maintenance" work, another reason why timing and setting are so crucial at times in the administration of reproof.[86]

He illustrated the concept with examples: "Joseph Smith knew what it was to be corrected by the Lord (see D&C 10:1–3). So did Oliver Cowdery (see D&C 9:7). Their reproofs were not vague but very specific: the Prophet Joseph Smith's for not following original instructions concerning the Book of Mormon manuscript, and Oliver Cowdery's for not continuing as he had commenced and for thinking he merely needed to ask for revelations without making intellectual effort."[87]

> **Reproof should be early, specific, inspired, and accompanied by credible reassurances of love.**

One of Elder Maxwell's concerns was the second part of the verse:

In the 121st Section of the Doctrine and Covenants we are all given clear instructions in this regard. When we are reproving betimes with sharpness, clearly he who is the reproof-giver has the responsibility to demonstrate an increase in the love shown for him who has been reproved. So many times as leaders we give out criticism without providing even the basic reassurances, to say nothing of the need to give added assurances. Those we seek to lead will venture more in testing and developing their strengths and skills, if the climate we provide is one in which our love and trust is clear, and the risks of their losing our love are low.[88]

Elder Maxwell also took note of the motivation for the reproof: "But sharp reproof should come as a matter of inspiration, not to meet an ego need which requires putting someone else in his place!"[89]

For Elder Maxwell, Doctrine and Covenants 121:43 means that reproof should be early, specific, inspired, and accompanied by credible reassurances of love. It is this form of reproof that can serve as a guardrail, preventing the plunge over the cliff.

Rescue of the Lost Lamb, by Minerva K. Teichert. President Howard W. Hunter said, "The Lord, our Good Shepherd, expects us to be his undershepherds and recover those who are lost." Courtesy of churchofjesuschrist.org.

IF THEY LEAVE, WHAT THEN?

For many, prevention is too late. They have already lost their faith. What does one do in that case? How do they regain faith? Unfortunately, this is an area with little good research. The NSYR provides some elements of hope after faith has been lost.

The first thing to realize is that unbelief is the least stable of intellectual positions.[90] Another reason for hope is that the home environment in which children grow up has a greater effect on youth and young adults than any other influence—even peers. (Of course, if the home environment has not been faithful, this is cold comfort.)

President Howard W. Hunter addressed this issue: "The Lord, our Good Shepherd, expects us to be his undershepherds and recover those who are lost. *We can't tell you how to do it*, but as you become involved and seek inspiration, success will result from efforts in your areas, . . . stakes, and wards."[91]

Going back to A. E. Housman's analogy that a dog hunting fleas using statistical methods would never find any, in this case we are looking for individual fleas, and individuals have to be dealt with as individuals; masses can be handled by statistics, but not individuals. As Elder Maxwell noted, "This work of reactivation often involves group study and socials, but, essentially, it is done a soul at a time, quietly and with dignity. It is done less 'by the numbers' and more 'by the Spirit.' It is less technique than genuine caring, more extending a helping hand than writing new handbooks."[92]

Very little social science work has been done on the processes for reclaiming the lost. This is another unfortunate example of the observation that "the current research agenda in the field of religion is at best uneven and at worst distorted."[93] The work that has been done holds some interest. We know, for example, among those who lose their faith in their teens or early twenties, that "the mean age of return to religion among apostates is around 28."[94] Nationally, over time, we see the following general pattern among all religions (given as percentages, numbers do not add up due to rounding errors).[95]

TABLE 8.1. COMPARATIVE FREQUENCY OF CHURCH ATTENDANCE AS TEENAGERS AND AS YOUNG ADULTS

	Attendance in late twenties (%)		
Attendance as adolescent	Weekly	1–3 times/month	Nonattending
Weekly	27.2	25.5	47.5
1–3 times per month	14.2	23.0	62.9

Those who attended church on a weekly basis as adolescents were significantly more likely to attend church in their late twenties. A small drop in consistency of attendance as a youth made a big increase in the likelihood of not attending as an adult. What this data hides is that about half of those who attended weekly as adolescents and in their late twenties went through a period in which they attended either less frequently or not at all. So a period of inactivity is not unusual. I remember being surprised to hear a friend, whom I had always viewed as steady and stalwart, recount how she had gone through a period of inactivity in her youth.

Although "overall levels of religious return are not high in absolute terms,"[96] as individuals marry and begin to have children, some return.[97] "Marrying a religious spouse often leads nonreligious individuals to increase their participation,"[98] but the reverse can also be true. Marrying in the faith with someone of similar religious attitudes and commitments "promotes a greater degree of marital happiness and more stable and satisfying marriages."[99]

Who is most likely to return? This is not necessarily predictable.[100] Those who believe there is only one true religion are more likely to convert,[101] and the same would apply to those returning. Noteworthy among the findings on conversion is the emphasis on choice.[102] What Latter-day Saints call agency plays a tremendous role in conversion and reconversion.

Because the conversion experience is, in the long term, a positive experience, we expect that it will be a positive experience all the way through. "Modern theorizing about spirituality has focused mostly on positive aspects of spirituality such as contentedness and gratitude, to the relative exclusion of negatively valenced emotions. Nevertheless, . . . emotions such as anxiety, sadness, and pain are central to religious and spiritual experiences"—including conversion.[103]

> "Nevertheless, God will be merciful unto many; and our children shall be restored, that they may come to that which will give them the true knowledge of their Redeemer" (2 Nephi 10:2).

In longitudinal studies of conversion, factors associated with both preserving religion and conversion are communication with parents, trusting parents, and social competence.[104] The causal directions of these correlations are ambiguous. Does communication between parents and children facilitate conversion of the children to their parents' religion, or are children who apostatize from their parents' religion more likely to cut off communication, or perhaps some of both? It is best at this point simply to note the correlation without specifying the causation. Looking more closely at the correlation between youth who convert to their parents' religion (as opposed to those who apostatize from it), one can look at the causation in one of two ways: either the youth convert to their parents' religion because they can trust them, or conversion to their parents' religion causes youth to trust their parents more. On the chance that the former is the case, it is important to know how we can regain our youth's trust. Trust is regained by living lives of character (or integrity) and competence. If we want to regain trust, we need to make our lives conform more to the values and principles that we espouse and increase our competence in doing so.[105] If parental trust factors into bringing children back to the Church and parents want to bring their children back, then parents need to live in harmony with the teachings of the Church and not excuse their children's behavior or attitudes that pull them away from living the teachings of the Church. The faithfulness of family and friends who surround them seems to have a positive influence on those who have lost faith and inclines them more toward belief.[106]

Nephi, having previously watched his brothers leave the faith of his fathers, learned with sorrow that eventually all of his descendants would fall away. "O the pain, and the anguish of my soul," he writes. "For I, Nephi, have seen it, and it well nigh consumeth me" (2 Nephi 26:7). He recalls, "I was overcome because of my afflictions, for I considered that mine afflictions were great above all, because of the destruction of my people, for I had beheld their fall" (1 Nephi 15:5). His brother Jacob, however, still held out hope: "as it has been shown unto me that many of our children shall perish in the flesh because of unbelief, nevertheless, God will be merciful unto many; and our children shall be restored, that they may come to that which will give them the true knowledge of their Redeemer" (2 Nephi 10:2).

The good news is that wayward children can repent and return; however, prevention has better results.

NOTES

1.   Mark D. Regnerus and Jeremy E. Uecker, "Finding Faith, Losing Faith: The Prevalence and Context of Religious Transformations during Adolescence," *Review of Religious Research* 47, no. 3 (2006): 231–32.

2. Regnerus and Uecker, "Finding Faith, Losing Faith," 231. Some factors, such as obesity, play no role whatsoever. Lee Ellis and David Biglione, "Religiosity and Obesity: Are Overweight People More Religious?," *Personality and Individual Differences* 28, no. 6 (2000): 1119–23.

3. Christian Smith and Patricia Snell, *Souls in Transition: The Religious and Spiritual Lives of Emerging Adults* (Oxford: Oxford University Press, 2009), 215, 218, 259.

4. Based on Smith and Snell, *Souls in Transition*, 116.

5. Smith and Snell, *Souls in Transition*, 304.

6. The lower figure includes the "regular," who are still attending church a few times a month and are otherwise slightly less valiant (Doctrine and Covenants 76:79) than the "devoted" (Smith and Snell, *Souls in Transition*, 259, 304).

7. Sam A. Hardy, Michael A. Steelman, Sarah Coyne, and Robert D. Ridge, "Adolescent Religiousness as a Protective Factor against Pornography Use," *Journal of Applied Developmental Psychology* 34, no. 3 (2013): 137.

8. Carol Markstrom-Adams, Greta Hofstra, and Kirk Dougher, "The Ego-Virtue of Fidelity: A Case for the Study of Religion and Identity Formation in Adolescence," *Journal of Youth and Adolescence* 23, no. 4 (1994): 467.

9. Ezra Taft Benson, "To the 'Youth of the Noble Birthright,'" *Ensign*, May 1986, 43–45; see Benson, "To the Young Women of the Church," *Ensign*, November 1986, 81–83.

10. Markstrom-Adams, Hofstra, and Dougher, "Ego-Virtue of Fidelity," 466.

11. Ying Chen and Tyler J. VanderWeele, "Associations of Religious Upbringing with Subsequent Health and Well-Being from Adolescence to Young Adulthood: An Outcome-Wide Analysis," *American Journal of Epidemiology* 187, no. 11 (2018): 2357.

12. *Relationships in America Survey* (Austin: The Austin Institute for the Study of Family and Culture, 2014), 14–15.

13. Brandon C. Martinez, "Is Evil Good for Religion? The Link between Supernatural Evil and Religious Commitment," *Review of Religious Research* 55, no. 2 (2013): 321.

14. Martinez, "Is Evil Good for Religion?," 333; *Relationships in America Survey*, 12.

15. R. David Hayward and Neal Krause, "Changes in Religious Group Affiliation during Older Adulthood: Evidence from an 11-Year Longitudinal Study," *Review of Religious Research* 56, no. 4 (2014): 552.

16. *Relationships in America Survey*, 7–8.

17. Baylor Religion Survey wave 4 data, data courtesy of Association of Religion Data Archives.

18. *Relationships in America Survey*, 9.

19. *Relationships in America Survey*, 9.

20. NSYR wave 1 data.

21. NSYR wave 3 data.

22. NSYR wave 3 data.

23. R. David Hayward and Neal Krause, "Patterns of Change in Prayer Activity, Expectancies, and Contents during Older Adulthood," *Journal of the Scientific Study of Religion* 52, no. 1 (2013): 24.

24. Jeremy E. Uecker and Christopher G. Ellison, "Parental Divorce, Parental Religious Characteristics, and Religious Outcomes in Adulthood," *Journal of the Scientific Study of Religion* 51, no. 4 (2012): 789.

25. Hayward and Krause, "Patterns of Change in Prayer Activity," 19.

26. Hayward and Krause, "Patterns of Change in Prayer Activity," 24–25.

27. Chen and VanderWeele, "Associations of Religious Upbringing," 3–6.

28. Frank D. Fincham, Steven R. H. Beach, N. Lambert, T. Stillman, and S. Braithwaite, "Spiritual Behaviors and Relationship Satisfaction: A Critical Analysis of the Role of Prayer," *Journal of Social and Clinical Psychology* 27, no. 4 (2008): 362–88.

29. Luke 18:1; 21:36; Acts 10:2; Ephesians 6:18; Colossians 1:3; 4:12; 1 Thessalonians 1:2, 11; Philemon 1:4; 2 Nephi 32:9; 3 Nephi 18:15, 18–19, 21; Moroni 8:3; Doctrine and Covenants 10:5; 32:4; 33:17; 61:39; 75:11; 81:3; 88:126; 90:24; 93:49–50.

30. Doctrine and Covenants 19:38; 32:4; 88:126; 10:5; 75:11; 90:24; 20:33 (3 Nephi 18:15, 18); 31:12 and 61:39; 93:49; 10:5; and 93:50.

31. NSYR wave 1 data.

32. NSYR wave 3 data.

33. Baylor Religion Survey wave 4 data.

34. Martinez, "Is Evil Good for Religion?," 321: "Biblical literalism is a frequently used measure of religious beliefs that has proven to be predictive of religious commitment."

35. NSYR wave 1 data.

36. NSYR wave 3 data.

37. Baylor Religion Survey wave 4 data.

38. Emily Sigalow, Michelle Shain, and Meredith Bergey, "Religion and Decisions about Marriage, Residence, Occupation, and Children," *Journal for the Scientific Study of Religion* 51, no. 2 (2012): 312-13.

39. Chen and VanderWeele, "Associations of Religious Upbringing," 9.

40. Wilford W. Andersen, "The Music of the Gospel," *Ensign*, May 2015, 54.

41. Michael R. Woodford, Denise Levy, and N. Eugene Walls, "Sexual Prejudice among Christian College Students, Denominational Teachings, and Personal Religious Beliefs," *Review of Religious Research* 55, no. 1 (2013): 122-24.

42. Bruce C. Hafen, *A Disciple's Life* (Salt Lake City: Deseret Book, 2002), 169-70.

43. Neal A. Maxwell, "A Brother Offended," *Ensign*, May 1982, 37.

44. Christian Smith, Kyle Longest, Jonathan Hill, and Kari Christoffersen, *Young Catholic America: Emerging Adults In, Out of, and Gone from the Church* (Oxford: Oxford University Press, 2014), 262.

45. Smith et al., *Young Catholic America*, 262.

46. Plato, *Republic* II.

47. Louis Midgley, "Theology," in *Encyclopedia of Mormonism*, ed. Daniel H. Ludlow (New York: Macmillan, 1992), 4:1475.

48. Midgley, "Theology," 1475.

49. Carl Olson, *The Allure of Decadent Thinking: Religious Studies and the Challenge of Postmodernism* (Oxford: Oxford University Press, 2013), 144; Walter H. Capps, "Religious Studies and Creative Reflection," *Soundings: An Interdisciplinary Journal* 71, nos. 2-3 (1988): 373-74.

50. James T. Burtchaell, *The Dying of the Light: The Disengagement of Colleges and Universities from Their Christian Churches* (Grand Rapids, MI: Eerdmans, 1998), 534.

51. Olson, *Allure of Decadent Thinking*, 6-7.

52. Olson, *Allure of Decadent Thinking*, 9.

53. Burtchaell, *Dying of the Light*, 494.

54. Joseph Bulbulia and Edward Slingerland, "Religious Studies as a Life Science," *Numen: International Review for the History of Religions* 59, nos. 5-6 (2012): 567.

55. Bulbulia and Slingerland, "Religious Studies as a Life Science," 569.

56. Bulbulia and Slingerland, "Religious Studies as a Life Science," 569; Olson, *Allure of Decadent Thinking*, 3–4; Herman te Velde, "The History of the Study of Ancient Egyptian Religion and Its Future," in *Egyptology at the Dawn of the Twenty-First Century*, ed. Zahi Hawass and Lyla Pinch Brock (Cairo: The American University in Cairo Press, 2003), 2:43–44; Robert N. McCauley, *Why Religion Is Natural and Science Is Not* (Oxford: Oxford University Press, 2011), 145–221.

57. Se-Woong Koo, "Death of the Humanities," Inside Higher Ed, http://www.insidehighered.com/views/2013/10/21/essay-real-death-humanities.

58. Olson, *Allure of Decadent Thinking*, 3.

59. David Frankfurter, "The Satanic Ritual Abuse Panic as Religious-Studies Data," *Numen: International Review for the History of Religions* 50, no. 1 (2003): 111–12.

60. Olson, *Allure of Decadent Thinking*, 6, 15.

61. Frankfurter, "Satanic Ritual Abuse Panic," 111.

62. Olson, *Allure of Decadent Thinking*, 81, 131.

63. te Velde, "Ancient Egyptian Religion," 2:43.

64. Bulbulia and Slingerland, "Religious Studies as a Life Science," 570–71.

65. Olson, *Allure of Decadent Thinking*, 80.

66. Frankfurter, "Satanic Ritual Abuse Panic," 111–12.

67. Olson, *Allure of Decadent Thinking*, 80.

68. Burtchaell, *Dying of the Light*, 483.

69. Olson, *Allure of Decadent Thinking*, 146.

70. Craig L. Blomberg, *Can We Still Believe the Bible? An Evangelical Engagement with Contemporary Questions* (Grand Rapids, MI: Brazos, 2014), 240n79, says, "One of the true scandals of the modern academy, apparently almost entirely unaddressed in the guild, involves the number of instructors in religious studies promoting, in their classes, Dan Brown's wholly fictitious claims about what took place at Nicaea as if they were actually based on historical fact. Yet in the past decade, one of the most recurring questions I have been asked by students on university campuses where I have spoken is how the Council of Nicaea determined the NT canon. When I explain that this wasn't what Nicaea was about, they stare in disbelief or reply that one of their professors taught them that it was."

71. Olson, *Allure of Decadent Thinking*, 148.

72. Olson, *Allure of Decadent Thinking*, 133.

73. Burtchaell, *Dying of the Light*, 482–83, 494–95.

74. McCauley, *Why Religion Is Natural and Science Is Not*, 212.

75. Chip Heath and Dan Heath, *Made to Stick: Why Some Ideas Survive and Others Die* (New York: Random House, 2007), 205–6.

76. Heath and Heath, *Made to Stick*, 237.

77. Olson, *Allure of Decadent Thinking*, 139.

78. Heath and Heath, *Made to Stick*, 237.

79. Heath and Heath, *Made to Stick*, 206.

80. Arthur C. Brooks, *Love Your Enemies: How Decent People Can Save America from Our Culture of Contempt* (New York: Broadside Books, 2019), 140.

81. Heath and Heath, *Made to Stick*, 244.

82. Neal A. Maxwell, *Wherefore, Ye Must Press Forward* (Salt Lake City: Deseret Book, 1977), chapter 4.

83. Neal A. Maxwell, "Insights from My Life," in *The Inexhaustible Gospel* (Provo, UT: Brigham Young University Press, 2004), 43.

84. Neal A. Maxwell, *A More Excellent Way: Essays on Leadership for Latter-day Saints* (Salt Lake City: Deseret Book, 1967), 90.

85. Neal A. Maxwell, *Meek and Lowly* (Salt Lake City: Deseret Book, 1987), 40.

86. Maxwell, *More Excellent Way*, 94.

87. Neal A. Maxwell, *A Wonderful Flood of Light* (Salt Lake City: Bookcraft, 1990), 113.

88. Maxwell, *More Excellent Way*, 40.

89. Neal A. Maxwell, *A Time to Choose* (Salt Lake City: Deseret Book, 1975), 78.

90. Lisa D. Pearce and Melinda Lunquist Denton, *A Faith of Their Own* (Oxford: Oxford University Press, 2011), 101.

91. *Teachings of the Presidents of the Church: Howard W. Hunter* (Salt Lake City: The Church of Jesus Christ of Latter-day Saints, 2015), 171–72; emphasis added.

92. Neal A. Maxwell, "A Brother Offended," *Ensign*, May 1982, 37.

93. Grace Davie, "Thinking Sociologically about Religion: Implications for Faith Communities," *Review of Religious Research* 54, no. 3 (2012): 281.

94. Jeremy E. Uecker, Damon Mayrl, and Samuel Stroope, "Family Formation and Returning to Institutional Religion in Young Adulthood," *Journal of the Scientific Study of Religion* 55, no. 2 (2016): 388.

95. Adapted from Uecker, Mayrl, and Stroope, "Family Formation and Returning to Institutional Religion," 393.

96. Uecker, Mayrl, and Stroope, "Family Formation and Returning to Institutional Religion," 386.

97. Jeremy E. Uecker, Mark D. Regnerus, and Margaret L. Vaaler, "Losing My Religion: The Social Sources of Religious Decline in Early Adult Years," *Social Sources* 85, no. 4 (2007): 1678–81.

98. Uecker, Mayrl, and Stroope, "Family Formation and Returning to Institutional Religion," 386.

99. Sigalow, Shain, and Bergey, "Religion and Decisions," 306.

100. C. Harry Hui, Sing-Hang Cheung, Jasmine Lam, Esther Yuet Ying Lau, Livia Yuliawati, and Shu-Fai Cheung, "In Search of the Psychological Antecedents and Consequences of Christian Conversion: A Three-Year Prospective Study," *Psychology of Religion and Spirituality* 9, no. 2 (2017): 226.

101. Hui et al., "Psychological Antecedents and Consequences," 226–27. There are some who claim that believing in one true religion is a bad thing for society; for example, Jean-Marc Ferry, "Conviction religieuse et responsabilité politique: La question d'une implication des religions dans nos espaces publics," *Philosophie et religion* 169 (2015): 118.

102. Gregory S. Longo and Jungmeen Kim-Spoon, "What Drives Apostates and Converters? The Social and Familial Antecedents of Religious Change among Adolescents," *Psychology of Religion and Spirituality* 6, no. 4 (2014): 285.

103. Adam B. Cohen, June Gruber, and Dacher Keltner, "Comparing Spiritual Transformations and Experiences of Profound Beauty," *Psychology of Religion and Spirituality* 2, no. 3 (2010): 134.

104. Longo and Kim-Spoon, "What Drives Apostates and Converters?," 288–89.

105. Steven M. R. Covey and Rebecca R. Merrill, *The Speed of Trust: The One Thing That Changes Everything* (New York City: Free Press, 2006), 303, 310–11.

106. Tim Clydesdale and Kathleen Garces-Foley, *The Twenty-something Soul: Understanding the Religious and Secular Lives of American Young Adults* (Oxford: Oxford University Press, 2019), 151–54.

Youth leave the Church or stay in it because of personal choices, but there are things that others do that can influence those choices. Courtesy of Pexels/Pixabay.

9 | THE MOST IMPORTANT WORK

Every youth who leaves the Church or stays in it does so because of personal choices, but there are things that others do that can influence those choices in subtle and perhaps unexpected ways. "Few teen problems in fact are invented or promoted by teenagers. Most are prevalent in and developed, modeled, and handed down to teens by the adult world."[1] Not all adults in the world, however, have equal footing with others. The NSYR concluded that "parents have an important influence on the shape of their teenager's religious lives. Teens are more likely to be religiously devoted—as measured by this conglomeration of variables—who have more highly religious parents, who have positive and loving relationships with their parents, and whose parents are married."[2] Another researcher stated it more bluntly: "The greatest predictor of the religious lives of youth is the religious lives of their parents."[3]

Elder Neal A. Maxwell once asked:

> When the real history of mankind is fully disclosed, will it feature the echoes of gunfire or the shaping sound of lullabies? The great armistices made by military men or the peacemaking of women in homes and in neighborhoods? Will what happened in cradles and kitchens prove to be more controlling than what happened in congresses? When the surf of the centuries has made the great pyramids so much sand, the everlasting family will still be standing, because it is a celestial institution, formed outside telestial time.[4]

The influence of the family and family patterns over and above official dogma was illustrated in a surprising fashion, using a seemingly innocuous and obscure phenomenon in Arabic grammar. Two researchers reported on this phenomenon. In classical Arabic grammar, nonhuman plurals are treated as feminine grammatical singulars, even in the pronouns referring back to them. In earliest Arabic that was not always the case. A thousand years ago, classical Arab grammarians (who were not native speakers of the language) decreed it should always be the case. Classical Arab authors dutifully followed the dogmas of the nonnative grammarians. The native speakers, however, followed their parents and over a millennium later still follow patterns of speech that mirror the oldest Arabic texts in spite of the dictates of the official grammatical rules.[5] The shaping sounds of lullabies wins, and there are ways of helping the shaping become more effective.

THE TYPE OF FAMILY

One of the biggest ways that parents can shape their children is by the type of family they create. Simply, the basic structure of the family can have a great deal of impact on the religiosity of youth. One researcher used the National Study of Youth and Religion to study the effects of family structure on youth religiosity.[6]

In his first hypothesis test, he found that the most significant positive impact on the religiosity of youth was parental religiosity (1.10). The second most significant positive impact was if their parent was a Latter-day Saint (0.64). The third most positive impact was if their

The most significant positive impact on the religiosity of youth was parental religiosity. Courtesy of churchofjesuschrist.org.

parent was a conservative Protestant (0.61). The most negative impacts were if the parents were cohabiting, that is living together without being married (-0.39), if the parent was single without ever being married (-0.35), or if the parents owned their own home (-0.34).[7] No attempt was made to explain how owning one's own home has a negative impact on the religiosity of youth.

In another hypothesis test, the researcher found that besides parental religiosity, the most important things were "family religious practices" (0.84), which meant: "Youth are considered to engage in religious practices with their family if they had prayed together with their family in the past year and talked with their family about religious things at least once a week."[8] In a context for families belonging to The Church of Jesus Christ of Latter-day Saints, that would include family prayer, family scripture study, and family home evening. Note that the bar was set pretty low: yearly instead of daily family prayer and talking about religious things once a week, but these turned out to be the most significant factors.

The researcher also tested for religious salience, that is, how important religion is for the youth.[9] The most important positive factors were parental religiosity (0.61), if the parent is a conservative Protestant (0.48), and if the parent is a Latter-day Saint (0.46). The three most detrimental elements were having a single parent who had never married (-0.24), living in a stepfamily (-0.20), and having a child who is a different race from their parent (-0.17).

When this researcher tested for factors that make youth feel close to God, the most important thing was family religious practices (0.36), while the most detrimental aspect was divorce (-0.28).

Here are some of this researcher's conclusions: Unsurprisingly, "parental religiosity was a strong predictor of youth religiosity; youth were less likely to be religious when raised by parents with low levels of religiosity and vice versa." We will return to this point later. The influence of family structure is more indirect, and other things can help to compensate for a less than ideal family structure. "Overall, religious transmission in nontraditional families appears to be less effective for religious participation and religious salience among youth, and these differences are most pronounced at higher levels of parental religiosity. That is, youth raised in nontraditional families with highly religious parents have lower levels of religious participation and religious salience than those raised by highly religious married parents." The more religious the parents, the more important family structure is. "Consistency in religious affiliation among family members and engaging in religious behavior as a family are important in predicting youth religiosity."[10] This harks back to "The Family: A Proclamation to the World": "Children are entitled to birth within the bonds of matrimony, and to be reared by a father and a mother who honor marital vows with complete fidelity. Happiness in family life is most likely to be achieved when founded upon the teachings of the Lord Jesus Christ."[11]

But other factors influence the outcomes as well. "Those with religiously heterogeneous or less religious parents are known to be less religious themselves and more prone to religious switching or disaffiliation."[12] "Adults who had parents with different religions altogether, one unaffiliated parent, and two unaffiliated parents have much higher odds of disaffiliation than those with two parents who had the same religious affiliation."[13] This is simply another way of stating an old Egyptian proverb: "Don't marry a woman who is apostate, lest she give an apostate testimony to your children."[14] The same would apply if the genders were reversed.

> A few other family dynamics occurring when children are young later affect their religiosity as adults.

Parents who want to keep their children in the faith should be mindful of the following considerations:

- set a positive example by participating yourself[15]
- attend Church[16]
- be married to your spouse and stay married[17]
- have harmony in your marriage[18]
- hold family prayer and pray daily for your children[19]
- hold family home evening[20]
- teach your children chastity (sexual abstinence) rather than sexual safety[21]

None of this is particularly new to Latter-day Saints.

Another study noted a few other family dynamics occurring when children are young that later affect their religiosity as adults: "Children raised in acrimonious households are less likely to carry on with their parents' faith. Changing religions is more likely when the quality of the relationship between children and parents is poor. Similarly, [some researchers suggest] that people who spend less time with relatives are more likely to switch religions."[22]

Where do families come into this? "Families where parents are high in religiosity seem to foster in adolescent children a rapid growth in religious salience and (especially) attendance, as well as to prevent rapid loss of either form of religiosity. . . . Family structure plays a more powerful role in rapid religious decline than in growth: youth in single-parent families appear much more likely to exhibit considerable decline in either type of religiosity when compared with adolescents in biologically intact, two-parent households. Adolescents in alternate family structures . . . are similarly more likely to display a considerable decline in church attendance."[23]

Two points for families come out of this research:

> Intact, two-parent families as well as step-families tend to provide religious stability for adolescents. [Other researchers] previously identified parental divorce as a predictor of apostasy or switching. . . . Adolescents living in a single parent family or in another family structure . . . appear to be at a higher risk of experiencing considerable religious decline.
>
> Finally, parents influence adolescent religious change through the quality of the parent-child relationship. Higher levels of family satisfaction boost the odds of a sharp increase in attendance and salience.[24]

Coming from a loving family also provides its own form of protection. "Even blue [politically liberal], irreligious respondents who've had the security of an intact family seem to fare much better in their relationships. They delay first sex longer, and they choose partners and a mate more wisely than do emerging adults who've experienced breakdown within their nuclear family unit."[25]

INVOLVEMENT

Parents make a difference by becoming involved in their children's lives. "Parents who attend religious services weekly are more likely to monitor whom their children associate with and to expect their children not to drink alcohol."[26] "Parents who attend religious services weekly are more likely to establish rules about which television shows can be viewed and to impose higher expectations about sexual morality," but this effect is moderated by orthodoxy: "orthodox parents . . . are more likely to keep a close eye on what TV shows/movies their

Parents need to be active not just in their children's lives, but in their church as well. Courtesy of churchofjesuschrist.org.

adolescent children are watching and to impose higher expectations about sexual morality. Conversely, progressive parents . . . are more lenient about sexual morality and what TV shows/movies their children watch."[27] This becomes important because the media that youth consume can change them. "Viewing R-rated movies is associated with an increased risk of using marijuana, and doubles the risk of smoking. Teens who watch more than three R-rated movies per month are five times more likely to drink alcohol compared to teens who do not watch R-rated movies. Other forms of media, such as violent video games, have been tied to drinking and drug use."[28] This is not to say that watching an R-rated movie will cause individuals to become drug addicts, but that frequent viewing increases the likelihood that that behavior will be seen as acceptable and then imitated. One study on the "frequency of media use on church attendance and salience of religious faith . . . showed that violent video games and pornography have direct and indirect effects on religious faith, often by affecting the internalization of prosocial values."[29] An NSYR study of the effects of viewing R-rated movies on faith showed that while frequently viewing R-rated movies decreased both church attendance and the importance of faith in a youth's life, "parental monitoring of media acted as a protective factor" in preserving the importance of faith in the youth and their attendance at church.[30]

Parents are more likely to monitor their children if they tend to be more orthodox in their beliefs. "When it comes to rules about bedtimes and normative controls related to skipping school, what mattered for parents was not how often they went to church, but where they went to church." The researchers warn, however, that the causation might be reversed: "more family-oriented parents could be attracted to religious institutions in general and religious orthodoxy in particular."[31]

"The transmission [of religiosity between generations] is strongest when there is a warm and positive parent-child relationship, when the child was raised by both biological parents, and if parents agree in their religiosity."[32]

Parents need to be active not just in their children's lives, but in their church as well. "The religious attendance of parents (individually) and couples (together) generally has a positive effect on child development. When measured as parents' worship service attendance . . . religion is good for kids."[33] But these effects, based on a large longitudinal study of children, are seen when parents are of the same religion and are both active in that religion: "Put differently, it is not simply generic homogamy (couple similarity regardless of religiosity) but rather the amount of religion (e.g., stocks of "religious capital") that a couple can jointly import into the family that bolsters child outcomes, particularly for child performance outside the home. In many of the developmental domains featured here, the children who are doing the best are in households where both parents attend worship services frequently."[34] Yet it is precisely parents who are active in their church lives who tend to be active in their children's lives: "Parents who attend religious services more often, believe in the full inspiration of their sacred text, and were highly influenced by religion in their childbearing decision all talk or read with their children more frequently about religion."[35]

In particular, parents need to practice religion, not just preach it: "The religiosity of parents must go beyond verbal assent to certain beliefs, but rather must be lived out on a consistent basis." Research has shown that "religious socialization more effectively takes place when parent–child relationships are stronger, and parents are not only vocal about their religious convictions, but are faithfully living those out in front of children."[36] Thus it is not surprising that consumption of pornography, particularly by fathers, interferes with passing on the faith to the next generation, in part because even if the behavior is clandestine, it is still behavior that goes against the faith that the parents

Simple things like eating together can make a big difference. Courtesy of churchofjesuschrist.org.

are trying to transmit to their children. Pornography consumption not only lessens the amount of time fathers spend socializing their children in religion, but it also negates any advantages that other behaviors like family prayer, family scripture study, and gospel discussion might bring.[37]

MAKING TIME

The NSYR observed that many facets of modern American life work against the family and its influence:

> Most of the structures and routines of American life actually pull families apart regularly and effectively. American work and education practices separate family members for most daytime hours of every weekday. Day care centers and preschools remove children from their parents at a very young age. After school, many parents, middle-class parents particularly, schedule their children's lives with so many programmed activities that they find themselves

with very little unstructured time simply to spend together as families. A minority of American families with teenagers eat most of their dinner meals together. . . . Contrary to our pro-family rhetoric, an alien anthropologist might have good reason to conclude that members of American families actually have little interest in spending time together.[38]

Simple things like eating together can make a big difference. One can talk about quality time versus quantity time, but sometimes talk about quality time can be merely an excuse for not having quantity time. The chances of quality time occurring increase with the amount of time spent. Elder Dallin H. Oaks explains:

> In choosing how we spend time as a family, we should be careful not to exhaust our available time on things that are merely good and leave little time for that which is better or best. A friend took his young family on a series of summer vacation trips, including visits to memorable historic sites. At the end of the summer he asked his teenage son which of these good summer activities he enjoyed most. The father learned from the reply, and so did those he told of it. "The thing I liked best this summer," the boy replied, "was the night you and I laid on the lawn and looked at the stars and talked." Super family activities may be good for children, but they are not always better than one-on-one time with a loving parent.[39]

THE PARENTAL ROLE IN THE LOSS OF FAITH IN YOUTH

Ultimately, children have their agency and make their own decisions about whether to keep their faith, dwindle in unbelief, or rebel. However, parents can unintentionally contribute to the loss of faith in youth.

The NSYR used qualitative comparative analysis to look at "combinations of causal factors most likely shifting the more highly religious teenagers into the least religious emerging adult religious groups within five years."[40] They found three different combinations of factors (or pathways) to loss of faith (one of which we have previously examined).

The first combination of factors includes:

- lower parental religious service attendance and importance set on faith
- lower importance of religious faith for the teen
- the teen prays and reads scriptures less frequently
- the teen has some doubts about his or her faith
- the teen has few adults in the congregation to whom he or she can turn for help

The second pathway includes:

- lower parental religious service attendance and importance set on faith
- lower importance of religious faith for the teen
- the teen has fewer personal religious experiences
- teen prays and reads scriptures frequently
- the teen has many adults in the congregation to whom he or she can turn for help

The third combination of factors includes:

- lower parental religious service attendance and importance set on faith
- lower importance of religious faith for the teen
- the teen has fewer personal religious experiences
- the teen prays and reads scriptures less frequently
- the teen has no doubts about his or her faith[41]

The NSYR notes: "Altogether, 60 percent of teens who experienced one of these three combinations of factors ended up as emerging adults in the low religious categories. And 56 percent of all those higher religious teenagers who did end up as emerging adults in a low religion category got there by following one of these three paths."[42]

Two factors appear in each of these pathways: (1) religion and church attendance is not that important to the parents, and (2) neither are they all that important to the teen. The two factors are probably related. Elder Oaks discusses how parents can subtly send the message that the Church is not really that important to them:

The amount of children-and-parent time absorbed in the good activities of private lessons, team sports, and other school and club activities also needs to be carefully regulated. Otherwise, children will be overscheduled, and parents will be frazzled and frustrated. Parents should act to preserve time for family prayer, family scripture study, family home evening, and the other precious togetherness and individual one-on-one time that binds a family together and fixes children's values on things of eternal worth. Parents should teach gospel priorities through what they do with their children.[43]

Our concern is with what parents do or can do for their youth. What does it mean for parents to have lower religious service attendance and importance set on faith? Among Latter-day Saints it might be manifest by the following (not an exhaustive list by any means):

- using stake or general conference as an excuse for a vacation
- giving athletic or other recreational events a higher priority than attendance at a Young Men or Young Women activity
- not holding family home evening if it is not convenient
- treating youth conference as an optional activity
- frequently missing Sunday meetings
- causualness in following the Church's *Come, Follow Me* initiative

This is not to say that legitimate reasons to miss stake conference, family home evening, or a Young Women meeting do not exist. But when it becomes a regular occurrence, parents might ask themselves what sort of message they are sending their children.[44] Elder Jeffrey R. Holland gave another example in a general conference talk in 2003:

> Parents simply cannot flirt with skepticism or cynicism, then be surprised when their children expand that flirtation into full-blown romance. If in matters of faith and belief children are at risk of being swept downstream by this intellectual current or that cultural rapid, we as their parents must be more certain than ever to hold to anchored, unmistakable moorings clearly recognizable to those of our own household. It won't help anyone if we go over the edge with them, explaining through the roar of the falls all the way down that we really did know the Church was true and that the

keys of the priesthood really were lodged there but we just didn't want to stifle anyone's freedom to think otherwise. No, we can hardly expect the children to get to shore safely if the parents don't seem to know where to anchor their own boat. . . .

I think some parents may not understand that even when they feel secure in their own minds regarding matters of personal testimony, they can nevertheless make that faith too difficult for their children to detect. We can be reasonably active, meeting-going Latter-day Saints, but if we do not live lives of gospel integrity and convey to our children powerful heartfelt convictions regarding the truthfulness of the Restoration and the divine guidance of the Church from the First Vision to this very hour, then those children may, to our regret but not surprise, turn out not to be visibly active, meeting-going Latter-day Saints or sometimes anything close to it.

> "Some parents seem to feel that they can ease up a little on the fundamentals without affecting their family or their family's future. But if a parent goes a little off course, the children are likely to exceed the parent's example."

Not long ago Sister Holland and I met a fine young man who came in contact with us after he had been roaming around through the occult and sorting through a variety of Eastern religions, all in an attempt to find religious faith. His father, he admitted, believed in nothing whatsoever. But his grandfather, he said, was actually a member of The Church of Jesus Christ of Latter-day Saints. "But he didn't do much with it," the young man said. "He was always pretty cynical about the Church." From a grandfather who is cynical to a son who is agnostic to a grandson who is now looking desperately for what God had already once given his family! What a classic example of the warning Elder Richard L. Evans once gave.

Said he: "Sometimes some parents mistakenly feel that they can relax a little as to conduct and conformity or take perhaps a so called liberal view of basic and fundamental things—thinking that a little laxness or indulgence won't matter—or they may fail to teach or to attend Church, or may voice critical views. Some parents . . . seem to feel that they can ease up a little on the fundamentals without affecting their family or their family's future. But," he observed, "if a parent goes a little off course, the children are likely to exceed the parent's example."

To lead a child (or anyone else!), even inadvertently, away from faithfulness, away from loyalty and bedrock belief simply because we want to be clever or independent is license no parent nor any other person has ever been given. In matters of religion a skeptical mind is not a higher manifestation of virtue than is a believing heart, and analytical deconstruction in the field of, say, literary fiction can be just plain old-fashioned destruction when transferred to families yearning for faith at home. And such a deviation from the true course can be deceptively slow and subtle in its impact.[45]

Now, the NSYR's statistics on pathways to disbelief cover a majority of the cases, but 40% do not follow the three pathways. What factors were present in those cases, the NSYR did not specify; we cannot know whether or not parental attendance at church was a factor; but in at least three out of five cases it was. Parents would be foolish not to take it into consideration.

Parents would also be wise to avoid either making or accepting some form of the argument that religion should be adopted because it promotes good values and leads to good results. Those are important benefits but lousy reasons for adopting religion. Religion should be adopted because it is true, not because it is useful. "Contemporary emerging adults' positive valuation of religion primarily because of the practical benefits it bestows on individual lives in the form of moral behaviors also has cultural roots in American evangelicalism."[46] The NSYR points out that

communities of faith would also do well, we think, to become more aware that a primarily instrumentalist view of faith is a double-edged sword. For many parents, religious congregations are good and valuable because they produce good outcomes in their children. . . . But making this into religion's key legitimating focus easily degenerates into a church-is-good-because-it-will-help-keep-my-kid-off-drugs-and-increase-their-seatbelt-use mentality. This obviously undermines larger and deeper questions of truth, tradition, discipleship, and peoplehood that matter to communities of faith.[47]

Sociologically the two positions lead to different results: "People who are extrinsically religious use their religion to achieve instrumental goals, such as social integration, whereas intrinsically religious people have internalized the teachings of their religion."[48] Pretending to value religion because it is useful actually devalues it. Taking a purely instrumentalist approach shows a distinct lack of faith. In fact, "pretending to value religion—or treating it with this sort of instrumentalism—is an insult to people of faith."[49] As one political philosopher and intellectual historian explains:

> When the content of faith is seen as merely salutary—a kind of noble lie or a soothing, controlling, or even necessary pharmakon—even its obvious usefulness is thereby radically compromised. For the myth to work its wonders, it cannot be considered merely salutary but must be seen simply as true. So the utility argument surrenders much of its utility, and hence its attractiveness, when it becomes the locus of loyalty and is thereby known for what it is.[50]

For individuals who use faith primarily as a means to an end, "religion is largely utilitarian and expedient, and faith and belief are typically superficial."[51] They typically employ "relatively uncritical acceptance of the doctrines of one's religion." In fact, they "tend to uncritically accept not just religious precepts and doctrines but nonreligious ideas and claims" and show a "lack of interest in and enjoyment of thinking through religious issues and ideas." Their "implicit orientation toward outward appearance (e.g., their participation in religion primarily for extrinsic reasons)" is "inversely related to the preference for internal consistency."[52] It also backfires in the end. Recall that "religious/spiritual beliefs and practices are effective deterrents of pornography use only insofar as they are practiced for their intrinsic value or meaning rather than their extrinsic or social value."[53]

> Pretending to value religion because it is useful actually devalues it.

On the other hand, those who see religion as an end in itself "tend to lead purposeful lives closely structured around their religious beliefs and institutions."[54] They tend to focus "not on the truth or validity of the religion," preferring to emphasize "the meaning of religion and its implications for one's life."[55]

The fruits of a third possibility, however, prove problematic. Those who "view religion as an open-ended process in which questioning basic religious tenets and doctrines is integral . . . are willing to tackle existential questions without reducing their complexity, are open to changing their religious beliefs and practices, and embrace religious doubt as positive and useful."[56] They "appear to more carefully examine the evidence of religious claims before accepting their veracity," "tend to examine existential and religious problems without reducing their complexity and do not unquestionably accept religious practices and doctrines handed down by their religious organizations." They are also afraid of being wrong, however, and thus "they tend to vacillate among the options, hesitating to commit to any particular option."[57] Thus embracing religious doubt as useful seems to undermine commitment.

MALACHI'S PROMISE

The NSYR has consistently noted that the family has the biggest impact of any institution on shaping the lives and especially the religious lives of teenagers and emerging adults: greater than teachers, greater than schools, greater than churches, greater than peers, greater than either the parents or the youth even realize.[58] This effect still remains a significant pull even years after young adults have left home.

At the end of the book of Malachi is a rather ominous promise: "Behold, I will send you Elijah the prophet before the coming of the great and dreadful day of the Lord: And he shall turn the heart of the fathers to the children, and the heart of the children to their fathers, lest I come and smite the earth with a curse" (Malachi 4:5–6). We are familiar with those verses and properly refer to them often in the context of genealogical work. But Elijah came not just to turn the hearts of the children to the fathers (genealogical work) but also "of the fathers to the children." We need to be concerned about our children as well as our ancestors.

The family has the biggest impact of any institution on shaping the lives and especially the religious lives of teenagers and emerging adults. Courtesy of churchofjesuschrist.org.

And then there is the matter of that curse spoken of. We usually take it to be a generic curse because the English word is generic. The Hebrew word translated "curse," ḥerem, however, is specific, not generic. The term is translated as "devoted" in the King James Version of certain passages in the Pentateuch.[59] The ancient Israelite conquest of Jericho is specifically labeled as ḥerem: "the city shall be accursed [ḥerem], even it, and all that are therein, to the Lord: only Rahab the harlot shall live, she and all that are with her in the house" (Joshua 6:17). "And they utterly destroyed all that was in the city, both man and woman, young and old, and ox, and sheep, and ass, with the edge of the sword" (Joshua 6:21). The Israelites were specifically not supposed to bring any property into their house but were to abhor it (Deuteronomy 7:26) and allow nothing to adhere to the hand (Deuteronomy 13:17). When Achan did (Joshua 7:1), he was "burnt with fire" (Joshua 7:15). The most explicit example of ḥerem is that of King Saul. He was commanded to "go and smite Amalek, and utterly destroy all that they have, and spare them not; but slay both man and woman, infant and suckling, ox and sheep, camel and ass" (1 Samuel 15:3). In this passage the term ḥerem is translated "the things which should have been utterly

283

destroyed" (1 Samuel 15:21). When Moroni quoted the Malachi passage to Joseph Smith he said that for those who do not turn their hearts, "If it were not so, the whole earth would be utterly wasted at his coming" (Doctrine and Covenants 2:3). The curse for not turning our hearts to our children is heavy.

These scriptures show the necessity of paying attention to our children, turning our hearts to them, and turning their hearts to God. Besides demonstrating our own faith that saves, we need to do what we can to save their faith.

NOTES

1. Christian Smith and Melinda Lundquist Denton, *Soul Searching: The Religious and Spiritual Lives of American Teenagers* (Oxford: Oxford University Press, 2005), 188.
2. Smith and Denton, *Soul Searching*, 111-12.
3. Melinda Lundquist Denton, "Family Structure, Family Disruption, and Profiles of Adolescent Religiosity," *Journal for the Scientific Study of Religion* 51, no. 1 (2012): 43; compare Laura B. Koenig, Matt McGue, and William G. Iacono, "Rearing Environmental Influences on Religiousness: An Investigation of Adolescent Adoptees," *Personality and Individual Differences* 47 (2009): 655.
4. Neal A. Maxwell, "The Women of God," *Ensign*, May 1978, 10-11.
5. R. Kirk Belnap and John Gee, "Classical Arabic in Contact: The Transition to Near Categorical Agreement Patterns," in *Perspectives on Arabic Linguistics VI*, ed. Mushira Eid, Vicente Cantarino, and Keith Walters (Amsterdam: John Benjamins, 1994), 121-49.
6. Richard J. Petts, "Parental Religiosity and Youth Religiosity: Variations by Family Structure," *Sociology of Religion* 76 (2015): 95-120. My page numbers will refer to the online publication.
7. Petts, "Parental Religiosity and Youth Religiosity," 13-14.
8. Petts, "Parental Religiosity and Youth Religiosity," 13-14, 8-9.
9. Petts, "Parental Religiosity and Youth Religiosity," 16-17.
10. Petts, "Parental Religiosity and Youth Religiosity," 19, 22, 23.
11. "The Family: A Proclamation to the World," *Ensign*, November 2010, 129, paragraph 7.

12. Jeremy E. Uecker and Christopher G. Ellison, "Parental Divorce, Parental Religious Characteristics, and Religious Outcomes in Adulthood," *Journal of the Scientific Study of Religion* 51, no. 4 (2012): 778.

13. Uecker and Ellison, "Parental Divorce," 787.

14. P. Onch. 25/17, in S. R. K. Glanville, *The Instructions of Onchsheshonqy* (London: British Museum, 1955), pl. 25.

15. Uecker and Ellison, "Parental Divorce," 789; Donna Freitas, *Sex and the Soul: Juggling Sexuality, Spirituality, Romance, and Religion on America's College Campuses* (Oxford: Oxford University Press, 2008), 36.

16. Lisa D. Pearce and Melinda Lunquist Denton, *A Faith of Their Own* (Oxford: Oxford University Press, 2011), 70; Christopher G. Ellison, Anthony B. Walker, Norval D. Glenn, and Elizabeth Marquardt, "The Effects of Parental Marital Discord and Divorce on the Religious and Spiritual Lives of Young Adults," *Social Science Research* 40 (2011): 548.

17. Pearce and Denton, *Faith of Their Own*, 71; Uecker and Ellison, "Parental Divorce," 786; Ellison et al., "Effects of Parental Marital Discord," 548.

18. Ellison et al., "Effects of Parental Marital Discord," 548.

19. Pearce and Denton, *Faith of Their Own*, 70.

20. Petts, "Parental Religiosity and Youth Religiosity," 8–9.

21. Mark Regnerus, *Forbidden Fruit: Sex and Religion in the Lives of American Teenagers* (Oxford: Oxford University Press, 2007), 181, 71.

22. Hsien-Hsein Lau and Nicholas H. Wolfinger, "Parental Divorce and Adult Religiosity: Evidence from the General Social Survey," *Review of Religious Research* 53, no. 1 (September 2011): 86–87, references omitted.

23. Mark D. Regnerus and Jeremy E. Uecker, "Finding Faith, Losing Faith: The Prevalence and Context of Religious Transformations during Adolescence," *Review of Religious Research* 47, no. 3 (2006): 230–31.

24. Regnerus and Uecker, "Finding Faith, Losing Faith," 233.

25. Mark Regnerus and Jeremy Uecker, *Premarital Sex in America* (Oxford: Oxford University Press, 2011), 222.

26. Young-Il Kim and W. Bradford Wilcox, "Religious Identity, Religious Attendance, and Parental Control," *Review of Religious Research* 56, no. 4 (2014): 573.

27. Kim and Wilcox, "Religious Identity," 573.

28. Phil Davignon, "The Effects of R-Rated Movies on Adolescent and Young Adult Religiosity: Media as Self-Socialization," *Review of Religious Research* 55, no. 4 (2013): 617–18.

29. Davignon, "Effects of R-Rated Movies," 618.

30. Davignon, "Effects of R-Rated Movies," 622, 624.

31. Kim and Wilcox, "Religious Identity," 573, 575.

32. Jasper van de Pol and Frank van Tubergen, "Inheritance of Religiosity among Muslim Immigrants in a Secular Society," *Review of Religious Research* 56, no. 1 (2014): 88.

33. John P. Bartkowski, Xiaohe Xu, and Martin L. Levin, "Religion and Child Development: Evidence from the Early Childhood Longitudinal Study," *Social Science Research* 37 (2008): 31.

34. Bartkowski, Xu, and Levin, "Religion and Child Development," 33.

35. Samuel L. Perry, "Pornography Consumption as a Threat to Religious Socialization," *Sociology of Religion* 76, no. 4 (2015): 447.

36. Perry, "Pornography Consumption," 440–41.

37. Perry, "Pornography Consumption," 451–52.

38. Smith and Denton, *Soul Searching*, 190.

39. Dallin H. Oaks, "Good, Better, Best," *Ensign*, November 2007, 105.

40. Christian Smith and Patricia Snell, *Souls in Transition: The Religious and Spiritual Lives of Emerging Adults* (Oxford: Oxford University Press, 2009), 230.

41. Smith and Snell, *Souls in Transition*, 230.

42. Smith and Snell, *Souls in Transition*, 230.

43. Oaks, "Good, Better, Best," 105.

44. Compare Jeffrey R. Holland, "Behold, the Lamb of God," *Ensign*, May 2019, 45: "There will be others who unavoidably find their ox in the mire on a Sabbath morning. However, to this latter group we say an *occasional* tardiness is understandable, but if the ox is in the mire *every* Sunday, then we strongly recommend that you sell the ox or fill the mire."

45. Jeffrey R. Holland, "A Prayer for the Children," *Ensign*, May 2003, 86.

46. Smith and Snell, *Souls in Transition*, 291.

47. Smith and Denton, *Soul Searching*, 270.

48. Kathryn A. Johnson, Adam B. Cohen, and Morris A. Okun, "Intrinsic Religiosity and Volunteering during Emerging Adulthood: A Comparison of Mormons with Catholics and Non-Catholic Christians," *Journal for the Scientific Study of Religion* 52, no. 4 (2013): 842.

49. Arthur C. Brooks, *Who Really Cares* (New York: Basic Books, 2006), 181.

50. Louis Midgley, "The Utility of Faith Reconsidered," in *Revelation, Reason, and Faith: Essays in Honor of Truman G. Madsen*, ed. Donald W. Parry, Daniel C. Peterson, and Stephen D. Ricks (Provo, UT: Foundation for Ancient Research and Mormon Studies, 2002), 179.

51. Daniel W. Barrett, Julie A. Patock-Peckham, Geoffrey T. Hutchinson, and Craig T. Nagoshi, "Cognitive Motivation and Religious Orientation," *Personality and Individual Differences* 38 (2005): 462–63.

52. Barrett et al., "Cognitive Motivation," 464, 471.

53. Myles Chisholm and Terry Lynn Gall, "Shame and the X-rated Addiction: The Role of Spirituality in Treating Male Pornography Addiction," *Sexual Addiction & Compulsivity* 22 (2015): 263.

54. Barrett et al., "Cognitive Motivation," 471, 463.

55. Barrett et al., "Cognitive Motivation," 464.

56. Barrett et al., "Cognitive Motivation," 463.

57. Barrett et al., "Cognitive Motivation," 470–71.

58. Smith and Denton, *Soul Searching*, 111–12; van de Pol and van Tubergen, "Inheritance of Religiosity," 87–88.

59. Leviticus 27:21, 28–29; Numbers 18:14.

The Church of Jesus Christ of Latter-day Saints is doing a much better job than other religions at keeping our youth in the faith. We are doing some things—probably many things—right. Courtesy of Jess Foami/Pixabay.

10 | **FAITH TO SAVE**

ooking back on what we have learned from our survey of published data from the National Study of Youth and Religion, we can draw the following conclusions:

- The Church of Jesus Christ of Latter-day Saints is doing a much better job than other religions at keeping our youth in the faith. We are doing some things—probably many things—right. While there is still room for improvement, we should not let our desire for improvement undercut the things that we are already doing right.
- Of those youth that we keep, more are active and faithful than in any other religion. We have over twice the activity rate and close to four times the faithfulness rate of the next closest religion. Again, we are doing some things right.
- We lose just over a third of our youth. Almost three quarters of those are lost to secularism. Sectarianism (different sects

of Christianity), while it poses some threat, is a minor threat compared to secularism.

- Most of the reasons why youth leave the Church have to do with either events that disrupt routines (for example, divorce, moving) or behaviors (for example, drugs, drink, sex, or sin), not intellectual issues.
- Doubts generally play a role only when combined with other factors. Specifically listed are (1) a lack of commitment to and importance set on the Church in the teenage years on the part of the parents, (2) a lack of commitment to and importance set on the Church by the youth, and (3) a failure by the youth to do one or more of the four statistically effective factors for retaining their faith.
- The only four statistically effective factors for individuals to retain their faith are (1) daily prayer, (2) regular scripture reading, (3) weekly Church attendance, and (4) keeping the law of chastity.
- Intellectual issues have more to do with accepting superficial counterfeits to the gospel rather than the gospel itself. The most prevalent intellectual issue undermining faith is the acceptance of various forms of relativism.

Based on my readings of the NSYR data, I think we, as a Church, are doing the following things right:

- At the beginning of the 1970s, the Church began to emphasize the family heavily. One can see this emphasis among many things: in the Homefront ads, blocking out one evening a week (Monday) for family home evening, the proclamation on the family, and the emphasis on teaching the gospel in the home with the new *Come, Follow Me* curriculum. Since no other institution has as much impact in shaping the lives of youth than the family, this emphasis has to be considered something that we have been doing right.
- Along with the emphasis on the family, the Church has also emphasized not postponing marriage unduly. (The Church has been very careful with how it treats this very personal, intimate, and important decision.) The NSYR literature does

President Gordon B. Hinckley told the Primary children of the Church, "Don't ever forget to pray." Courtesy of churchofjesuschrist.org.

point out that marriage in the early twenties tends to correlate with retaining faith and postponing it tends to correlate with losing faith. It also points out that Latter-day Saints tend to marry earlier than the national average.

- Basing the Sunday School curriculum for everyone in the Church over the age of eight (and the seminary curriculum as well) on the scriptures and emphasizing reading one's scriptures started in the 1970s and has been a very good thing for the Church. Regular scripture reading is one of the four things statistically proven to help youth (and others) retain their faith. The NSYR statistics show that we do not follow national trends in this area.
- The Church has emphasized daily prayer. When President Gordon B. Hinckley was asked by the General Primary Presidency what one thing he wanted the Primary children of the Church to know, he told them, "Don't ever forget to pray."[1] Daily prayer is also one of the four things statistically proven to help youth (and others) retain their faith.

- Encouraging weekly Sunday Church attendance, as well as attendance at youth activities, seminary, institute, etc., has been a longstanding emphasis of the Church. Those who attend Church weekly are more likely to keep their faith through their college years. Those who attend more than once a week are even more likely. The NSYR statistics for Latter-day Saints appear very different than other religions because we have significantly higher attendance.
- The Church has emphasized chastity before marriage and fidelity after marriage. This is also one of the important things that help youth retain their faith. Semiannual interviews with the youth, temple recommend interviews, and continuing ecclesiastical endorsements all help in this regard. As we have seen, this is one area where the statistics about Latter-day Saints in the NSYR vary greatly from national trends.
- The Church involves adults in the lives of the youth as teachers and youth leaders. If the handbooks are being followed, every child should have contact with two adult Sunday School teachers at least twice a month. Every teenager should have at least weekly contact with two Sunday School teachers, a Young Men or Young Women presidency member, a Young Men or Young Women teacher, and a seminary teacher. The NSYR emphasizes that getting other adults in the congregation to have a mentoring relationship with the youth is beneficial to the youth. Bishopric members should also conduct at least semiannual interviews to discuss worthiness.
- Emphasizing agency and accountability has been a consistent teaching in the Church. It is not just the right or ability to choose but the responsibility for those choices that is important. Many so-called intellectuals in the Church will emphasize the choices or agency,[2] but the Church emphasizes the accountability along with the choices. That emphasis makes a huge difference.

There are other things that we are doing right as well, but I have limited myself to items I found backed by the NSYR data. Amid all this discussion about ways to improve the situation, it is worth remembering what we are doing well already.

> **It is worth considering an actual case of the circumstances when people were leaving their church in droves.**

Most of the concrete recommendations that come from the NSYR are things that prophets and apostles have been telling the Church for decades. There is nothing new in that information, but the NSYR shows that the narrative about why youth (and others) are leaving the Church is not based on actual data.

A Historical Note

In context of the narrative about people leaving the Church in droves, it is worth considering an actual case of the circumstances when people were leaving their church in droves. Over the course of the eighth and ninth centuries, the Coptic Church (the branch of Christianity in Egypt) lost over half of its members.[3] Though Muslims had taken over Egypt in the seventh century, their religion did not initially make extensive inroads into the Christian faith at that time. A number of factors converged to effect the change.

Although in theory the Islamic leaders officially tolerated the Christians, in practice it all depended on the whims of whoever was in charge.[4] Official positions of tolerance did not prevent persecution.

Some Christians found it economically advantageous to leave their faith.[5] When the choice was between God and Mammon, they chose Mammon; they literally left their faith for a tax break.[6]

When Muslim scholars began challenging their faith intellectually, beginning in the mid-eighth century,[7] "the Copts produced very few apologetic works with regard to the teachings of Islam."[8] They would not defend their own faith, and those defenses of the faith that they did produce did not address the criticisms raised.

In an effort to bolster flagging faith, some Copts fabricated narratives to try to keep people in the churches, to give them reasons not to leave. Fictitious and forged accounts flourished.[9] The expressed purpose for promoting fictional stories was to instill courage.[10] These fictional accounts were not sufficient to encourage enough people to keep the faith in times of trial and persecution.

Lacking the courage of their convictions, the more intellectual classes, such as scribes and bureaucrats, simply assimilated to the surrounding elite culture.[11] One of the ironies of the situation is that the rise of Arabic science did not begin in Baghdad until half a century later;[12] the intellectual system to which intellectuals had defected was defective.

Coptic Church leaders tried to appease outsiders and ended up supporting outside interests rather than the faith of their adherents,[13] which proved disastrous for the faith.[14] Not only did the appeasement not work—in the Bashmuric revolts thousands of Copts were slaughtered[15]—but it undercut the moral authority of the clergy,[16] which was already damaged by lapses in integrity.[17]

We could look at what happened to the Coptic Church in the eighth century through the words of a scripture in the Book of Mormon: "For the time speedily shall come that all churches which are built up to get gain, and all those who are built up to get power over the flesh, and those who are built up to become popular in the eyes of the world, and those who seek the lusts of the flesh and the things of the world, and to do all manner of iniquity; yea, in fine, all those who belong to the kingdom of the devil are they who need fear, and tremble, and quake; they are those who must be brought low in the dust; they are those who must be consumed as stubble; and this is according to the words of the prophet" (1 Nephi 22:23). When the society was seeking power (the bureaucrats), gain (the tax converts), popularity (the intellectuals), the lusts of the flesh, and the vain things of the world (some of the clergy), then people did leave the ancient Coptic Church in droves and the church was brought low in the dust. A lack of interest in providing a saving faith failed to save faith.

FAITH WORTH SAVING

What sort of faith saves and is worth saving?

In English, monosyllabic terms are usually indicative of native Anglo-Saxon vocabulary, while polysyllabic terms are generally loanwords from another language, but the term *faith* is actually a loanword into English. It came into English in the thirteenth century from French *feid*, which came in turn from Latin *fides*. *Fides*, "like its etymological cognate Gr[eek] πιστις, which it renders in the N[ew] T[estament], had the following principle senses: 1. Belief, trust. 2. That which produces belief, evidence, token, pledge, engagement. 3. Trust in its objective aspect, troth; observance of trust, fidelity."[18] It has these connotations because it is related to the Latin term *foedus* which means "treaty, agreement, covenant."[19] Its first usage in English (mid-thirteenth century) was "loyalty to a person to whom one is bound by promise or duty, or to one's promise or duty itself,"[20] which is preserved in the sense of "the duty of fulfilling one's trust; allegiance owed to a superior, fealty."[21] By the beginning of the fourteenth century, it had acquired the sense of "confidence, reliance, trust."[22] At about the same time, it had acquired the meaning of "a system of religious belief," especially Christianity.[23] It is only at the end of the fourteenth century that it came to mean "belief in the truths of religion."[24] It is the last meaning that tends to be the most popular in modern times, but the meanings of both "trust" and "loyalty" should not be forgotten. The meaning of "loyalty" survives in the modern English term *faithful*. All three meanings are implicit in the expression *faith in Jesus Christ*, which implies believing he exists and is the son of God, trusting in him and his atonement, and being loyal to him by keeping the covenants we have made with him and that bind us to him.

In English the term *faith* replaced the earlier term *belief*, which was first used in the twelfth century to mean "trust, dependence, reliance, confidence, faith."[25] This in turn replaced the older form *geleáfa*, by replacing the *ge-* prefix (meaning "together") with the prefix *by-*. The older form was cognate with German noun *Glaube* and the verb *glauben*, which originally meant "the friendly reliance of a man on divinity," but the sense later softened to assenting that something is true.[26] The English term *faith* also replaced Old English *treów*, or *trúwa*, and the variant forms *geðtrywð*, *getriwð*, and *getrýwð*. The former forms survive as an adjective (originally a noun) *true*, which originally meant a person who was "loyal,"[27] and the archaic verb *to trow* meaning "to trust."[28] The latter survive as the archaic word *troth*, originally meaning "one's faith

Faith is both the trust and confidence in God that impels us to make the covenants in the first place and the loyalty that enables us to keep them. Courtesy of churchofjesuschrist.org.

as pledged or plighted in a solemn agreement or undertaking."[29] All of this English vocabulary originally had covenant connotations.

Faith is thus connected with the making and keeping of covenants. It is both the trust and confidence in God that impels us to make the covenants in the first place, and the loyalty that enables us to keep them. It is this sort of faith that we want for ourselves and for the youth of the Church. This sort of faith is worth saving.

Covenants

We need to give youth and young adults reasons to believe rather than reasons not to leave.

In that sense, though statistics can illuminate areas in which we can improve, the focus on statistics can be a distraction. This is not about changing the Church so that atheist determinists or moral relativists (or followers of whatever wind of doctrine) can feel comfortable coming to church, but about changing ourselves so that we will feel comfortable when we come into the presence of God (see Mormon 9:3–4). This is not about keeping people in the pews but about keeping covenants. Covenants are not something that get in the way of what we are trying to do; they are what we are trying to do.

The Church is a group of individuals who have made sacred covenants with God through his divine authority. When individuals cease to keep those covenants, they remove themselves from the Church whether or not the Church formally removes them from the rolls. We need to help youth, young adults, and ourselves make sacred covenants in the waters of baptism and the temple. We need to remember those covenants by reviewing records of those covenants (scripture study) and communicating with the author of those covenants (prayer). We need to form our families by covenants and center them in covenants. We need to renew those covenants by regularly partaking of the sacrament. We need to keep those covenants and repent when we stray from those covenants. And we need to endure in those covenants. If we keep our covenants, the statistics will take care of themselves.

NOTES

1. Gordon B. Hinckley, "Don't Ever Forget to Pray," *Friend*, April 2006, 11.

2. For example, James B. Mayfield, "Poverty, Population, and Environmental Ruin," in *New Genesis: A Mormon Reader on Land and Community*, ed. Terry Tempest Williams, William B. Smart, and Gibbs M. Smith (Salt Lake City: Gibbs Smith, 1999), 61–62; Terryl L. Givens, *People of Paradox: A History of Mormon Culture* (Oxford: Oxford University Press, 2007), 5–8; Patrick Q. Mason, *Planted: Belief and Belonging in an Age of Doubt* (Provo, UT: Neal A. Maxwell Institute for Religious Scholarship; Salt Lake City: Deseret Book, 2015), 26, 33, 93, 108–9, 114, 116, 153, 161, 197; Michelle Chaplin Sanchez, "Wrestling with Language: Exploring the Impact of Mormon Metaphysics on Theological Pedagogy," *Mormon Studies Review* 3 (2016): 114; Fenella Cannell, "Mormonism and Anthropology: On Ways of Knowing," *Mormon Studies Review* 4 (2017): 13; Rosalynde Welch, "The New Mormon Theology of Matter," *Mormon Studies Review* 4 (2017): 70–72; Adam S. Miller, *Letters to a Young Mormon*, 2nd ed. (Provo, UT: Neal A. Maxwell Institute for Religious Scholarship; Salt Lake City: Deseret Book, 2018), 1–5. As a discussion of agency, Miller's treatment is both confused and incoherent.

3. Sam I. Gellens, "Egypt, Islamization of," in *The Coptic Encyclopedia* (New York: Macmillan, 1991), 3:936; *History of the Patriarchs* 1.17, in *Patrologia Orientalis*, 5:51–52; Siegfried Richter, "Vom mönchischen Leben: Entwicklungslinien des Mönchtums in Ägypten," in *Christen in Ägypten*, ed. Heike Behlmer and Martin Tamcke (Wiesbaden: Harrassowitz, 2015), 39: "Der Steuerduck war so groß, dass wahrscheinlich schon im 9. Jh. so viele Christen Mohammedaner geworden waren, dass diese in der Überzahl waren." Compare Otto F. A. Meinardus, *Christian Egypt: Life and Faith* (Cairo: The American University in Cairo Press, 1970), 346: "During the reign of al-Mutawakkil (847–861 A.D.) many Christians denied the Lord Jesus Christ, some denied Him on account of the worldly possessions which they loved, and others, on account of the poverty which they suffered."

4. Meinardus, *Christian Egypt*, 345.

5. Gellens, "Egypt, Islamization of," 936, 938; Meinardus, *Christian Egypt*, 347.

6. Meinardus, *Christian Egypt*, 346; *History of the Patriarchs* 1.18, in *Patrologia Orientalis*, 5:116–17, 189; Mark N. Swanson, *The Coptic Papacy in Islamic Egypt: The Popes of Egypt* (Cairo: American University in Cairo Press, 2010), 20.

7. Maged S. A. Mikhail, "The Early Islamic Period (641–1517): From the Arab Conquest through Mamlūk Rule," in *The Coptic Christian Heritage: History, Faith, and Culture*, ed. Lois M. Farag (London: Routledge, 2014), 42.

8. Meinardus, *Christian Egypt*, 360.

9. Antonia St. Demiana, "*In Michaelem*: The Encomium on Michael the Archangel Attributed to Severus of Antioch," *Bulletin de l'Institut français d'archéologie orientale* 113 (2013): 396; Tito Orlandi, "Coptic Literature," in *Coptic Encyclopedia*, 5:1456–58.

10. Apa Stephanos, *Encomium on Saint Helias*, fol. 44r, in Geo. P. G. Sobhy, *Le martyre de Saint Hélias et l'encomium de l'éveque Stéphanos de Hnès sur Saint Hélias* (Cairo: IFAO, 1919), 87.

11. Meinardus, *Christian Egypt*, 347; Gellens, "Egypt, Islamization of," 938.

12. Jim Al-Khalili, *The House of Wisdom: How Arabic Science Saved Ancient Knowledge and Gave Us the Renaissance* (New York: Penguin, 2010), 12–17.

13. *History of the Patriarchs* 1.18, in *Patrologia Orientalis* 5:162; Meinardus, *Christian Egypt*, 353, 355–59, 361.

14. Meinardus, *Christian Egypt*, 347.

15. Mounir Megally, "Bashmuric Revolts," in *Coptic Encyclopedia*, 2:350–51; Gellens, "Egypt, Islamization of," 938; al-Maqrizi, *Taqi al-Din*, in *A Short History of the Copts and Their Church*, trans. S. C. Malan (London: D. Nutt, 1873), 81–82.

16. *History of the Patriarchs* 1.18, in *Patrologia Orientalis* 5:162; Meinardus, *Christian Egypt*, 353.

17. *History of the Patriarchs* 1.16–19, in *Patrologia Orientalis* 5:22–23, 25–26, 32–34, 36–37, 43–45, 59–60, 80–81, 103, 105, 107, 118, 123–24, 202–3, 205; 10:362–64, 420, 454; W. E. Crum, *The Monastery of Epiphanius at Thebes* (New York: Metropolitan Museum of Art, 1926), 2:11 (#51), 36 (#111), 41 (#141), 44 (#154), 45 (#162), 70 (#269), 103 (#459), 193 (#157), 193–94 (#158). Otto F. A. Meinardus, *Monks and Monasteries of the Egyptian Deserts*, 2nd ed. (Cairo: The American University of Cairo Press, 1992), 191. W. E. Crum, *Short Texts from Coptic Ostraca and Papyri* (Oxford: Oxford University Press, 1924), 11 (#33); W. E. Crum, *Coptic Ostraca* (London: Egypt Exploration Fund, 1902), pl. 19 (#83), pl. 90 (Ad 13).

18. *Oxford English Dictionary*, s.v. "faith."

19. I'd like to thank Jacob Mackey for bringing this to my attention.

20. *Oxford English Dictionary*, s.v. "belief," definition 1.

21. *Oxford English Dictionary*, s.v. "faith," definition 9.

22. *Oxford English Dictionary*, s.v. "faith," definition 1.

23. *Oxford English Dictionary*, s.v. "faith," definition 4.

24. *Oxford English Dictionary*, s.v. "faith," definition 3.

25. *Oxford English Dictionary*, s.v. "belief," definition 1.

26. "Das freundschaftliche Vertrauen eines Menschen zur Gottheit." Günther Drosdowski and Paul Grebe, *Duden 7: Das Herkunftswörterbuch* (Mannheim: Dudenverlag, 1963), 225.

27. *Oxford English Dictionary*, s.v. "true."

28. *Oxford English Dictionary*, s.v. "trow."

29. *Oxford English Dictionary*, s.v. "troth."

INDEX

competency, 9–14

conduct, moral relativism and code of, 148

contraceptives, 213

conversion
from The Church of Jesus Christ of Latter-day Saints, 36–38
factors influencing, 34–36, 258–59

Cook, Quentin L., 1

Coptic Church, 293–94

correction, 253–55

Council of Nicaea, 263n70

covenants, 55, 70, 87, 128, 152, 239, 240, 242, 295–97

Cowdery, Oliver, 255

creationism, 79

crisis of faith, 67–68

cynicism, 103–6

D

Dartmouth College, 144–45

David, King, 97–98

death as disruption leading to disaffiliation, 82

differentiation as reason for disaffiliation, 84–85

disaffiliation, 75–76. See also apostasy
disruptions to routine as reason for, 76–82
distractions as reason for, 83–84
doubt as driver of, 62–63, 71, 290
and doubt in combination with other factors, 63–65
honoring diversity as reason for, 86–88
keeping options open as reason for, 89–90
loss of trust as reason for, 103–6
Moralistic Therapeutic Deism and, 126–27
partying as reason for, 91–92
politics as reason for, 95–97
pornography as reason for, 97–103
reactivation following, 256–59
self-confidence in self-sufficiency as reason for, 90–91

disagreement equated with intolerance, 140

disruptions to routine as reason for disaffiliation, 76–82

distractions as reason for disaffiliation, 83–84

diversity, honoring, as reason for disaffiliation, 86–88

divorce
among evangelicals, 206–7
cohabitation and, 184–85
as disruption leading to disaffiliation, 79–82

Doctrine and Covenants, 250

doubt
in combination with other factors, 63–65
defending against, 65–66
delaying, 67–70
as driver of disaffiliation, 62–63, 71, 290
embracing, 282
encouraging, 70–71
as reason for loss of faith, 61, 106–7

drug use, 94–95, 273

Dunning–Kruger effect, 9–14

Duty to God, 239, 242

E

economics
and cohabitation, 186, 187–88
and sexual activity, 181–84, 219–20n67

Einstein, Albert, 149

Elijah, 282

estrous cycle, 172–73

evangelicals, 158–59, 205–7

Evans, Richard L., 279–80

evolutionism, 79

F

fairness under Moralistic Therapeutic Deism, 127–28

faith. See also belief; disaffiliation
acting before knowing as act of, 243–44
building, 69, 73n17
chastity and, 241
church attendance and, 235–37

moral compromises, 159–60
moral dilemmas, 159
moral individualism, 132–46
moral instincts and happiness,
 157–59
Moralistic Therapeutic Deism,
 122–30, 164n11, 165n23
moral relativism, 146–52, 158–59,
 290
moral sources, 153–57
other, 131
interstitial nucleus of the anterior
 hypothalamus, third (INAH-3),
 191–92
intolerance, 139, 140–41, 145
irreligion, 141–42

J

Jericho, Israelite conquest of, 283
Jerusalem, Lehi's judgment of, 133–34
Jesus Christ
 atonement of, 125, 148, 295
 church of, 149
 divinity of, 159
 faith in, 295
 gospel of, 70, 96, 130, 136–37, 151,
  152, 248, 250
 as head of the Church, 97
 remembering, 236
 on theology, 245
 parables of, 51–52, 67, 83, 250
 story of, 250
 teachings of, 51–52, 67–68, 79, 83, 98,
  125, 128, 136–37, 146, 244, 270
judging others, 133–38
 tolerance and, 138–46
justness, 128

K

Kael, Pauline, 9
karma, 156
Kuyper (Kuijper), Abraham, 142–43

L

Laman and Lemuel, 12, 133–34
Law, William, 88
laws, obedience to civic, 156
learning, seeking, 69, 73n17

Lee, Harold B., 244
Lehi, 133–34
Lewis, C. S., 130, 183
life, purpose of, 129
life transitions and disturbances as reasons for disaffiliation, 76–82
love
 of God, 125, 164n15
 romantic, 183–84
 sexual activity and building, 179–80

M

Malachi's promise, 282–84
marriage. See also divorce
 age at first, 85, 110n55
 among evangelicals, 206–7
 and church activity, 258
 cohabitation and, 184–86
 postponing, 85–86, 290–91
 sexual activity of LDS youth before,
  209–10
materialism, 84
Maxwell, Neal A.
 on heeding warnings, 253
 on heeding words of prophets, 90
 on influence of parents, 268
 on intervention, 68
 on irreligion, 141–42
 on leading others astray, 70–71
 on memorability in gospel teaching,
  244
 on reactivation, 257
 on reproof, 253, 254–55
mean, 2
media, 273. See also pornography
median, 2
memorability, 244–53
mode, 2
modion, 67–68
Monson, Thomas S., 70–71
moral compromises, 159–60
moral dilemmas, 159
moral individualism, 132–46
Moralistic Therapeutic Deism, 122–30,
 164n11, 165n23
morality. See also abstinence; chastity;
 promiscuity; sexual activity;
 virginity
 and acting on instinct, 157–59

morality (*continued*)
 attention given to, 131–32
 and sex education, 213–14
 shift in American, 179
 sources of, 153–57
moral reasoning, 160–63
moral relativism, 146–52, 158–59, 290
"Mormon effect," 210–11
Moroni's promise, 251
mortality, purpose of, 129

N

National Longitudinal Study of Adolescent to Adult Health, 199–200
National Study of Youth and Religion (NSYR) data
 advantages and disadvantages of, 4–5
 alcohol consumption in, 93
 categories of faithfulness in, 43–50
 conversions in, 34–35
 disaffiliation in, 75–76, 78–79
 doubt in, 62–65
 effective teaching in, 245
 family togetherness in, 275–76
 on instrumentalist view of faith, 280–81
 intellectual issues in, 122–24, 126, 153–57, 159, 160–61, 162
 parental role in loss of faith in, 276–77
 purpose of, 15, 122
 religiosity in, 39–40
 statistics on youth retention in, 20–21
natural man, 172–84
Nelson, Russell M., 90
New Testament, 250, 263n70
Nicaea, Council of, 263n70
niceness under Moralistic Therapeutic Deism, 127–29
Noah, King, 134–35
nones, 17–19
normal distribution of data, 2–3

O

Oaks, Dallin H., 276, 277–78
obedience
 cafeteria approach to, 89–90

Moralistic Therapeutic Deism and, 128
 morality and, 156
offense, taking, 104–5
optimism, 12. See also Dunning–Kruger effect
options, keeping open, as reason for disaffiliation, 89–90
overoptimism, 9–14

P

Packer, Boyd K., 70, 148–49
Paglia, Camille, 190–91
parables, 250
parents. See also family
 and doubt and faith, 64, 65–66
 and homosexuality, 192
 influence of, 267–68, 282–84
 and reactivation of youth, 259
 role in loss of faith, 276–82
 and sexual activity, 208, 212–14, 230n265
 as teachers of Moralistic Therapeutic Deism, 125–26
partying as reason for disaffiliation, 91–94
Pauline Kael Syndrome, 8–9
Personal Progress program, 239, 242
petting, heavy, 209, 214
politics as reason for disaffiliation, 95–97
pornography
 consumption by user type, 118n154
 consumption in religious states, 116n127
 and homosexuality, 193–94
 influence of parent's consumption of, 274–75
 men's susceptibility to, 174
 rates for unintentional exposure to, 115n117
 as reason for disaffiliation, 97–103
poverty of children in cohabiting households, 187
prayer, 238–39, 291
promiscuity, 171–72. See also abstinence; chastity; sexual activity; virginity
 and cohabitation, 184–88

and homosexuality, 188–200
LDS youth as outliers regarding, 207–15
and natural man, 172–84
protection of young adults. See youth retention
psychology, relativism in, 149–50
puberty, 173
public speaking, 252–53
pure love of Christ, 136

R

reactivation, 256–59
relativism, 149–52. See also moral relativism
religion
    church attendance and changing, 236
    instrumentalist view of, 280–81
    as protection against pornography, 102–3
    tolerance and, 140–44
    and youth retention, 20–23
religiosity. See also spirituality
    associations between homosexuality and, 190
    correlation between sexual activity and, 171–72, 200–207, 215
    decline in, 39–40
    and family's influence on youth retention, 268–72
    parental involvement and, 272–74
    pornography's effects on, 102
    statistics on, 14–20
religious instruction as factor in youth retention, 34
religious studies, 246–48, 263n70
repentance, 151–52
reproof, 253–55
righteousness, overestimation of, 12–14
routine, disruptions to, as reason for disaffiliation, 76–82
R-rated movies, 273

S

sacrament, 236
Saul, King, 283–84
science, relativism and, 149, 150–51

scriptures. See also Bible; Book of Mormon; Doctrine and Covenants
    injunctions to pray in, 239
    neglecting, 241
    as stories, 250
    tolerance in, 143, 145–46
scripture study, 239–42
secularism / secularization, 16–17, 38–39, 289–90
self-assessment, Dunning–Kruger effect and, 9–14
selfishness and sexual activity, 181
self-sufficiency, self-confidence in, as reason for disaffiliation, 90–91
sex education, 213–14, 230n265
sexual abuse, 195–97
sexual activity. See also abstinence; chastity; promiscuity; virginity
    correlation between religiosity and, 171–72, 200–207, 215
    economics of, 181–84, 219–20n67
    emotional consequences of, 176–78
    by faithfulness category, 56
    gender and, 172–74
    as reason for disaffiliation, 91–92, 95
    regrets concerning, 175–76
    relationship of alcohol to, 94
sexual orientation. See homosexuality
shame culture, 48–49
Smith, Hyrum, 240–41
Smith, Joseph, 69, 121–22, 129, 255
smorgasbord Saints, 47, 55
snowball sampling, 8–9
social-contract theory, 155–56
social desirability bias, 99–100, 116n127, 116n135
socialization as factor in youth retention, 32–34
social media, 84
spiritual but not religious, 17–19, 46, 48–50, 171, 210
spirituality. See also religiosity
    pornography's effects on, 102
    versus religion, 18–19
statistics
    advantages and disadvantages of, 2–9
    of The Church of Jesus Christ of Latter-day Saints, 1, 4

CITATION INDEX

ABOUT THE AUTHOR

JOHN GEE has degrees from Brigham Young University, the University of California at Berkeley, and Yale University. A research professor at Brigham Young University since 1998, Gee is currently the William (Bill) Gay Research Professor in the Department of Asian and Near Eastern Languages at Brigham Young University.